ADVANCE PRAISE FOR *THE BOILING MOAT*

"With *The Boiling Moat*, Matt Pottinger becomes Taiwan's Paul Revere, warning the world of the likelihood of a PRC escalation across the Taiwan Strait. He and his contributors give us a lucid, informative, and yet spellbinding menu of unwelcome scenarios from which Xi Jinping will choose to 'reunify the motherland' and advance his 'China Dream.'"

—ORVILLE SCHELL, author of *Wealth and Power: China's Long March to the Twenty-First Century*

"If you are concerned about the looming conflict with China over Taiwan, read this book and ask those in positions of leadership to heed its recommendations with a sense of urgency."

—H.R. McMASTER, former US national security advisor

"*The Boiling Moat* is a one-of-a-kind book that lays out precisely how we can deter the catastrophic war that China's dictator is planning."

—MIKE POMPEO, former US secretary of state and CIA director

THE BOILING MOAT

THE BOILING MOAT

URGENT STEPS TO DEFEND TAIWAN

Edited by
MATT POTTINGER

HOOVER INSTITUTION PRESS
STANFORD UNIVERSITY   STANFORD, CALIFORNIA

hoover.org

Hoover Institution Press Publication No. 738
Hoover Institution at Leland Stanford Junior University,
Stanford, California 94305-6003

Cover and interior illustrations by Badiucao

First printing 2024
30 29 28 27 26 25 24   7 6 5 4 3 2 1

Manufactured in the United States of America
Printed on acid-free, archival-quality paper

Library of Congress Cataloging-in-Publication Data
Names: Pottinger, Matt, editor.
Title: The boiling moat : urgent steps to defend Taiwan / edited by Matt Pottinger.
Other titles: Urgent steps to defend Taiwan | Hoover Institution Press publication ; 738.
Description: Stanford, California : Hoover Institution Press, Stanford University, 2024. | Series: Hoover Institution Press publication ; no. 738 | Includes bibliographical references and index. | Summary: "Military and political leaders map out a workable strategy for Taiwan, the United States, and their allies to deter China from pursuing acts of aggression against Taiwan"— Provided by publisher.
Identifiers: LCCN 2024010359 (print) | LCCN 2024010360 (ebook) | ISBN 9780817926458 (paperback) | ISBN 9780817926465 (epub) | ISBN 9780817926489 (pdf)
Subjects: LCSH: National security—Taiwan. | Taiwan—Military policy. | United States—Foreign relations—Taiwan. | Taiwan—Foreign relations—United States. | United States—Military policy. | Taiwan—Foreign relations—China. | China—Foreign relations—Taiwan.
Classification: LCC UA853.T28 B65 2024 (print) | LCC UA853.T28 (ebook) | DDC 355/.033551249—dc23/eng/20240326
LC record available at https://lccn.loc.gov/2024010359
LC ebook record available at https://lccn.loc.gov/2024010360)

邊城之地，必將嬰城固守，皆為金城湯池，不可攻也。

—《漢書·蒯通傳》

*Cities along the frontier must resolutely fortify
their defenses; protected by metal ramparts and
boiling moats, they become impregnable.*

**— *THE BOOK OF HAN: BIOGRAPHY OF KUAI TONG,*
FIRST CENTURY CE**

*To be prepared for war is one of the most
effectual means of preserving peace.*

**— GEORGE WASHINGTON, FIRST ANNUAL ADDRESS
TO CONGRESS, JANUARY 8, 1790**

CONTENTS

FOREWORD

Over the last decade, and especially since the February 2022 launch of the latest and biggest phase of Russia's war on Ukraine, resurgent military aggression and various other forms of authoritarian power projection have changed the face of world politics. Even before it was fully formed, the hope that the end of the Cold War would usher in a new era of interstate peace was belied by Saddam Hussein's invasion and occupation of Kuwait. That should have been enough reminder of the timeless adage—written so frequently in blood across the pages of history—that power-hungry tyrants pose grave threats to their neighbors. By now, the illusions of a new, more peaceful and rule-bound era of world order have been shattered. Over the last three decades, Europe (along with the broader arc of post-Soviet space) and the Middle East have been the principal strategic theaters of authoritarian belligerence. But there is good reason to believe that in the coming decade, the greatest threat will come from Asia and the world's most powerful autocracy, the People's Republic of China (PRC).

As Matt Pottinger and his coauthors make clear in this brilliant and urgently important book, no country in recent decades has been expanding its military might with greater speed, intensity, and foreseeable consequence than China. This is not simply a general military buildup to buttress China's rise as a global superpower. It is quite specifically designed to achieve coercively—through military invasion, strangulation by blockade, or some sequence of the two—what the Communist leaders in Beijing term "unification of Taiwan with the motherland." As this book elucidates in chilling detail, China's mega-lomaniacal dictator, Xi Jinping, is increasingly warning his Communist Party cadres, and the nation, to prepare for war—and quite specifically, a war for Xi to achieve the crowning victory that would elevate him above even Mao Zedong in the pantheon of China's Communist leaders. Moreover, the authors show, it is not only through rhetoric and military expansion that China is preparing for a war of annexation against Taiwan. China is also restructuring its economy to insulate it from potential economic sanctions, escalating information warfare and gray-zone military exercises, and rapidly building and repositioning infrastructure in ways that signal preparation for a bold military exercise across the Strait of Taiwan, and even a "great struggle," if that is what it takes to prevail.

This is hardly the first time that a dictator has given the world notice of his intent to aggress against a neighbor. Adolf Hitler did just that with his headlong pace of military modernization in the 1930s, and then his march of twenty thousand Wehrmacht troops into the Rhineland in 1936, in brazen violation of the Treaty of Versailles and the Locarno Pact. Europe's democracies did nothing in response to Hitler then. What followed were repeated failures to deter Hitler's thirst for conquest. The most famous of these was the 1938 Munich agreement, in which Britain and France, hoping to prevent the war that Hitler threatened, yielded to his territorial demand to annex a German-speaking part of Czechoslovakia, the Sudetenland. So naïve and calamitous was the Anglo-French concession to the German dictator that the Munich agreement has become synonymous with delusional appeasement of tyrants seeking to aggrandize their power, wealth, and territory.

Now it is Taiwan that is in the crosshairs of totalitarian aggressive ambition. And what today's powerful democracies do or fail to do to deter the potential aggressor, China, will be every bit as consequential for the future of world peace and order. It is not merely that Taiwan—like Czechoslovakia in the 1930s—is a democracy in a difficult neighborhood. In Taiwan's case, it is also perhaps the most liberal democracy in Asia and one of the most successful results of the post-1974 "third wave" of democratization. That should be reason enough to resolve, as we should have done in the 1930s, that we cannot allow a democracy to be swallowed by a power-hungry dictator without endangering all democracies.

There are also, as Pottinger and his coauthors enumerate, other powerful reasons why deterring China from forcibly annexing Taiwan is vital to world order. As this book explains, it is difficult to overstate the strategic importance of Taiwan to the world economy, to the free flow of goods throughout the Indo-Pacific, and to the national security of the United States. In conquering Taiwan, China might gain a chokehold over the global supply of semiconductors, especially at the advanced nodes. Or in the heat of battle, the development and fabrication facilities that produce over half of the world's chips (and over 90 percent of the most advanced chips) might be damaged or destroyed, sending the world economy into a deep tailspin, if not an outright global depression. Beyond this, if China captures Taiwan, it could reposition its submarines and numerous other military assets to the island and use that strategic location (between Japan and the Philippines in the so-called First Island Chain) to hold the rest of East Asia hostage to its demands. With China already using relentless coercion and intimidation to press its baseless claims to most of the South China Sea, the US commitment to maintain a free and open Indo-Pacific would be fatally undermined. Democracies throughout Asia (and perhaps beyond) would abandon strategic confidence in the United States. And the stage would be set for the biggest shift in world power since the end of World War II.

It is still possible to prevent this scenario from happening. But as Pottinger and his colleagues argue (echoing George Washington and many other strategic thinkers), to maintain the peace, democracies must prepare for war. They must show they have not only the means but also the will to fight effectively, and that in launching a needless war, China would face a probability of defeat. With his economy stagnating, his entrepreneurial and scientific talent fleeing, and the society (and even many Communist Party members) disillusioned with his rule, Xi would be courting personal ruin if he launched a war and lost it. Taiwan's job now, America's job now, Japan's job now, and Australia's and Europe's job now is to persuade China's leaders that using military force to resolve the Taiwan question would likely be disastrous—both for all these nations and for all of China.

In the pages that follow, Pottinger and his remarkable coauthors spell out the urgent steps that Taiwan, the United States, and their strategic partners must take to be able to hold off, repel, and ultimately defeat a PRC attempt at coercive annexation. They make clear that it is only through such strength, resolve, and readiness that a PRC attack on Taiwan will be deterred. We must hope that policymakers and democratic publics take their message to heart before it is too late.

LARRY DIAMOND
William L. Clayton Senior Fellow, Hoover Institution
Mosbacher Senior Fellow in Global Democracy,
    Freeman Spogli Institute for International Studies
Stanford University

ACKNOWLEDGMENTS

I am indebted to Larry Diamond for planting the idea for this book in late 2022. Larry provided constant encouragement as my project mentor from start to finish. I am also indebted to all my coauthors for their contributions. Three of them—Robert Haddick, Ivan Kanapathy, and Michael A. Hunzeker—deserve a special shout-out for providing smart suggestions and edits beyond the chapters they wrote. Semper Fidelis.

Several colleagues at the Hoover Institution provided helpful feedback, including Nadia Schadlow, Matt Turpin, Glenn Tiffert, H.R. McMaster, Jim Ellis, and Philip Zelikow. The Hoover Institution is one of the country's finest bastions of free and critical research, and I am privileged to be a part of it. I'm also grateful to the Foundation for Defense of Democracies, whose can-do CEO Mark Dubowitz suggested we bring a delegation of Israeli national security leaders to Taiwan last summer. The trip yielded fascinating exchanges that helped inspire portions of this book, especially chapter 4, "A New Military Culture for Taiwan."

Lin Yang provided me with the Han dynasty reference that inspired the title of the book. Badiucao provided the original artwork that went inside the book and onto its cover. Abi Kim and Brandon Holt provided indispensable administrative support. Graham Allison hosted a round table at Harvard University to sharpen the book's arguments. I'm grateful to all of them. I'm also grateful to all my colleagues at the research firm Garnaut Global LLC. There isn't a more talented band of China-focused researchers assembled under one roof.

One of my pleasures of 2023 was getting to meet the great Australian writers Geoffrey Blainey and Ann Blainey over a meal in their hometown of Melbourne. Geoffrey's book *The Causes of War*, with its deeply investigated and frequently counterintuitive insights, electrified me when I read it as a White House official. It also inspired chapter 3, which Geoffrey was kind enough to review. The chapter is dedicated to him.

Barbara Arellano, Alison Law, and Danica Michels Hodge at the Hoover Institution Press worked speedily to publish the book, with the editorial expertise of David Sweet. I'd also like to thank the Taipei Economic and Cultural Office (TECO SF) in San Francisco for generously providing financial support for the project. TECO SF neither reviewed the manuscript in advance nor influenced its content in any way.

Most important of all is the support and love I received from my family throughout this project, which makes it all worthwhile. My siblings and parents looked at draft excerpts between cups of eggnog over Christmas. And Yen and the boys remained cheerful (and patient) during the final sprint to get it done. This book is dedicated to them.

MATT POTTINGER
Stanford, California, 2024

PART I
Overview

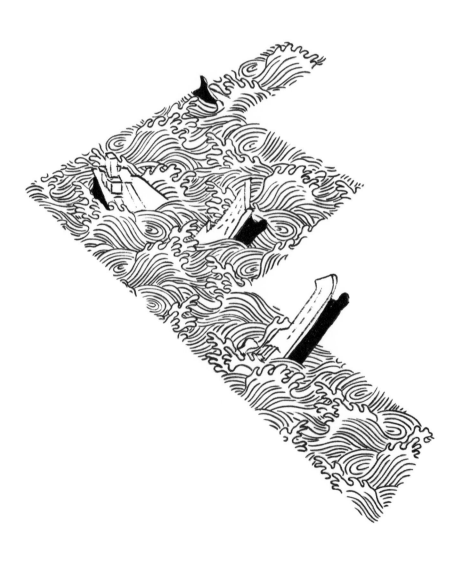

CHAPTER 1

"The Stormy Seas of a Major Test"

MATT POTTINGER

Deterrence is unlikely to be achieved by accident.

—ROSS BABBAGE

If just one lesson could be drawn from Russia's invasion of Ukraine, it must be that deterrence would have been a lot cheaper than war. Yet democracies seem to be getting worse at deterrence. The record of the past two years is marred with failures and signs of trouble:

- Vladimir Putin, unfazed by Washington's threats of sanctions, assaulted the capital of Ukraine and plunged Europe into its most destructive conflict since World War II.
- Iran equipped Hamas to initiate a war with Israel and, once the war had started, mobilized several of its other terrorist proxy groups, in Lebanon, Yemen, Syria, and Iraq, to rocket Israel, attack commercial shipping in the Red Sea, threaten US warships, and strike US military positions across Iraq and Syria.[1]
- Beijing intensified its long-standing campaign to impose Chinese sovereignty over the South China Sea, home to some of the world's most important international sea-lanes and fishing grounds. China is using its coast guard to block and ram Philippine vessels tasked with sustaining or regaining Manila's administrative

control of offshore islets that Beijing claims for itself, in defiance of international norms and court rulings.

- Venezuela's dictator, who may have concluded that Washington's bark is worse than its bite, has threatened to annex much of Venezuela's oil-rich neighbor, Guyana.[2] In a bold reprisal of Soviet mischief in the Americas during the Cold War, Beijing is expressing sympathy for Venezuela's position while also developing Chinese intelligence facilities and a plan for a military base on Cuba.[3]

- North Korea, undaunted by United Nations Security Council resolutions or American sanctions, resumed testing intercontinental ballistic missiles (ICBMs) for the first time in more than five years and became a supplier of arms and munitions for Russia's war in Ukraine.[4]

Looming on the horizon is the specter of a conflict more consequential than all these flashpoints combined: Chinese supreme leader Xi Jinping has vowed to "reunify" Taiwan with mainland China through force of arms if necessary. Indeed, Xi's public statements about a coming "great struggle" against China's enemies provide a window into his intentions—one the world would be unwise to ignore.

More than once, Xi has described unification with Taiwan as a prerequisite for achieving his broader objectives for China on the world stage, a vision he calls "the Chinese dream for the great rejuvenation of the Chinese nation."[5] In a 2017 address to the 19th Party Congress in Beijing, Xi said that "complete national unification is an inevitable requirement for realizing the great rejuvenation of the Chinese nation."[6] In 2019 in Beijing, at the Meeting Marking the 40th Anniversary of the Issuance of the Message to Compatriots in Taiwan, he said: "The rejuvenation of the Chinese nation and reunification of our country are a surging popular trend. It is where the greater national interest lies, and it is what the people desire."[7] In October 2021, he delivered an address about Taiwan at the Great Hall of the People in Beijing in which he uttered the word "rejuvenation" more than two dozen times.[8] The implication is hard to miss: Xi is equating a failure to subsume Taiwan with a failure to enact his overarching goals as China's leader.

Although Xi has been less concrete—at least in public—about a timeline, he has exhibited an impatience that distinguishes him from his predecessors. "The issue of political disagreements that exist between the two sides must reach a final resolution, step by step, and these issues cannot be passed on from generation to generation," Xi told an envoy from Taiwan in October 2013.[9] This and similar statements by Xi are a far cry from then paramount leader Deng Xiaoping's famous line, in 1984, that China could wait "1,000 years" to unify with Taiwan if necessary.

And whereas Xi's more immediate predecessors, Jiang Zemin and Hu Jintao, framed war as something Beijing would wage in response to a declaration of independence by Taiwan, official propaganda under Xi has gone further by suggesting that force may be used to *compel* unification, not just to respond to a Taiwanese bid for formal independence.

Xi seemed to confirm this in his face-to-face meeting with US president Joe Biden in San Francisco in November 2023. According to a senior US official who briefed reporters after the summit, Xi said his "preference was for peaceful reunification but then moved immediately to conditions that the potential use of force could be utilized."[10] When Biden responded by "assuring Xi that Washington was determined to maintain peace in the region," Xi's response was blunt. Per the US official:

> President Xi responded: "Look, peace is . . . all well and good, but at some point we need to move toward resolution more generally."[11]

In other words, Xi appeared to elevate the goal of unification above the goal of peace. His tough signaling extended to China's official readout of the meeting, which quoted Xi as follows:

> The United States should embody its stance of not supporting "Taiwan independence" in concrete actions, stop arming Taiwan, and support China's peaceful reunification. China will eventually be reunified and will inevitably be reunified.[12]

That may have been the first time Xi publicly called for US "support" for unifying China and Taiwan. Such language marks a fundamental revision of Beijing's long-standing demand that Washington refrain from supporting Taiwan independence. Simply put, and contrary to the assumptions of many Western analysts, Xi's moves aren't aimed at maintaining the decades-old status quo in the Taiwan Strait but at ending it.

Xi knows this may require war. In key speeches over the past few years, he has admonished his party and its armed wing, the People's Liberation Army, to prepare for a major conflict.

"In the face of major risks and strong opponents, to always want to live in peace and never want struggle is unrealistic," Xi said in his November 2021 speech to the Sixth Plenum of the 19th Party Congress in Beijing.[13] "All kinds of hostile forces will absolutely never let us smoothly achieve the great rejuvenation of the Chinese nation. Based on this, I have repeatedly stressed to the entire Party that we must carry out a great struggle."[14]

In this seminal address, kept secret for two months before being published in a Chinese-language journal (where it was missed by Western journalists and many scholars), Xi praised then paramount leader Mao Zedong's decision to enter the Korean War in 1950. "Facing the threat and provocation of the United States," Mao and his comrades made the brave decision to go to war, Xi said. As he put it:

> The Party Central Committee and Comrade Mao Zedong, with the strategic foresight of "by starting with one punch, one hundred punches will be avoided," and the determination and bravery of "do not hesitate to ruin the country internally in order to build it anew," made the historical policy decision to "resist America and aid Korea" and protect the nation.[15]

The language shows Xi framing Mao's move as a preemptive attack to avoid what Xi called "the dangerous situation of 'invaders camping at the gates.'" Xi's choice of words was surely meant to signal his own preparedness to wage war under analogous circumstances

Xi Jinping gestures to his audience in Tiananmen Square during a July 2021 speech celebrating the one hundredth anniversary of the Chinese Communist Party. Xi vowed in his speech that any foreign forces trying to bully China would have their heads bashed bloody against a Great Wall of steel. *Ju Peng/Xinhua via Getty Images*

and, chillingly, his tolerance for risking national "ruin" as the price of victory over China's enemies. "No matter how strong the enemy is, how difficult the road, or how severe the challenge, the Party is always completely without fear, never retreats, does not fear sacrifice, and is undeterrable," he said.[16]

While the speech's description of the United States as an enemy was made in a historical context, Xi has more recently cast Washington as China's explicit, present-day adversary. "Western countries headed by the United States have implemented containment from all directions, encirclement and suppression against us, which has brought unprecedented severe challenges to our country's development," Xi said in a March 2023 address.[17] That address was one of four made by Xi that month in which he underscored the need to prepare for war.[18]

In the first of the addresses, to delegates of the National People's Congress on March 5, Xi said China must end its reliance on imports of grain and manufactured goods. "In case we're short of either, the international market will not protect us," Xi declared. In a speech the following day, he urged his listeners to "dare to fight, and be good at fighting."[19] On March 8, he unveiled to an audience of generals a National Defense Education campaign to unite society behind the military, invoking as inspiration the Double Support Movement, a 1943 campaign for society-wide militarization.[20] In the fourth speech, on March 13, Xi announced that the "unification of the motherland" was the "essence" of his great rejuvenation campaign—a formulation that exceeded even his previous statements calling unification a "requirement" for China's rejuvenation.[21]

In light of all this, the world should regard gravely Xi's exhortation, contained in his "work report" to the 20th Party Congress in October 2022, that the Chinese Communist Party must prepare to undergo "the stormy seas of a major test."

These statements, it is important to understand, weren't propaganda meant for Western ears. They were authoritative instructions delivered by Xi to the Chinese Communist Party. They are taken seriously by the country's governing apparatus. We should give them at least the same weight that analysts ascribe to leaked Oval Office conversations about war and peace.[22]

This book offers practical and feasible steps that democracies should pursue urgently to deter Xi from triggering a catastrophic war over Taiwan.

The book focuses mainly on the military dimension. This isn't because economic, financial, informational, and diplomatic tools are unimportant when trying to dissuade adversaries; it's because they have little chance of succeeding in the absence of credible hard power—the sine qua non for effective deterrence.[23]

The book singles out Xi Jinping personally as the object of deterrence and for good reason: After more than a decade of consolidation and centralization of power, no other decision maker counts nearly so much as Xi when it comes to questions of war and peace. His personal assumptions about China's chances in a conflict, and about the intentions and capabilities of Taiwan and the United States and its allies, are key variables informing his calculus on whether to wage war. As the Australian strategist Ross Babbage reminds us in chapter 12, "deterrence involves using one's actions to deliver the strongest possible psychological impact on the opposing decision-making elite so as to persuade them to desist, delay, or otherwise alter their operations to one's advantage." In today's China, the "decision-making elite" more or less boils down to one man.

The steps called for in this book are meant to be adopted *now*. The coauthors call for marshaling technologies and weapons systems that, for the most part, already exist in the arsenals of the United States and its partners or have been developed and tested and are eligible for production and procurement. The biggest challenges are

1. insufficient stockpiles of munitions, such as antiship missiles, and the means to produce more of them rapidly; and
2. insufficient planning, training, rehearsals, and coordination within and between the United States, Taiwan, and other threatened democracies.

The coauthors believe that if democracies rush to implement the recommendations in this book over the next twenty-four months, we will have a better shot at deterring a Taiwan war through the end of this decade, after which newer weapons systems may enter democratic arsenals that can, if we play our cards wisely, deepen the allied "offset" of China's growing military juggernaut.

If we do succeed at deterring Xi for the remainder of the 2020s, it will be thanks largely to "legacy" military systems—not futuristic programs that have yet to bear fruit. General Christopher G. Cavoli, America's senior military officer in Europe, said one of the lessons of the Ukraine war is that "kinetic effects are what determine results . . . and the majority of kinetic effects are from legacy systems. So don't 'sunset' legacy systems prematurely while awaiting the 'sunrise' of next-generation capabilities. Otherwise, we'll be left stranded at midnight."[24]

This means democracies must increase their defense spending sharply to keep key legacy systems working and to scale up the production of munitions while we research and develop new systems. The US military has a smaller active-duty force today than at any time since the early stages of World War II.[25] The US defense budget, adjusted for inflation, is shrinking at a time when wars are proliferating. As a percentage of GDP, US annual defense spending today (at 3.1 percent) is less than half what it was at the peak of the Reagan administration (6.8 percent), which presided over the most decisive decade of the Cold War without the need for a direct conflict with the Soviet Union.[26] These statistics suggest Washington is forgetting the hardest lessons of the twentieth century—the ones that were written in blood.

Bolstering deterrence in the face of China's *Wehrmacht* can appear daunting. Yet China's vulnerabilities are many. It may now have the world's largest navy, but its surface vessels (without which it cannot secure military control of Taiwan) would be ripe targets in a war—not only for American attack submarines, but for US heavy bombers that can reach the Western Pacific in hours and launch fusillades of anti-ship missiles from a relatively safe distance. (This is why, in chapter 7, we argue for the US Air Force to prepare for a more central role in a Taiwan contingency than its current priorities suggest.)

China may have a large arsenal of antiship ballistic missiles to keep US aircraft carriers at bay, but Washington has formidable allies in the region that could help thwart Beijing's war aims if they joined an effort to defend Taiwan. This is why we argue, in chapter 10, for Tokyo to publicly embrace the near inevitability that it would be compelled to fight in the event China attacks Taiwan. A clear statement of intentions by Japan now, in peacetime, would reduce the odds of a war by helping to dispel wishful thinking in Beijing that Tokyo would remain passive.

China may be physically close to Taiwan, but geography offers asymmetric advantages for the defender too. Taiwan's mountainous coastline, poor landing beaches, and urban sprawl present foreboding challenges for an invader. A favored metaphor in Taiwan is that it should adopt the strategy of a porcupine, making itself unappetizing or, if that fails, fatal to a hungry predator.

But the real blessing for Taiwan is the strait that separates it from China. The Han dynasty statesman Kuai Tong advised that even a powerful army should refrain from attacking well-defended border cities protected by "metal ramparts and boiling moats." Taiwan, the United States, and key US allies should embrace a "boiling moat strategy." The Chinese military's center of gravity in a Taiwan war would be its naval forces. The Taiwan Strait would be its graveyard. This book encapsulates that approach.

Some related themes run throughout this book.

1. The future of democracy, sovereignty, and prosperity in Taiwan matters for the future of democracy, sovereignty, and prosperity in Asia and beyond.

It is tempting to imagine that the ripple effects from Beijing subjugating Taiwan could be contained, especially if the island were coercively annexed without a wider and highly destructive war. After all, there were dire predictions in the 1960s and 1970s about what a US loss in Vietnam would spell for the future of Asia and for American power in the region—predictions that never came to pass. "Domino theory" didn't play out and communism didn't spread from Indochina. In the decades after Saigon fell in the spring of 1975, US economic and political influence actually *grew* in Asia, even as Washington's military footprint decreased in the region.

But this is the wrong analogy. A more apt precedent would be Imperial Japan's aggression and brief domination of the Asia-Pacific in the first half of the 1940s as Tokyo foisted its Greater East Asia Co-Prosperity Sphere upon hundreds of millions of unwilling subjects. Xi Jinping, in a landmark speech in Shanghai in 2014, even declared, "It is for the people of Asia to run the affairs of Asia, solve the problems of Asia, and uphold the security of Asia"—a formulation eerily similar to the "Asia for Asians" slogan Tokyo adopted in 1940 when it set out to impose its concept of a self-contained, regional economic and security bloc controlled by Japan.[27]

As Gabriel B. Collins, Andrew S. Erickson, and I argue in chapter 2, "Taiwan: The Stakes," the subjugation of the island nation by Beijing would have profound ramifications for geopolitics, trade, nuclear proliferation, and technology. Taipei's fall would represent much more than a mere Vietnam-style unification; it would herald the dawn of a new empire—one that would suit Beijing's brand of muscular authoritarianism and strongly disfavor the interests of the United States and its fellow democracies. The coercive annexation of Taiwan, even in the absence of an American intervention, would not alleviate Sino-American tensions but would supercharge them.

2. Long-term deterrence won't be achieved haphazardly as a by-product of other defense objectives; it will be achieved when it is the primary goal.

A long and sorry tradition of underestimating Beijing's capabilities and intentions is giving way to sober new analyses in Taipei, Tokyo, Canberra, and Honolulu, home to the US Indo-Pacific Command. In Washington, the bromide that "war isn't in Beijing's interest" is also finally, if slowly, beginning to subside.

Even so, the coauthors of this book—who hail from seven democracies and include former elected leaders, policymakers, flag officers, combat veterans, strategists, and scholars—are alarmed by what we see as deficient planning, training, equipping, and coordinating for a crisis over Taiwan. The often parochial and ill-coordinated defense budgets requested by allied military services and voted on by our legislatures leave the impression that deterrence is at best a secondary objective, something leaders evidently hope to achieve by accident or on the cheap. This thinking must change, and fast.

So must the absence of top civilian leaders from tabletop exercises and other rehearsals for war. The decisions that the president of the United States makes in the first few hours of a Taiwan war could be decisive, as Robert Haddick, Mark Montgomery, and Isaac "Ike" Harris argue in chapter 7. As commander in chief, the president, along with his top aides, should participate in exercises covering a wide range of scenarios to test the consequences of various decisions so the president can be confident and swift in wartime. The elected leaders of Taiwan, Japan, Australia, and other democracies should follow suit.

We believe that Xi Jinping, contrary to his declaration that the Chinese Communist Party is "undeterrable," can be persuaded that a decision to wage war over Taiwan would be a grave miscalculation. Xi has demonstrated an appetite for risk, but his record isn't that of a reckless gambler. Even so, we believe time is running short to halt—and hopefully reverse—the erosion of deterrence.

3. The United States and its allies must urgently expand their capacity for making munitions.

Taiwan and its partners must have enough munitions not only to deny Beijing a speedy victory but also to continue fighting in case Xi chooses to wage a protracted war. At present, democracies may lack sufficient munitions for *either* scenario. The preexistence of industrial capacity for making these weapons will be a crucial element of effective deterrence.

One silver lining is that in war, time tends to be a better friend to the defender than to the aggressor. "An offensive war requires above all a quick, irresistible decision," the Prussian strategist Carl von Clausewitz wrote in his classic *On War*. "Any kind of interruption, pause, or suspension of activity is inconsistent with the nature of offensive war." If Beijing stumbles in its initial onslaught, Taiwan will have a much better chance at winning a conflict. It would be a shame for Taiwan to make it that far only to fail in a follow-on, protracted phase of war because democracies didn't have the foresight to invest enough in military manufacturing.

Admiral Yoji Koda, author of chapter 11 and a former commander of the Japanese fleet, told me that Americans often consider the June 1942 Battle of Midway to be the decisive naval engagement of World War II. Japanese military historians don't all see it that way, he said. Rather, it was the months of sea battles that followed, many of them without names, during which the US armed forces decisively wore down the Imperial Japanese Navy thanks to superior production of ships, munitions, aircraft, and incremental technologies, such as those that gave the Americans an edge in nighttime combat. This "War of the Destroyers," as Koda calls it, was more costly to Japan than the Battle of Midway. The United States and Japan—now great allies—should be aiming together for a capacity to win wars, not just battles. The deterrence of Beijing depends on it.

4. A Nation's will to fight is the great "X factor" in war, and it can be strengthened by courageous leaders.

Ukrainians have demonstrated what a people can accomplish when they and their leaders embrace the will to fight. They repelled Russian armored columns in early 2022 that friends and enemies alike assumed would overrun Kyiv in a matter of days, and they have persevered in holding off their much larger foe for more than two years since then. But the will to fight is less tangible than bombers and antiship missiles, submarines and torpedoes, sea mines and combat drones. In advance of war, national will is hard to measure.

This book argues that Taiwan must adopt a new military culture. Although the United States can and should play a leading role assisting Taiwan with this cultural transition, the US military shouldn't be the model Taiwan aspires to. Taiwan would do better transplanting cultural elements from other nations that, like itself, face steep odds. Think Estonia, Finland, Ukraine, and Israel.

In June 2023, I accompanied Israeli retired military officers and national security officials to Taiwan for exchanges with senior military officers and civilian leaders. The Israelis described how young men and women in Israel participate in multiyear compulsory military service. They described a reserve force that is much smaller than Taiwan's but that serves as the mainstay of Israel's defense, with more frequent and realistic training than takes place in Taiwan's reserves. They described how military service is held in high esteem across Israeli society. Israel has, without any formal alliances, won every war it has fought since the 1940s, despite facing numerically superior and technologically sophisticated enemies.

Since the Hamas attacks of October 7, 2023, the benefits of Israel's warrior ethos have been on display again as Israelis have unified, despite bitter domestic political differences, to wage a war to destroy Hamas. The authors of chapter 4, including an Israeli combat veteran whose children are fighting today against Hamas and Hezbollah, argue for Taiwan to compensate for its lack of geographic depth by cultivating greater *social* depth—that is, a more strategic culture.

Taiwan's partners need to be clear-eyed, too, about what would be required of them to break a Chinese blockade or repel an invasion. What the American people must sacrifice to win a Taiwan war will be far greater than the indirect support they have, to date, provided to Ukraine. There is simply no realistic hope that Taiwan can hold out for long against China without America committing directly to the fight. If America's support for Ukraine today is analogous to its indirect support for the United Kingdom and other allies through its Lend-Lease program in 1941, US support for Taiwan amid a Chinese attack would be more akin to its direct participation in the 1950–53 Korean War.

This makes preventing war all the more desirable and important. Yet the 1930s-style isolationism that has infected pockets of the political discourse in America and Europe bodes ill for deterrence. The only antidote for isolationism—other than war—is morally courageous leadership. In this sense, it isn't only Taiwan that has some soul-searching to do. Fortunately, America can look to its own history to find inspirational episodes and archetypal leaders: the America of the early 1940s under Roosevelt; the America of the late 1940s under Truman; the America of the 1950s under Eisenhower; the America of the early 1960s under Kennedy; and the America of the 1980s under Reagan.

A closing word about deterrence in the context of multiple, simultaneous conflicts.

On October 19, 2023—at a moment when Israel was fighting on multiple fronts, US forces and Iranian proxies were exchanging fire in Syria and Iraq, Ukraine was approaching the two-year mark of its war for national survival, and North Korea was funneling arms and munitions into Putin's war machine—President Biden summarized the stakes in a sobering Oval Office address. "We're facing an inflection point in history—one of those moments where the decisions we make today are going to determine the future for decades to come," he said in his opening line.[28]

Biden made no mention of China in the speech. Yet Beijing serves as a propaganda engine for, and the primary economic and diplomatic sponsor of, the revanchist autocracies that Biden did single out in his address: Russia, Iran, and North Korea.

While Beijing often hides the extent of its support for Moscow, Tehran, and Pyongyang, the fig leaf is wearing thin. The aims and actions of these four regimes are increasingly interrelated, as exemplified by Xi's "no-limits" pact with Putin on the eve of Russia's 2022 reinvasion of Ukraine, and by Moscow's "trilateral" meeting with senior leaders from Iran and the terrorist group Hamas less than three weeks after the massacre of more than 1,200 Israelis on October 7, 2023.

Whether Xi is acting opportunistically or according to a grand design (or, more likely, both), it is clear he sees advantage in the compounding crises on multiple continents—crises that run the risk of exhausting the United States and its allies and setting the table for a possible move on Taiwan.

Indeed, Xi has made statements over the past few years that suggest he would agree with Biden that the world has reached a historic inflection point. The difference is that, from Xi's perspective, this is good news.

"Since the most recent period, the most important characteristic of the world is, in a word, 'chaos,' and this trend appears likely to continue," Xi told a seminar of high-level officials in January 2021.[29] Xi made clear that this was a useful development. "The times and trends are on our side," Xi continued. "Overall the opportunities outweigh the challenges."

Official texts make clear that this is a moment Xi has been long preparing for. A 2018 military textbook on Xi Jinping Thought, stamped "internal use only," states the following:

> The world is now undergoing a transition so massive that nothing like it has ever been seen before. At its core, this transition is being driven by the following changes: The United States is becoming weak. China is becoming strong. Russia is becoming aggressive. And Europe is becoming chaotic. . . . The Chinese

nation-state is rising and the Chinese ethnos is resurgent. This is an historic turning point.[30]

Xi has since cast himself not just as a beneficiary of the current situation but as an *architect*. In March 2023, more than a year into Russia's full-scale assault on Ukraine, Xi visited Moscow to strengthen his cooperation with Vladimir Putin. As he bade farewell to Putin at the Kremlin, Xi was captured on video telling his host: "Right now there are changes, the likes of which we haven't seen for 100 years, and we are the ones driving these changes together."[31]

Any realistic and effective strategy for deterring Beijing cannot be crafted in a silo, isolated from the conflicts in Europe and the Middle East. Because the crises are interrelated, so must be the responses to them. That deterrence failed in Ukraine and Israel means it stands a greater chance of failing in Taiwan. Some will argue that effective deterrence of Beijing must entail de-prioritizing US support for Ukraine or Israel or other partners. No doubt, prioritization (and de-prioritization) are the essence of strategy.[32] Given the stakes involved, along with the fact that US forces would have to intervene directly and fight to prevent Taiwan's defeat in a war, there should be little question that the preponderance of American military focus should be on acquiring the means to deter and, if necessary, defeat China in war.

But any strategy that underplays the conflicts in Europe and the Middle East risks inadvertently deepening those crises and inviting aggression elsewhere. That would leave us with more of the global "chaos" that Xi clearly values and would fuel perceptions of democratic weakness. It would be hard for even the most robust China-centric defense policy to remain credible under such conditions.

There is an opportunity now to thread this strategic needle. To the fortune of democracies everywhere, the people of Ukraine and Israel have demonstrated their will and ability to fight their wars without asking any third country to sacrifice their own troops. Robust support for them by fellow democracies, through financial assistance and the provision of weapons and ammunition, would seem both economical and prudent, particularly when contrasted with the far greater costs—in lives and treasure—that would be required if either of those nations fell.

By raising defense spending (calculated as a percentage of GDP) to the average levels of the Cold War, the United States, Europe, Japan, South Korea, Australia, and other allies can serve as a new Arsenal of Democracy, counterbalancing the arsenals of autocracy played by Iran, North Korea, and, above all, China. Using government spending to catalyze private industry in unorthodox ways could result in a rapid scaling up of munitions and armaments production, much as Washington's 2020 Operation Warp Speed collaboration with private companies produced hundreds of millions of COVID-19 vaccines in record time.

Such an undertaking would have the benefit of resupplying our partners for their defensive wars in Europe and the Middle East, while simultaneously creating the military stockpiles needed to deter Beijing. There is evidence already that US support for Ukraine has in some respects *improved* US procurement for a war with China, by forcing the Department of Defense to kick-start manufacturing lines and replace old munitions and equipment with new inventory.[33]

The clock is ticking. While diplomacy and public statements have an important place in a well-crafted policy of deterrence, unmistakable strength in the form of military hard power is the key to persuading China to refrain from setting off a geopolitical catastrophe over Taiwan. This is what kept the Cold War cold in the last century. This is what can keep Xi from rolling the iron dice of war in this one.

NOTES

1. Michael R. Gordon, Nancy A. Youssef, and Gordon Lubold, "Iranian-Backed Militias Mount New Wave of Attacks as U.S. Supports Israel," *Wall Street Journal*, updated October 24, 2023; Lara Seligman, "US Officials Frustrated by Biden Administration's Response to Attacks in the Red Sea," *Politico*, December 4, 2023; Lara Seligman, "Pentagon Chief Heads to Middle East as Attacks on US Forces Spike," *Politico*, December 13, 2023.
2. Alexandra Sharp, "Why Is Venezuela Threatening a Land-Grab War in Latin America?," *Foreign Policy*, December 7, 2023; Kejal Vyas, "Venezuela Ramps Up Threat to Annex Part of Guyana," *Wall Street Journal*, December 5, 2023;

Kiana Wilburg, Vivian Sequera, and Julia Symmes Cobb, "Guyana, Venezuela Agree to Not Use Force or Escalate Tensions in Esequibo Dispute," Reuters, December 14, 2023.

3. 凤凰卫视，"#委内瑞拉就与圭亚那领土争端举行公投#，委方：争议领土150年前被不当掠夺，" *Weibo*, December 3, 2023, https://archive.ph/Jw3e5; "美国介入？外媒：美军南方司令部将与圭亚那国防军举行联合空中军演，" *Global Times*, December 8, 2023, https://archive.ph/Vz02k; Ministry of Foreign Affairs, "2023年12月6日外交部发言人汪文斌主持例行记者会，" December 6, 2023, https://archive.ph/FLZAr; Ministry of Foreign Affairs, "2023年12月15日外交部发言人毛宁主持例行记者会，" December 15, 2023, https://archive.ph/kSZTt; Warren P. Strobel, Gordon Lubold, Vivian Salama, and Michael R. Gordon, "Beijing Plans a New Training Facility in Cuba, Raising Prospect of Chinese Troops on America's Doorstep," *Wall Street Journal*, updated June 20, 2023.

4. Jeff Mason, "White House Accuses North Korea of Providing Russia with Weapons," Reuters, October 13, 2023.

5. The Chinese phrase 中华民族 (*zhonghua minzu*), often translated as "Chinese nation," is central to modern Chinese nationalism, simultaneously connoting a national, ethnic, and racial community. The Chinese Communist Party uses the phrase to encompass people within China and people of Chinese descent worldwide. In his speeches, Xi distinguishes between the terms 民族 (*minzu*), or "nation," and 国家 (*guojia*), which means "state" or "nation-state."

6. At the 19th Party Congress, Xi said: "实现祖国完全统一，是实现中华民族伟大复兴的必然要求." Communist Party Members Network, "习近平：决胜全面建成小康社会 夺取新时代中国特色社会主义伟大胜利—在中国共产党第十九次全国代表大会上的报告，" October 18, 2017, http://archive.today/MGZKr.

7. "现场实录）习近平：在《告台湾同胞书》发表40周年纪念会上的讲话，" Xinhua News Agency, January 2, 2019, http://archive.today/fwH4r.

8. See "习近平在纪念辛亥革命110周年大会上的讲话（全文），" October 9, 2021, archived at http://archive.today/u0CxM.

9. "两岸长期存在的政治分歧问题终归要逐步解决，总不能将这些问题一代一代传下去，" 习近平：政治问题不能一代一代传下去，" *China News*, October 7, 2013, archived at http://archive.today/pVrSw.

10. Jeff Mason and Trevor Hunnicutt, "Xi Told Biden Taiwan Is Biggest, Most Dangerous Issue in Bilateral Ties," Reuters, November 15, 2023.

11. Mason and Hunnicutt, "Xi Told Biden."

12. Ministry of Foreign Affairs, "习近平同美国总统拜登举行中美元首会晤，" press release, November 16, 2023, https://archive.ph/OJ9JW.

13. Xi Jinping, "以史为鉴、开创未来　埋头苦干、勇毅前行，" *Qiushi*, January 1, 2022, https://archive.ph/3kxGX.

14. Xi, "以史为鉴."

15. Xi, "以史为鉴."

16. Xi, "以史为鉴."

17. John Pomfret and Matt Pottinger, "Xi Jinping Says He Is Preparing China for War," *Foreign Affairs*, March 29, 2023.

18. Pomfret and Pottinger, "Xi Jinping Says."

19. Pomfret and Pottinger, "Xi Jinping Says."

20. Pomfret and Pottinger, "Xi Jinping Says."

21. Pomfret and Pottinger, "Xi Jinping Says."

22. Matt Pottinger, Matthew Johnson, and David Feith, "Xi Jinping in His Own Words: What China's Leader Wants—and How to Stop Him from Getting It," *Foreign Affairs*, November 30, 2022.

23. For a useful and creative exploration of new financial tools the United States could develop to strengthen deterrence of Beijing, see Hugo Bromley and Eyck Freymann's forthcoming report "On Day 1: An Economic Contingency Plan for a Taiwan Crisis," expected from Hoover Institution Press in 2024.

24. General Christopher G. Cavoli, private presentation attended by author, May 2023. The quotation is used with permission of General Cavoli.

25. Leo Shane III, "Amid Recruiting Woes, Active Duty End Strength to Drop Again in 2024," *Military Times*, December 14, 2023.

26. The Center for Strategic and Budgetary Assessments (CSBA) puts Department of Defense spending in FY 1983–85 at 6.7 percent of GDP, and the Office of Management and Budget historical tables put FY 2022 defense and international spending at 3.4 percent of GDP. Katherine Blakely, "Defense Spending in Historical Context: A New Reagan-esque Buildup?," Center for Strategic and Budgetary Assessments, November 8, 2017; Office of Management and Budget, "Table 14.5—Total Government Expenditures by Major Category of Expenditure as Percentages of GDP: 1948–2022," Historical Tables, accessed December 22, 2023.

27. "Criticising 'Asia for Asians,' Jaishankar Says 'Narrow Asian Chauvinism' against Regional Interests," *The Wire*, August 30, 2022.

28. White House, "Remarks by President Biden on the United States' Response to Hamas's Terrorist Attacks Against Israel and Russia's Ongoing Brutal War Against Ukraine," press release, October 20, 2023.

29. Xi Jinping, "把握新发展阶段, 贯彻新发展理念, 构建新发展格局," *Qiushi*, April 30, 2021, https://archive.ph/negvH#selection-73.1-73.24.

30. Ren Tianyou and Zhao Zhouxian, eds., *Strategic Support for Achieving the Great Chinese Resurgence* (Beijing: National Defense University Press, 2018), 217. Originally cited, with a slightly different translation, in Ian Easton, *The Final Struggle: Inside China's Global Strategy* (Manchester, UK: Eastbridge Books, 2022), 115.

31. "China's Xi Tells Putin of 'Changes Not Seen for 100 Years," Al Jazeera, March 22, 2023.

32. For an exploration of strategic de-prioritization in statecraft, see A. Wess Mitchell, Jakub Grygiel, Elbridge A. Colby, and Matt Pottinger, *Getting Strategic Deprioritization Right*, prepared by the Marathon Initiative for the Office of Net Assessment, US Department of Defense, June 26, 2023.

33. Marc A. Thiessen, "Ukraine Aid's Best-Kept Secret: Most of the Money Stays in the U.S.A.," *Washington Post*, November 29, 2023.

CHAPTER 2

Taiwan: The Stakes

GABRIEL B. COLLINS, ANDREW S. ERICKSON, AND MATT POTTINGER

*The domination of Formosa by an unfriendly power
would be a disaster of utmost importance to the United States,
and I am convinced that time is of the essence.*

—DOUGLAS MACARTHUR, JUNE 14, 1950

Washington and its allies face many potential geopolitical disasters over the next decade, but nearly all pale in comparison to what would ensue if the People's Republic of China (PRC) coercively annexed Taiwan.

For such a small place, Taiwan carries outsized geostrategic, economic, and ideational importance. The ramifications of its subjugation by Beijing would be surprisingly far-reaching. Whether one cares about the future of democracy in Asia or prefers to ponder only the cold math of realpolitik, Taiwan's fate matters. Whether one's preferences on international trade are laissez-faire or protectionist, a PRC annexation of Taiwan would pose essential problems. Whether one believes that Taiwan's semiconductor fabs would be successfully resuscitated by Beijing after an invasion or kept idle by Western sanctions,

---

A version of this chapter also appeared in *Foreign Affairs*. See Andrew S. Erickson, Gabriel B. Collins, and Matt Pottinger, "The Taiwan Catastrophe: What America—and the World—Would Lose If China Took the Island," *Foreign Affairs*, February 16, 2024.

industrialized democracies would face severe economic predicaments. The coup de grâce would be a race among nations to develop new or expanded nuclear arsenals, resulting from the diminished credibility of America's "extended deterrence" guarantees.

On June 14, 1950, General Douglas MacArthur, supreme commander for the Allied powers in Japan, wrote a top secret memorandum to Washington arguing that it was a matter of "utmost importance" that Taiwan (then still referred to as Formosa) remain in the hands of a friendly, or at least neutral, government. That Communist insurgencies were seething in Southeast Asia and trouble was brewing on the Korean Peninsula only served to underscore the island's strategic significance. "Formosa in the hands of the Communists can be compared to an unsinkable aircraft carrier and submarine tender ideally located to accomplish Soviet offensive strategy and at the same time checkmate counteroffensive operations by United States Forces based on Okinawa and the Philippines," MacArthur wrote. He explained how Imperial Japan had used Taiwan as "a springboard for military aggression" beyond East Asia and warned that Communist forces could do the same. He also raised the ideological and "moral implications" if Taiwan fell into Beijing's hands, saying Taiwan's people should be offered "an opportunity to develop their own political future in an atmosphere unfettered by the dictates of a Communist police state." He even highlighted Taiwan's importance as a net exporter of food in postwar Asia and as a future "prosperous economic unit."[1]

Remarkably, the dynamics MacArthur highlighted in 1950 are still relevant today, some more than ever.

In the decades since MacArthur's memo, Taiwan's citizens have indeed seized the opportunity "to develop their own political future" by building a full-blown democracy off the coast of the PRC, which only raises the strategic stakes if such a government were snuffed out. The world is currently "mired in a deep, diffuse, and protracted democratic recession," argues the democracy scholar Larry Diamond. "If conquest looks inevitable or if Taiwan eventually falls, most regional states will opt to ride the wave of China's hegemonic ascent rather than be drowned by it," Diamond writes.[2] Beijing would have erased the world's first liberal democracy whose founders include many people of Chinese heritage—and, with it, living proof that there is a workable and appealing alternative to Beijing's totalitarian governance.

Taiwan's economic and technological heft today is likewise far greater than what MacArthur would have imagined three-quarters of a century ago. A PRC strengthened by the annexation of Taiwan would hold sway over global semiconductor manufacturing—the backbone of most strategic industries in the twenty-first century. If Taiwan's fabs remained intact and operational, Beijing would control virtually the entire world's supply of the most advanced semiconductors. If, on the other hand, Taiwan's fabs struggled to resume operations, the world would have to settle for inferior older-generation chips—of which the PRC is on course to become the largest producer. Beijing, whose explicit strategy is to acquire leverage over other nations through dominating high-tech supply chains, would impose adverse economic and trade realignments that would diminish American power and the industrial might of other industrialized democracies.[3]

Certainly, China's economy would suffer a major setback if Taiwan's high-end chips disappeared from the world market. But so would the economies of the rest of the industrialized world. Beijing's Marxist-Leninist rulers, who regard power as zero-sum, may consider this as a price worth paying—especially if China ultimately emerged as the world's leading producer of chips.

Moreover, from a geopolitical standpoint, the fall of Taiwan would rob US alliances of much of their credibility. America would be at risk of losing the forward military and commercial access that enable it to be a global power. PRC forces would stand ready to fill the vacuum. The ensuing proliferation of nuclear weapons among untrusting allies and adversaries alike could reap whirlwinds of instability.

Even if Beijing achieved Taiwan's involuntary subjugation through something less than a full-scale war, the ripple effects would be highly consequential.

Employing steps that fall below the threshold of sustained, high-intensity combat may be Beijing's best strategy because it leverages ambiguity, allows for face-saving retreats from ineffective actions under most circumstances short of Taiwan formally declaring de jure independence, and puts Taiwan, the United States, Japan, and others on the horns of a dilemma: either confront Beijing's actions and invite accusations of "destabilizing" behavior or remain passive as Beijing consolidates changes to the status quo that strengthen its hand vis-à-vis Taiwan. Such an approach would also allow Beijing to capture industrial and technological infrastructure intact.[4] Accordingly, Beijing is trying first to employ United Front tactics—including the use of what it calls the "three warfares": public opinion warfare, psychological warfare, and legal warfare—to undermine Taiwan's democracy and the public will to resist in pursuit of "peaceful reunification" and "winning without fighting."[5]

Whether through outright war or quasi war, PRC success in annexing Taiwan against the will of its people would disrupt and reconfigure the global order in ways unlike anything since World War II, making concrete the "changes unseen in a century" that PRC commander-in-chief-of-everything Xi Jinping keeps foreshadowing in his speeches. With Xi now in his early seventies and facing limited time to pursue his grand ambitions, the following consequences of PRC aggression against Taiwan merit urgent examination.[6]

Key Impact #1: Dark Clouds for Democracy in Asia and Beyond

In 1996, Taiwan citizens voted for the first time to directly elect their president. Four years later, they elected an opposition-party candidate as president, ending the Kuomintang's decades-old political monopoly over Taiwan. Democracy has since deepened its roots in ways that have allowed not only for an orderly transition of political power every four to eight years, but also for remarkable economic and social achievements.

- Taiwan enjoys freedom of speech and freedom of association and is ranked by the Economist Intelligence Unit as the world's eighth most "fully democratic" polity, ahead of every other country in Asia as well as the United Kingdom and the United States.

- Taiwan has one of the most economically equitable societies in the world, with a relatively low disparity in income distribution despite having among the highest median incomes. Taiwan's per capita GDP overtook Japan's in 2023.[7]
- Taiwan's gender equality is the sixth highest in the world, according to the United Nations Development Programme's Gender Inequality Index. Women account for more than 40 percent of Taiwan's legislators, the highest percentage in Asia and well ahead of the United States, where women account for 28 percent of members of the US Congress. And not only have Taiwanese twice elected a woman to the highest office in the land, but several of Taiwan's leading cities are led by female mayors. Taiwan's respect for the rights of indigenous and minority groups stands out too. In 2019, it became the first place in Asia to pass a same-sex marriage law.

Taiwan is a democratic standout in another important respect: its faith in democracy is growing at a time when some democracies are indulging in cynicism about self-government. A Taiwan Foundation for Democracy poll in 2022 found that three-quarters of Taiwanese respondents believe that although there are problems with democracy, it is still the best system.[8] And, in a refreshing contrast with the United States, the younger the demographic in Taiwan, the more prevalent the trust in democracy.[9]

It is difficult to overstate the significance of all this in the context of the politics just across the Taiwan Strait, where more than a billion people who share a linguistic and cultural heritage with so many Taiwanese nonetheless remain subject to autocratic—even totalitarian—rule. Millions of PRC citizens draw inspiration from the political model in Taiwan, which flips Chinese Communist Party tropes about political legitimacy on their head.

Whereas leaders in Beijing have long tried to caricature Taiwan as slavishly imitating Western forms of government, it is actually Beijing that plagiarized an early-twentieth-century European political model that Europe has long since rightly discarded. As a PRC street protester caught on video in late 2022 put it, after he and fellow protesters were accused of being manipulated by foreign forces: "Excuse me, but what 'foreign forces' are you referring to? Is it Marx and Engels? Is it Stalin? Is it Lenin?"[10]

The loss of Taiwan as a democratic alternative would end the experiment with popular, multiparty self-government by a predominantly ethnic Chinese society, with bad tidings for the possibility of democracy in the PRC and beyond.

Key Impact #2: PRC Achieves Hegemony Regionally—and Bids for It Globally

Would Beijing stop after annexing Taiwan? Vladimir Putin's war in Ukraine reminds us that revanchist powers aren't known for having small appetites. The PRC is actively challenging Japan's administrative control of the Senkaku (Diaoyu) Islands in the East China Sea as well as the territorial claims of five other governments in the South China Sea. Ominously, PRC maps and official propaganda question the legitimacy of Japanese sovereignty over the Ryukyu island chain—including Okinawa—and of Russia's control over parts of its far east.

The Ryukyu dynamics already bear watching. In 2013, soon after Xi came to power, a commentary in the authoritative *People's Daily* suggested that the Ryukyus "belonged neither to China nor Japan," sparking recriminations between Tokyo and Beijing.[11] One of the authors, Li Guoqiang, has since been installed by Xi to serve as deputy head of the Chinese Academy of History, which Xi visited in 2023.[12]

In March 2023, China's new ambassador to Japan met with the deputy governor of Okinawa and encouraged Okinawa's "independent diplomacy."[13] Then, in May 2023, the former deputy chief of the Joint Staff Department of the PLA, Admiral Sun Jianguo, told a delegation from Japan's Liberal Democratic Party: "I hope you consider that from the position of the Chinese government, Ryukyu was originally within the Chinese sphere. What would you think if I told you that it was to seek independence?"[14]

On June 4, 2023, *People's Daily* carried a front-page story on Xi visiting the National Archives of Publications and Culture to reflect on the "historical continuity" of China. According to the article, a curator pointed Xi to an ancient book, *Records of the Imperial Title-Conferring Envoys to Ryūkyū*, detailing a Ming dynasty (1368–1644) diplomatic mission. The curator told Xi that the ancient book plays "a politically important role" by showing that the Senkakus are part of Chinese territory.[15] On the same visit—in a scene reminiscent of Putin's inspections of historical maps and archives amid his invasion of Ukraine—Xi viewed a Qing dynasty map, *The Great Qing Dynasty's Complete Map of All Under Heaven*.[16] The map depicts the Ryukyus and Taiwan in a manner that could be interpreted to mean they were both parts of the Chinese empire.[17]

Japan would be in a far weaker position to defend its territory in the event Taiwan was controlled by Beijing. This is because Japan's defensive concept relies on its ability to hold at-risk PRC naval vessels and warplanes that venture near, through, and beyond what is informally known as the First Island Chain. For Japan's defensive posture to work, the full island chain, which includes the Japanese and Philippine archipelagoes as well as Taiwan at the center, must remain in the hands of friendly powers. If Taiwan became a PLA basing location—the "unsinkable aircraft carrier and submarine tender" that MacArthur warned of—Japan would become acutely insecure. PRC military doctrine stresses precisely this point, with a PLA Air Force textbook emphasizing:

> As soon as Taiwan is reunified with mainland China, Japan's maritime lines of communication will fall completely within the striking ranges of China's fighters and bombers. . . . Our analysis shows that, by using blockades . . . Japan's economic activity and war-making potential will be basically destroyed. . . . Blockades can cause sea shipments to decrease and can even create a famine within the Japanese islands.[18]

By establishing an indisputably dominant position in East Asia, Xi would be free to turn wholeheartedly to his bid for achieving PRC preeminence globally. The mighty military resources, planning, and

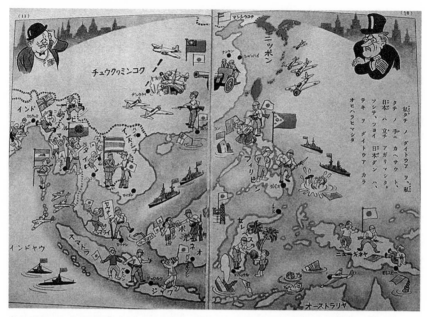

Japanese propaganda in the form of a 1943 map depicts Japanese forces "freeing" Asian nations from Western imperialism. Taiwan can be seen in the role MacArthur described in his cautionary memo years later as a "springboard" for aggressors. *CPA Media Pte Ltd/Alamy Stock Photo*

training that have long been almost single-mindedly concentrated on taking Taiwan could, following a successful invasion, be applied to projecting power throughout the Pacific, the Indian Ocean, and the Atlantic—where Beijing has already built, or apparently envisions, military bases in Argentina, West Africa, and even potentially Cuba. Beijing has already declared its goal of becoming a "world-class" military and to use its armed forces to defend its national interests wherever it asserts them around the world. And those interests are set to expand, as Beijing has recently unveiled a Global Security Initiative, a Global Development Initiative, and a Global Civilization Initiative—elements of a vision Xi calls "A Community of Common Destiny for Mankind."[19]

Herein lies a strategic danger that Franklin Delano Roosevelt warned about in 1939: "So soon as one nation dominates Europe, that nation will be able to turn to the world sphere."[20] East Asia is today the global center of economic and technological gravity that Europe was eighty-five years ago. Just as Europe has declined on the global economic stage, so America could decline in relative terms if its strategic interests were undermined by a hostile China. We contend that the Chinese capture of Taiwan poses a grave threat to America's strategic interests.

Key Impact #3: Greater Sway over Semiconductors and High Technology

Chips are today as important as oil was in the twentieth century. Approximately 600 billion dollars' worth of chips is now produced globally each year.[21] These are incorporated into physical items collectively worth multiple trillions of dollars, and the services delivered by these devices amount to tens of trillions of dollars annually.[22] Chips power smartphones, data centers, and high-performance computing applications like artificial intelligence (AI), as well as the electronic brains controlling systems in aircraft, cars, tools, machinery, and many other necessities.

Unlike oil, however, the very latest generation silicon chips (those with circuits 5 nanometers or smaller) are presently produced in only two places—Taiwan (by Taiwan Semiconductor Manufacturing Company Limited, or TSMC) and, to a much lesser extent, South Korea (by Samsung). Taiwan now accounts for more than half of global semiconductor foundry capacity and a much higher proportion—perhaps 90 percent of production—for the most advanced chips.[23] The aftermath of a coercive annexation of Taiwan would adversely impact Americans' security and well-being to a far greater degree than what would have happened had Operation Desert Storm failed in 1991 and Saddam Hussein retained control of Kuwait and with it greater influence over vital Persian Gulf energy resources—which then supported about 27 percent of total global oil production.[24] Taiwan's significance for semiconductor production, in short, is far greater than that of all members of the Organization of Petroleum Exporting Countries (OPEC) combined for oil.

If China captured Taiwan, it would command the dominant position regarding the most fundamental industrial input of the twenty-first century's technology economy. That could help to make the PRC much wealthier, provide it with consequential leverage over democracies that depend on its supplies, and catapult it into a position of global preeminence.

Much as cheap energy from Russia was a core catalyst for German economic power, abundant Taiwanese semiconductors have been a core catalyst for global technological progress.[25] Thanks largely to Taiwanese manufacturers' efficient scaling, transistors now cost only billionths of a cent apiece (or tens to hundreds of dollars for phenomenally powerful semiconductor chips). Yet unlike energy supplies, where a diversity of resources can substitute for one another to compensate for supply disruptions, no such fungibility exists for high-end semiconductors.

A major disruption of Taiwan-origin semiconductor supplies would likely decelerate human technological progress and cause an immediate global economic contraction followed by lower, slower growth for years thereafter. This is because chip production lines constructed elsewhere to replace damaged high-end chip facilities in Taiwan would take several years to bring into service, given the depth and complexity of multinational supply chains producing silicon wafers, chemicals like photoresists and exotic gases, and other critical inputs.[26] The length of time likely needed to reconstitute supply chains matters because chips are ubiquitous in everything from automobiles to high-performance computing facilities that power cutting-edge drug discovery and genomics research.[27]

Even if Taiwanese chip foundries were captured intact, they might struggle mightily to recover to prewar production levels. The disruptions to electricity, software updates, foreign equipment, maintenance, chemicals, and engineering—not to mention the likely flight overseas by many of Taiwan's most knowledgeable semiconductors experts—would have effects on Taiwan's fabs comparable to the effects of prolonged oxygen deprivation on a human brain. Many of these effects might be sustained for months or years through postwar sanctions regimes imposed by the world's democracies.[28]

The global economic convulsion that followed could well exceed that caused by the Great Recession of 2007–09 or the worst decline of economic output during the COVID pandemic's early phase in 2020. The Great Recession's cumulative losses ran as high as $22 trillion in the United States alone, according to estimates from the Government Accountability Office (GAO).[29] Some financial markets participants see a semiconductor disruption as causing still worse economic impacts. For instance, Citadel chief executive officer Kenneth Griffin stated at a November 2022 conference that he believed that "if we lose access to Taiwanese semiconductors, the hit to US GDP is probably in the order of magnitude of 5% to 10%. It's an immediate Great Depression."[30]

World War II caused the largest economic disruption for at least the past 120 years—imposing a peak global GDP loss of 6 percent between 1944 and 1945.[31] Yet America's economy increased in size by nearly 2.5 times between 1939 and 1945 as Americans rallied for war, mobilized industrial capacity idled by depression, and forged the Arsenal of Democracy.[32] This significantly decreased the economic downturn's severity on a net global basis. None of the positive prerequisites that existed in World War II, such as spare US industrial capacity, remain. A loss of Taiwanese semiconductors could thus realistically trigger an economic disruption reminiscent of World War II—with the downturn resounding potentially for several years, if not longer, as impacts compound upon each other.

Key Impact #4: Adverse Economic and Trade Realignments

More than a century ago, "the efficient functioning of the global trading system (and a high level of trade) was critical to the British Empire's prosperity and strength," the historian Nicholas Lambert observes.[33] While different in its domestic and international politics, in the present postimperial era the United States occupies an economic position that is analogous to the British Empire in its heyday. This helps explain why, despite periodic spasms of isolationism, US strategy on balance has recognized for decades that America's prosperity is tied to free and open access to the world and robust flows of trade. It is axiomatic that constrained access and exclusion of US exports would be disproportionately harmful to American power and position over time.

Reduced US trade flows with East Asia resulting from a post-Taiwan-invasion order would be especially impactful, given the region's current and future status as the largest, most dynamic global economic activity zone. East Asia and the Pacific account for one-third of global GDP in purchasing power parity terms, a share roughly twice that of the United States.

Curtailment of US access to economic opportunities in East Asia would be a very real prospect in the wake of a PRC coercive annexation of Taiwan. History shows a strong correlation between cementing hegemony and restricting rivals' economic prospects. In a 2018 *Foreign Affairs* article asking what "Life in China's Asia" might look like, the Dartmouth scholar Jennifer Lind points out, "Great powers typically dominate their regions in their quest for security. They develop and wield tremendous economic power. They build massive militaries, expel external rivals, and use regional institutions and cultural programs to entrench their influence."[34]

If, as described above, Japan would have a hard time defending itself after the fall of Taiwan, the situation facing the Philippines and other Southeast Asian nations would be even worse. PRC control of even part of the First Island Chain would put Beijing in a position to complicate US access to East Asia, Southeast Asia, and the Indian Ocean—the littoral of the most populous and economically active part of the world.

The United States could begin to resemble, in the words of the late Henry Kissinger, "an island off the coast of the world."[35]

A hegemonic PRC's intolerance of external rivals (among which the United States would be first) would probably drive economic and other coercion against Asian states that sought to continue robust trading and investment relationships with American entities. To that point, recent PRC behavior in the region is already consistent with an apparent effort to economically displace the United States. A well-placed Malaysian scholar recently noted that China is attempting to have Association of Southeast Asian Nations (ASEAN) states denominate more of their trade with other ASEAN states in yuan and that "this is being done to score points against the U.S., not to improve the way trade is conducted."[36]

Although ASEAN states would prefer not to be forced into a binary choice between the dollar and the renminbi, PRC actions and regional responses suggest Beijing would likely erase the prospects for a "middle course" in the wake of a successful coercive annexation of Taiwan and the presumptive diminishment of America's presence and role.

Key Impact #5: Nuclear Proliferation

The invariable lack of trust in US security commitments after an annexation of Taiwan would reinforce the incentives of key countries to develop their own nuclear weapons.

Multiple events tested the American nuclear umbrella during the past sixty years, including China's development of nuclear weapons; Washington's normalization of relations with Beijing beginning in 1972; the fall of Saigon and loss of the Vietnam War for the United States in 1975; President Jimmy Carter's 1976 campaign pledge to withdraw troops from the Korean Peninsula; and the acquisition of nuclear weapons by India, Pakistan, and North Korea. But American preeminence across the economic, technological, and military domains kept US power credible and conferred the leverage necessary to dissuade most East and Southeast Asian states from going nuclear, despite China and North Korea developing their own arsenals. Washington was able to offer the "carrot" of coverage by a first-class nuclear umbrella, while wielding the "stick" of economic, technological, and hard security exclusion against countries that insisted on pursuing nuclear weapons capability.

An East Asia reeling from the coerced annexation of Taiwan would present very different circumstances and might make nuclear weapons appear necessary to regional leaders. Japan would probably have the shortest path to developing nuclear weapons. It possesses a full onshore nuclear fuel cycle, including the world's third-largest commercial reprocessing plant, in Rokkasho.[37] Furthermore, it already possesses what is likely the world's largest plutonium stockpile (nearly forty-five tons at year-end 2021) with about nine tons of this held domestically under sovereign control. For perspective, one ton of plutonium could produce 162 "Fat Man" atomic bombs or 250 "pits" for a modern thermonuclear weapon.[38]

In February 2022, months before he was assassinated, former prime minister Shinzo Abe raised the idea of Japan engaging in "nuclear sharing" similar to the arrangements the United States has with Belgium, Germany, and the Netherlands, whereby nuclear weapons are stored in-country under US custody but are deliverable by nuclear-capable aircraft possessed by both the United States and the host country.[39] Abe also noted that had Ukraine retained nuclear weapons following the fall of the Soviet Union, Russia might have been deterred from invading.[40]

South Korea, meanwhile, has a world-class civilian nuclear program, with twenty-six reactors in service, but does not, for now, control the nuclear fuel cycle and lacks the domestic uranium enrichment or reprocessing ("plutonium recovery") facilities that would be required to build nuclear weapons.[41] Nevertheless, the question of whether to develop a nuclear arsenal is now openly debated by politicians in Seoul. If South Korea's world-class science complex and industrial base were mobilized under exigent strategic circumstances, it would be reasonable to assume Seoul could fashion deployable fission devices within a handful of years.[42]

One question is how China would respond to Japanese nuclearization. PRC leaders might conclude they need considerably more than the 1,500 warheads the 2022 and 2023 *China Military Power Reports* forecast China's nuclear arsenal will have by 2035.[43] That decision would have substantial ramifications for both American and Russian nuclear stockpile decisions. Recapitalization of the American stockpile would, in conjunction with a potential Sino-Japanese nuclear competition, raise at least two disturbing scenarios, neither of which existed during the Cold War. In the first, US planners would worry about Russia and China presenting a combined nuclear front against the United States and its allies. This concern was never realized during the Cold War because China pursued a minimum deterrence strategy with significant limitations regarding weapons technology, force structure, and posture and because of Sino-Soviet enmity.

India would also likely substantially expand its nuclear stockpile and deployment options. Warning signs already loom on the horizon. In December 2022, India tested an updated version of its *Agni-5* ballistic missile that allegedly now has a range of more than seven thousand kilometers—sufficient to reach all of China.[44] Geopolitical patterns persisting to the present suggest that Pakistan would likely seek parity if India expanded its nuclear warhead stockpile.[45]

Nuclear proliferation would also affect the Middle East. Iran continues to edge closer to breakout capability. Iranian acquisition of a nuclear weapon, in addition to inviting a preemptive attack by Israel, would probably induce Saudi Arabia to urgently acquire its own nuclear weapons, perhaps first through a stopgap sharing agreement with Pakistan and subsequently in-kingdom production drawing on foreign expertise. Riyadh has announced plans to build a substantial nuclear system with a full fuel cycle (including enrichment) that would use domestic uranium resources and thus be exempted from International Atomic Energy Agency (IAEA) safeguards.[46]

A baseline nuclear proliferation cascade following a PRC coerced annexation of Taiwan could potentially see hundreds of nuclear warheads added to stockpiles globally.

Conclusion

Taiwan is a beacon illuminating powerfully that Chinese heritage and culture is no barrier to democracy, rule of law, or freedom. Taiwan's wares underpin the modern economy worldwide. By helping Taiwan keep its flame of self-governance burning bright, we safeguard the world we want to inhabit for the next fifty years. Coercive annexation of Taiwan would not alleviate Sino-American tensions but rather would supercharge them. Should Taiwan be subjugated by the PRC because of US inaction or ineffective action, there will be serious global questioning of US claims about commitments to the security of allies and to defending democracy.

Accordingly, this chapter is a call to action to avert manifold disasters by spotlighting several of the most consequential. As the ongoing struggle intensifies, American policymakers must internalize the dire consequences of losing the pivotal techno-industrial, geostrategic, and political alternative and buffer that Taiwan represents to PRC coercive power. Isolationism shrouded in realpolitik may sound attractive from the back benches of legislative chambers, but it has repeatedly failed catastrophically, as in 1914 and 1941.

In addition to the severe economic and military consequences, a successful PRC coercive annexation of Taiwan would propel autocracy ahead in the global contest of systems, signaling a likely end to the US-led postwar order that underpinned so much improvement in the human condition over the past eighty years. An authoritarian, PRC-centric world would not only crush US foreign trade—it would also set the stage for future wars. It would limit India's development and crimp the future well-being of multiple middle powers, including key American allies and partners. Moreover, by strangling economic freedom, throttling freedom of action, and squandering untold resources and potential, the CCP's quest for domination abroad would substantially shrink prospects for China's own population. Enhancing American investment in deterrence—while simultaneously making clear to Beijing that Washington favors continuance of the peaceful status quo that most Taiwanese embrace—would signal three important things. One, our allies and partners are well placed in standing with Taipei and Washington. Two, we seek peace through strength. Three, for China and its people, today, tomorrow, and the next day are bad times to pursue war but good times to direct their energy toward peaceful endeavors. Taiwan is worth supporting and defending, the stakes are stark, and there's no time left to waste.

NOTES

1. Office of the Historian, "Memorandum of Conversation, by the Ambassador at Large (Jessup)," Subject: Korean Situation Foreign Relations of the United States, 1950, Korea, Volume VII (Washington, DC: US Department of State, June 25, 1950).

2. Larry Diamond, "All Democracy Is Global," *Foreign Affairs*, September 6, 2022.

3. Matt Pottinger, "Beijing Targets American Business," *Wall Street Journal*, March 26, 2021.

4. Bombardment risks hardening Taiwan's will to resist and would also likely simplify the US decision to intervene. Outright invasion would clarify the situation even further for Washington, Tokyo, Canberra, and other relevant regional capitals. Any scenario involving external military intervention on Taiwan's behalf would (1) stack the risk/reward ratio against Beijing by raising the risk that its invasion fails and (2) substantially increase the risk of a prolonged war between industrial powers that would unleash global economic devastation. See, for instance, David C. Gompert, Astrid Stuth Cevallos, and Cristina L. Garafola, *War with China: Thinking through the Unthinkable* (Santa Monica, CA: RAND Corporation, 2016). It would be far better for all concerned, however, if Washington and Taipei deterred any use of force in the first place through concerted preparations. See Andrew S. Erickson and Gabriel B. Collins, "Deterring (or Defeating) a PLA Invasion: Recommendations for Taipei," in *Chinese Amphibious Warfare: Prospects for a Cross-Strait Invasion*, ed. Andrew S. Erickson, Ryan D. Martinson, and Conor M. Kennedy (Newport, RI: Naval War College Press, forthcoming 2024).

5. For a hierarchy of CCP-preferred approaches applied directly to Taiwan, see the following article by Liu Jieyi, a prominent diplomat who served as director of the Taiwan Affairs Office of the State Council (2018–22) after serving as China's permanent representative to the United Nations (2013–17): 刘结 (Liu Jieyi), "坚持贯彻新时代党解决台湾问题的总体方略" (Adhere to the Party's Overall Strategy for Resolving the Taiwan Issue in the New Era), 求是 (Seeking Truth), *Qiushi*, December 1, 2022; Mark Stokes and Russell Hsiao, *The People's Liberation Army General Political Department: Political Warfare with Chinese Characteristics*, Project 2049 Institute (Arlington, VA), October 14, 2013.

6. Here the authors cite with appreciation and attempt to build on a pathbreaking special journal issue: David Santoro and Ralph Cossa, "The World after Taiwan's Fall," *Issues & Insights* 23, SR2, Pacific Forum (February 2023). See especially the lead article by Ian Easton, "If Taiwan Falls: Future Scenarios and Implications for the United States," 7–17.

7. Archyde.com, "Taiwan's Economic Success: A Deeper Look at the 2023 Per Capita GDP Ranking," December 23, 2023.

8. Olivia Yang, "2022 TFD Survey on Taiwanese View of Democratic Values and Governance," press release, Taiwan Foundation for Democracy, December 29, 2022.

9. Olivia Yang, "2021 TFD Survey on Taiwanese View of Democratic Values and Governance," press release, Taiwan Foundation for Democracy, December 29, 2021.

10. 鏡週刊, "男向白紙革命喊「反華勢力滲透」北京群眾怒轟: 外網都上不了哪來境外勢力? 月球嗎! | 鏡週刊," YouTube Video, 0:28, November 29, 2022, https://www.youtube.com/watch?v=UZGc9Zf6bII.

11. Wang Zhaokun, "Okinawa Discussion Aimed to Show Sovereignty over Diaoyu: Academics," *Global Times*, May 10, 2013.

12. 李国强, "中国历史研究院," archived June 21, 2023, https://web.archive.org/web/20230621003108/http://cah.cass.cn/zzjg/yld/201907/t20190723_4937729.shtml.

13. Ryukyu Shimpo, "沖縄県副知事が駐日中国大使と面談 デニー知事の中国訪問に協力要請 大使「地域の安定へ平和的な解決を」," March 31, 2023, https://archive.ph/aDCe4.

14. 市岡 豊大, "「沖縄が独立すると言ったら?」…中国軍元幹部が日本側に不穏当発言," *Sankei Shimbun*, May 27, 2023, https://www.sankei.com/article/20230527-DRDJOXQSLZLC3ODZ5C6F4LSA7E/photo/E3VAJJT3D5IC3AAWQBGIJL2HCI.

15. "习近平总书记考察中国国家版本馆和中国历史研究院并出席文化传承发展座谈会纪实," Xinhua News Agency, June 5, 2023, https://archive.ph/3yxsy.

16. "习近平出席文化传承发展座谈会并发表重要讲话," press release, 盘锦市住房公积金管理中心, Xinhua News Agency, June 8, 2023, https://archive.ph/RdeNU.

17. Harvard-Yenching Library, "皇朝一統與地全圖," accessed January 6, 2024, https://iiif.lib.harvard.edu/manifests/view/ids:53965145.

18. Yang Pushuang, ed., *The Japanese Air Self-Defense Force* (Beijing: Air Force Command College, 2013), 190–91; see also Ian Easton, *The Chinese Invasion Threat: Taiwan's Defense and American Strategy in Asia* (Manchester, UK: Camphor Press, 2017), 28.

19. "习近平新时代中国特色社会主义思想学习问答" (Questions and Answers on the Xi Jinping's Thought of Socialism with Chinese Characteristics in the New Era), The National People's Congress of the People's Republic of China, http://www.npc.gov.cn/npc/c1773/c2518/xjpxsdzgtsshzysxxxwd/index.html.

20. David M. Kennedy, *Freedom from Fear: The American People in Depression and War, 1929–1945* (New York: Oxford University Press, 2001), 421.

21. Robert Casanova, "Chip Sales Rise in 2022, Especially to Auto, Industrial, Consumer Markets," Semiconductor Industry Association, March 27, 2023.

22. Steve Blank, "The Semiconductor Ecosystem—Explained," Steve Blank (blog), January 25, 2022.

23. Tudor Cibean, "Taiwan Controls Almost Half of the Global Foundry Capacity, Other Governments Racing to Build More Fabs Locally," *TechSpot*, April 26, 2022.

24. Calculated using oil production data from *BP Statistical Review of World Energy 2022* (London: The Energy Institute, 2022).

25. When Russia withheld gas supplies, a regional and then globalized energy crisis promptly resulted. Gabriel Collins, Anna Mikulska, and Steven Miles, "Winning the Long War in Ukraine Requires Gas Geoeconomics," Research paper no. 08.25.22, Rice University's Baker Institute for Public Policy (Houston, TX), August 25, 2022; Gabriel Collins, Anna Mikulska, and Steven Miles, "Gas Geoeconomics Essential to Win the 'Long War' in Ukraine—and Asia," Baker Institute Research Presentation, September 2022.

26. Consider, for instance, the concern among semiconductor makers about shortages of neon gas resulting from Russia's assault on Ukraine. Vish Gain, "What a Neon Shortage in Ukraine Would Mean for the Chip Industry," *Silicon Republic*, March 15, 2022.

27. NVIDIA, "GTC 2023 Financial Analyst Q&A," March 21, 2023.

28. This assessment is derived from Matt Pottinger's conversations with Taiwanese and other semiconductor industry engineers and executives in 2022 and 2023.

29. US Government Accountability Office, *Financial Crisis Losses and Potential Impacts of the Dodd-Frank Act*, GAO-13-180, January 2013.

30. Steve Mollman, "Ken Griffin Warns U.S. Faces 'Immediate Great Depression' If China Seizes Taiwan's Semiconductor Industry," *Fortune*, November 18, 2022.

31. International Energy Agency, "Global Annual Change in Real Gross Domestic Product (GDP), 1900–2020," October 26, 2022. Note also that GDP's biggest fall—8.1 percent year-over-year (YoY)—occurred in 1946 as the war economy was wound down globally.

32. US Bureau of Economic Analysis, "Gross Domestic Product [GDPA]," retrieved from FRED, Federal Reserve Bank of St. Louis.

33. Nicholas Lambert, *Planning Armageddon: British Economic Warfare and the First World War* (Cambridge, MA: Harvard University Press, 2012), 23. Part of this efficiency was from British firms' position in directly handling and facilitating physical commerce flows via ownership and control of the world's largest merchant marine. But arguably even more important was London's role as the epicenter of shipping insurance and provider of deep, liquid, trusted capital markets that financed trade activity. The two roles proved mutually reinforcing.

34. Jennifer Lind, "Life in China's Asia," *Foreign Affairs* 97, no. 2 (March/April 2018): 71–82.

35. Henry Kissinger, conversation with Matt Pottinger, 2020.

36. "ASEAN Likely to Hedge Bets against De-Dollarisation Hysteria," *The Star* (Malaysia), May 21, 2023.

37. World Nuclear Association, "Processing of Used Nuclear Fuel," updated December 2020.

38. Atomic Heritage Foundation, "Little Boy and Fat Man," July 23, 2014; Arjun Makhijani, Howard Hu, and Katherine Yih, *Nuclear Wastelands: A Global*

Guide to Nuclear Weapons Production and Its Health and Environmental Effects (Takoma Park, MD: International Physicians for the Prevention of Nuclear War, Institute for Energy and Environmental Research, 1995), 58.

39. Jesse Johnson, "Japan Should Consider Hosting U.S. Nuclear Weapons, Abe Says," *Japan Times*, February 27, 2022.

40. Johnson, "Japan Should Consider."

41. World Nuclear Association, "Nuclear Power in South Korea," updated January 2024.

42. Elmer B. Staats, comptroller general of the United States, *Quick and Secret Construction of Plutonium Reprocessing Plants: A Way to Nuclear Weapons Proliferation?*, Report to Senator John Glenn, chairman, Senate Committee on Governmental Affairs: Energy, Nuclear Proliferation and Federal Services Subcommittee, END-78-104; B-151475, October 6, 1978; Rachel Oswald, "If It Wanted to, South Korea Could Build Its Own Bomb," *CQ Weekly*, April 11, 2018.

43. Office of the Secretary of Defense, *Military and Security Developments Involving the People's Republic of China 2022: Annual Report to Congress*, US Department of Defense, November 29, 2022, 98; Office of the Secretary of Defense, *Military and Security Developments Involving the People's Republic of China 2023: Annual Report to Congress*, US Department of Defense, October 19, 2023, 111.

44. "If India Wants, Agni Missiles Can Now Strike Targets beyond 7,000 kms," ANI News, December 17, 2022.

45. Hans Kristensen, Matt Korda, Eliana Johns, and Kate Kohn, "Status of World Nuclear Forces," Federation of American Scientists, March 31, 2023.

46. Ismaeel Naar, "Saudi Arabia Plans to Use Domestic Uranium for Entire Nuclear Fuel Cycle, Says Minister," *Gulf News*, January 11, 2023.

CHAPTER 3

The Myth of Accidental Wars

MATT POTTINGER AND MATTHEW TURPIN

*No wars are unintended or "accidental." What is
often unintended is the length and bloodiness of the war.
Defeat too is unintended.*

—GEOFFREY BLAINEY, *THE CAUSES OF WAR* (1988)

In this chapter, we challenge some myths about what causes wars, explore neglected variables that may be influencing Xi Jinping's calculus, and argue that some well-intentioned actions by Washington and its partners that are meant to avoid "provoking" Beijing into a war over Taiwan could, paradoxically, make Xi more optimistic about the utility and costs of war.

The Myth of Accidental Wars

"The only thing worse than a war is an unintentional war," Joe Biden told Xi more than a dozen years ago when they were both vice presidents.[1] Biden and members of his cabinet have repeated that phrase numerous times in recent years, including in the context of the Taiwan Strait, where US, Taiwanese, and Chinese warplanes and ships are coming into closer proximity to one another. "We've prioritized crisis communications and risk-reduction measures with Beijing" to help prevent an "unintended" conflict, Secretary of State Antony Blinken said in a major policy address about China in May 2022.[2]

Taking care to mitigate the risk of accidents is a reasonable aim. But a military mishap is a good example of something that might serve as a *pretext* for war but not a *cause*. "Wars have been called accidental or unintentional by many political scientists and a few historians," the Australian historian Geoffrey Blainey wrote in his seminal book *The Causes of War* after carefully examining the origins of nearly every war from the seventeenth through the twentieth centuries. "It is difficult however to find a war which on investigation fits this description."[3]

Western diplomats and journalists reflexively assume more hotlines and communication channels with Beijing are a key to preventing a mishap from spiraling into war. What they fail to recognize is that if war follows a military mishap, it wouldn't be because of a misunderstanding. Quite the opposite: it would be because Beijing has made a deliberate decision that the time is advantageous to fight a war it has spent decades equipping and rehearsing for. Leaders start wars when they believe war will pay strategic dividends that couldn't be obtained through peaceful means—not because their anger got the better of them on a particular afternoon or because they couldn't find a working phone number for the White House.

Consider previous military mishaps between the United States and China, such as when an American warplane mistakenly bombed China's embassy in Belgrade in 1999, or when a Chinese fighter pilot mistakenly steered his plane through the propellor of a US EP-3 spy plane in 2001. Those incidents resulted in fatalities and sharply increased bilateral tensions. But they produced no serious possibility of war. The exact same incidents, were they to occur today, would in and of themselves be equally unlikely to cause a war. But Beijing might be more inclined to use either incident as an elaborate excuse for a conflict if it had been aiming to launch one anyway.

Beijing understands this better than Washington does and uses Washington's misapprehension to its advantage. That may be why Chinese leaders, in contrast with American ones, rarely mention "accidental" or "unintentional" wars in their official statements, doctrine, and internal propaganda. The only examples we could find of commentators in the People's Republic of China (PRC) using the phrase "accidental war" were in articles pointing out that US leaders are pre-occupied with the concept. In their first call after Biden became president, Xi reportedly reintroduced the theme. "I remember during one of our conversations years ago, you told me your father once said, 'The only thing worse than conflict that one intends is a conflict one does not intend,'" Xi said, according to a recent book about the Biden presidency.[4] It is a reasonable bet Xi made the remark with a forked tongue, with the aim of stoking, rather than empathizing with, Biden's anxiety.

Moreover, it is conceivable that Washington's fixation on unintentional conflict and hotlines may have emboldened Beijing to undertake more aggressive behavior, such as increasing its tempo of dangerously close intercepts of US ships and planes in the South China Sea and the Taiwan Strait. In orchestrating these close encounters, Beijing enjoys a psychological advantage over Washington: it knows there is no such thing as an unintentional war. Thus, Beijing may have calculated that even a midair or at-sea collision with the US military carries limited downside risk and appreciable upside potential, since it might persuade Washington—ever fearful of that mythic accidental war—to reduce its military operations in the Western Pacific.

A clue that Beijing assigns low value to hotlines may be the fact that it has suspended military-to-military communication with the United States on several occasions since the turn of the century (Washington, by contrast, has initiated a brief suspension only once during that time, in 2021, as part of an unsuccessful attempt to establish a more senior-level Chinese counterpart for the US secretary of defense).[5] Beijing always restores military talks, typically in return for concessions from the United States, recycling what has become a form of manufactured leverage. If Washington adopted a similarly nonchalant attitude toward these communications channels, Beijing might be less inclined to suspend them in the first place.

An argument could be made that Taipei and Washington should be careful to avoid steps that would give Beijing even a pretext for starting a war. (Ivan Kanapathy explores this question in chapters 5 and 6 with respect to how Taipei should respond to Beijing's military activities near Taiwan.) But without a clear and common baseline understanding that accidents don't actually cause wars, Taipei and Washington are liable to be so tentative that they signal weakness or otherwise erode deterrence.

The "Provocation" Misconception

A close cousin of the accidental war fallacy is the widespread misconception that Taiwan might "provoke" a war by shoring up its national defenses. Beijing shrewdly weaponizes this misconception to dupe some politicians in Taipei, Tokyo, and Washington into second-guessing the wisdom of strengthening deterrence in the Taiwan Strait.

This playbook has been used before by Russia—and with catastrophic consequences. For years, the United States and its allies were too timid to provide defensive weapons to Ukraine, even after Russia first invaded the country in 2014. Washington eventually began providing such assistance in 2017. But it would periodically "freeze" weapons shipments to Ukraine, such as before a Biden-Putin summit in mid-2021, on the apparent assumption that withholding defensive articles might earn Putin's goodwill.[6] Judging by his full-on invasion of Ukraine in February 2022, Putin more likely viewed Washington's gestures as signs of weakness.

In a variation on this theme, autocrats in Beijing and Moscow also implicate the mere existence of alliances as "provocative." No doubt Moscow under Putin doesn't like the North Atlantic Treaty Organization (NATO) any more than his Soviet forebears did. He doesn't like the fact that NATO membership expanded to Russia's doorstep after the Cold War ended three decades ago either. But it would be a stretch to say that NATO, a defensive organization that has gone to war only once in its history (in response to the al-Qaeda terrorist attacks of September 11, 2001), provoked Russia to invade Ukraine. History suggests something more like the opposite: that NATO's existence helped maintain peace in Europe, exemplified by the fact that Russia has never attacked a NATO member since the alliance was founded in 1949. When Russia and Ukraine eventually transition from war to peace, key NATO countries will probably guarantee some form of security for Ukraine that ensures that the peace holds.

It is true that nations sometimes choose to go to war to prevent a rival from acquiring military capabilities that could pose a grave offensive threat over time. This dynamic fueled Israel's decision in 1981, and Washington's in 2003, to attack Iraq over its suspected development of nuclear weapons. But this is a less credible casus belli in cases where the aggressor already enjoys an overwhelming military advantage and faces little prospect of being threatened offensively by the country in question.

It is hard to conceive that Taiwan would choose to initiate a war with the PRC in coming decades. It is true that in the aftermath of the Chinese Civil War, Chiang Kai-shek and his followers dreamed of returning to the mainland from Taiwan and reversing the Communist victory of 1949. But today, Taiwan lacks anything like a capability to coerce, much less invade, the PRC. Its defense budget is about 10 percent that of China's publicly stated budget, a disparity comparable to that between Finland and Russia. Taiwan no longer harbors an ambition to build nuclear weapons. (Those dreams were definitively squelched decades ago by Washington, before Taiwan was a democracy.)

Granted, Beijing wants assurances from Taipei and Washington that Taiwan will not declare formal independence. But ever since Jimmy Carter and Deng Xiaoping established formal diplomatic relations in 1979, US policy has provided such assurances and balanced them with military deterrence of Beijing. As Xi's quotations in chapter 1 make clear, Beijing's goal—unlike Washington's and Taipei's—isn't to maintain the status quo in the Taiwan Strait but to change it. Secretary Blinken acknowledged as much at a speaking event at Stanford University in October 2022: "There has been a change in the approach from Beijing toward Taiwan in recent years," including "a fundamental decision that the status quo was no longer acceptable and that Beijing was determined to pursue reunification on a much faster timeline." This central fact must be kept front of mind in any serious policy discussion in or about Taiwan.

We must also acknowledge that Beijing's goals are bigger than annexing Taiwan. In much the way Putin has duped some Westerners into believing NATO's mere existence is an act of belligerence, Chinese officials are making a similar case today about US alliances in Asia.

American defense pacts have existed with Japan, South Korea, the Philippines, Thailand, and Australia dating back to the 1950s. It is a telling clue that Beijing is much more preoccupied with the "threat" posed by these treaties now, when China is strong, than it was in past decades when it was economically and militarily weak. This suggests Beijing views US alliances less as a threat to China's security than as an obstacle to its regional and global ambitions. Beijing's Global Security Initiative, launched in recent years, appears to be an effort to replace US alliances with a China-led security architecture for Asia.

As with Russia, Beijing's campaign to disintegrate US alliances appears to be in the service of building an empire.

The Myth of the Rogue General

Another variant of the "accidental war" shibboleth is the idea that rogue military leaders might initiate an external war for their own purposes, à la the character General Jack D. Ripper in the 1964 film *Dr. Strangelove*. Under this popular trope, warmongering military subordinates drag their countries into an overseas conflict against the wishes of their political leadership.

Blainey, in his investigation, found such cases to be rare as a cause of war during the last four centuries. It was true centuries ago that European empires granted generals and admirals a degree of independence in deciding whether to fight when they were far from their capitals.[7] But that was in the days before the telegraph, when communication between a monarch and his squadrons required weeks or months of transit time. A rare exception from the modern era that Blainey cites was the Imperial Japanese Army's decision in September 1931 to capture the city of Mukden (known today as Shenyang), followed by the rest of Manchuria, without receiving authorization from the government in Tokyo.[8] It was a rare case that, in any event, could hardly have been classified an "accidental" war, writes Blainey.

Could Chinese generals today go rogue and launch a war against Taiwan or Japan or the United States against Beijing's wishes? In the PRC, soldiers swear an oath not to a constitution but to the Chinese Communist Party, giving supreme leader Xi ultimate and unambiguous control of the gun. A ubiquitous new slogan chanted by Chinese soldiers goes as follows: "Obey Chairman Xi's commands, be responsible to Chairman Xi, and put Chairman Xi at ease."

Even during periods of domestic turmoil when PRC military chains of command broke down and some units fought one another inside China, such as during the Cultural Revolution (1966–76), the PRC's brief external conflicts (e.g., border clashes with India in 1967 and with the Soviet Union in 1969) were not the actions of rogue military commanders but campaigns authorized by Chairman Mao Zedong in Beijing.

In short, China has one of the most centralized systems of military command and control in the world—so much so that some foreign analysts view the lack of delegated authority as a liability for China during wartime. It seems improbable, then, that a Chinese general would go off the tracks and launch an external war. (Nor, we suspect, would he be likely to resist a command to fight if so ordered by Xi.)

Western statesmen should, in our view, worry less about potential mishaps or rogue soldiers and concentrate on addressing factors that might increase Xi Jinping's confidence that a war could be quick, relatively low cost, and victorious for Beijing.

Inflated Optimism: The Harbinger of War

World War I, because of its sheer scale and complex origins, is a favorite topic of study for scholars interested in war. Yet an easily overlooked fact about the Great War is that it was preceded by a high degree of *optimism* by so many of the main participants. True, there were some grim premonitions in the summer of 1914 that a collision between Europe's industrial giants would be highly destructive. It is also true that some leaders were influenced by their anxiety about longer-term national decline. But European leader after leader—regardless of what side he was on—expressed optimism that the war would be short and victorious for his respective side.[9]

"If the iron dice are now to be rolled, may God help us," said German imperial chancellor Theobald von Bethmann Hollweg on August 1, 1914, upon revealing to his federal council that Germany had sent its fateful ultimatum to Russia and France.[10] His use of the phrase "iron dice" signifies he was aware of the ever-present element of chance in war. But he also had conviction that the dice would roll in Germany's favor. He wasn't alone in his optimism. Some German military leaders estimated Germany would mostly or completely defeat France within four to six weeks and have enough forces left over to whip Russia too—regardless of whether Britain entered the war against Germany.

The short-war delusion was hardly unique to Germany. Most British ministers also expected a speedy outcome but with the roles of victors and losers reversed: they were optimistic that Germany would suffer a decisive defeat within months.[11] French leaders were confident that they had learned the lessons of the Franco-Prussian War of 1870–71 and that they could reverse the outcome with even faster mobilization and more élan in the attack. In Russia, the tsar was anxious about how a war might turn out, but his war minister, General Vladimir Soukhomlinov, publicly and privately conveyed his belief that Russia could trounce Germany within a few months. Most Russian ministers agreed.[12] There were recent precedents for short wars that fed the Europeans' prevailing sense of optimism, such as the six-month Franco-Prussian War.

But in 1914, the iron dice would roll quite differently than expected. The Great War would last more than four years and kill an estimated twenty million people, half of them civilians. Another twenty-one million would be wounded.[13] European leaders had entered the war with deliberate intention. As Blainey's research showed: World War I was no accident, only its consequences were.

Misplaced optimism of a quick and decisive victory precedes wars time and again throughout history. So confident in Russian military superiority was Vladimir Putin in February 2022 that he reportedly didn't inform many of his army commanders that they were being sent into war just days before the invasion began.[14] Russian battalions on Ukraine's border believed they were participating in a mere exercise and carried only a few days' rations.

 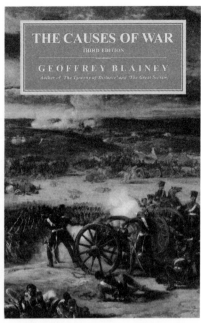

In *The Causes of War* (third edition, 1988), his pathbreaking study on what causes outbreaks of war and peace, Geoffrey Blainey found that overweening optimism is a recurring prelude to war—and that anything that dampens it is a cause of peace. *Photograph courtesy of the author; book cover courtesy of Simon & Schuster*

Autocracies and democracies alike are prone to such miscalculations. Estimations that "the troops will be home by Christmas" were indulged not only by German and other leaders in 1914, but also by American ones in Korea in 1950 and again in Afghanistan and Iraq in the early 2000s, as they calmly embarked on what would turn out to be multiyear conflicts.

Overweening optimism isn't merely an ironic footnote of history; *it is an indicator that war is near*—and a sign that deterrence is failing. "Why did nations turn so often to war in the belief that it was a sharp and quick instrument for shaping international affairs when again and again the instrument had proved to be blunt or unpredictable? This recurring optimism is a vital prelude to war," Blainey writes in *The Causes of War*. "Anything which increases that optimism is a cause of war. Anything which dampens that optimism is a cause of peace."[15]

Anger, of course, contributes to tensions in international affairs. Diplomatic slights, wounds to national pride, and other injuries can induce hostility or even hatred. But "rivalry and tension between countries can exist for generations without producing a war," Blainey observes.[16] It is optimism—specifically the optimism that important political objectives can be gained through war that cannot be gained through peace—that can actually result in a decision to wage war.

It should go without saying that public assessments by American military and intelligence officials that Beijing would *prefer* to achieve its goals peacefully should give us little comfort. In 1940, Adolf Hitler confidently made several peace overtures to London before having to fight the Battle of Britain. In 1941, Hitler also would have preferred it if Tokyo hadn't struck Pearl Harbor when it did. He made clear to adversaries and his inner circle alike that he would have preferred to attain many of his goals peacefully. But if warfare was needed, his goals were a higher priority than peace and, by his reckoning, worth the price of war.

This has been the case with democracies too. The United States has at numerous points in its history stated its preference for peaceful means to secure objectives that it nonetheless resorted to war to achieve. Xi's reported comment to Biden, while discussing Taiwan during their November 2023 summit in San Francisco, that "peace is . . . all well and good but at some point we need to move towards resolution more generally" carries similar overtones.[17]

Simply put, statements by or about Xi that he would prefer to annex Taiwan peacefully rather than through war should be regarded as rhetorical diet soda—cheap and calorie free.

Key Influences on a Decision for War

If Xi launches a war over Taiwan, it will be a consummate act of optimism on his part. To deter him, Taiwan and the United States and their friends should focus their efforts on eroding whichever of Xi's assumptions might contribute most to his sanguinity about war.

According to Blainey's study, national leaders, in deciding for war or peace, seemed to be strongly influenced by at least seven factors. We list those factors here and how they might impact Xi Jinping's calculus on whether to initiate a war.

1. Military Strength and the Ability to Apply That Strength Efficiently in the Likely Theater of War

This is probably a source of growing confidence for Xi Jinping. Beijing has been engaged in the most comprehensive peacetime military buildup of any nation since World War II, accumulating quantitative and qualitative advantages in traditional weapons like missiles, bombers, and warships, as well as advanced capabilities in space, electronic, information, and cyber warfare. Its nuclear weapons and missile expansion programs, despite reported setbacks, are growing so rapidly that China is expected to double its number of operational nuclear warheads to one thousand by the end of the decade.[18]

2. Predictions of How Outside Nations Will Behave If War Should Occur

The possibility that Washington enters a war over Taiwan is, in our view, Beijing's single greatest cause for hesitation. Beijing's main consideration in deciding whether to invade is probably its perception of (1) whether Washington would come to Taiwan's defense and (2) whether Washington could do so quickly enough to prevent Taiwan's fall. President Biden's public remarks—on four occasions—that the United States would defend Taiwan against a Chinese attack appear to be a calculated effort to strengthen deterrence. Future US presidents should at least match Biden's commitments or risk signaling a weakening in resolve to Beijing.

3. Perceptions of Whether There Is Internal Unity or Discord at Home and in the Lands of Their Enemies

Blainey's investigation shows that governments suffering from serious civil unrest preferred to avoid war if at all possible. Even for countries already at war, serious disunity at home was a powerful incentive to sue for peace. Think of Russia in 1905 and 1917, Germany in 1918, and the United States in the early 1970s. Even though China's economy is slowing, youth unemployment is high, Xi's handling of COVID was lackluster, and people are frustrated, there are few signs of the sort of social turmoil that make nations reluctant to pursue expeditionary wars. With the exception of a brief period in the fall of 2022, when street protests erupted in numerous Chinese cities against Xi Jinping's "zero-COVID" lockdowns, China appears to be socially stable. The United States, on the other hand, is facing its gravest political divisions since the Vietnam War and Watergate in the early 1970s. Leaders in Beijing are aware of these divisions (in fact, they expend significant resources to exacerbate them through disinformation operations on social media platforms). American disunity may encourage China's leaders to conclude that US politics are too fraught to forge a consensus to intervene in a Taiwan crisis. Beijing's activities to foment disunity within Taiwan, Japan, Australia, and Europe could similarly embolden Beijing and fuel its optimism about war.

4. Knowledge or Forgetfulness of the Realities and Sufferings of War

The Chinese People's Liberation Army hasn't seen significant combat since its costly punitive war against Vietnam in 1979. Contrary to conventional wisdom, this lack of recent combat experience could make a new generation of military officers more inclined to fight because they lack any visceral connection to the agony and unpredictability of war.

5. Nationalism and Ideology

Ideology in the era of Xi Jinping is laced with fatalism about the inevitability of struggle and confrontation. "Our struggle and contest with Western countries is irreconcilable, so it will inevitably be long, complicated, and sometimes even very sharp," Xi is quoted as saying in an internal military textbook.[19] Xi frequently states his confidence—overconfidence, we would argue—in the idea that Western democracies are in irrevocable decline. Xi, as mentioned in chapter 1, gave a major address in November 2021 in Beijing in which he said "no matter how strong the enemy is, how difficult the road, or how severe the challenge, the Party is always completely without fear, never retreats, does not fear sacrifice, and is undeterrable."[20] He also glorified a chilling quotation by the late chairman Mao Zedong: "Do not hesitate to ruin the country internally in order to build it anew." On the other hand, Xi's paragons—Mao and Stalin—weren't reckless in their use of military force during the Cold War. Stalin carefully read the odds and refrained from committing land troops to the war on the Korean Peninsula (1950–53). Mao sacrificed huge numbers of troops in that war after estimating (overoptimistically) that the United States could be pushed off the peninsula. But neither the Soviet nor Chinese communist parties directly fought the United States again for the duration of the Cold War.

6. The State of the Economy and Also Its Ability to Sustain the Kind of War Envisaged

China's economic dynamism is waning for reasons that are deeper than Xi's since-abandoned zero-COVID policy. Headwinds in the form of debt, unfavorable demographics, and a recentralization of economic decision making under Xi should, at first glance, auger stability in the Taiwan Strait over the long run. But first you have to make it to the long run. These economic headwinds could persuade Beijing to use its accumulated military advantages in the near term while it still enjoys them.[21] One of China's greatest advantages is its industrial capacity, which grew from half that of the United States at the turn of the century to twice America's just two decades later. China's shipbuilding capacity is more than two hundred times greater than that of the United States.[22] "Despite the economy, they are delivering significant warfighting capability," a senior US military officer told us in early 2024. The Ukraine war, meanwhile, has served to highlight the shortfalls in US weapons and munitions–manufacturing capacity.[23] Xi, as also mentioned in chapter 1, is also assembling the means to mobilize China for a major war.[24] Many of the steps his government is undertaking, including stockpiling food and other supplies and calling on individual families to do the same, might be a sign of preparation for a conflict.

7. The Personality and Experience of Those Who Shared in the Decision

Xi, who secured a third five-year term in power at the October 2022 Party Congress, is a paramount leader in the mold of Lenin, Stalin, and

Mao. He controls what he explicitly calls "the tools of dictatorship" to a degree his immediate predecessors rarely did. There is little question that Xi has the personal authority to decide whether and when to fight a war over Taiwan. But would he? Many of the seven factors discussed here lean unmistakably toward that possibility. But there are also important aspects of his personality that suggest he wouldn't wage war unless he was supremely confident of the outcome. For decades, Xi has shown he has a preternatural capability for strategic patience. He climbed the ladder of power carefully without revealing to his factional power brokers the extent of his political ambition and ruthlessness. Xi is someone who rarely makes U-turns (his COVID policy is the most notable exception). But he also proceeds cautiously—*zou yi bu, kan yi bu* (taking a step and observing before taking another step). He is a leader who has been careful to refrain from playing a card when he might lose, though he is willing to play one when he might not win. Xi's speeches consistently reveal that he relishes hardship and struggle in a ruling party that "forged vigor and qualities of not fearing strong enemies, daring to struggle, and daring to be victorious." But whereas Putin rolled the iron dice and may yet lose in Ukraine, Xi is probably weighing those dice more carefully.

Conclusion

One of Blainey's keenest insights in *The Causes of War* was that a true "balance of power" between rival nations is, contrary to the soothing image the phrase conjures, often a prelude to war. A lopsided balance of power, conversely, often promotes peace. In other words, it is when nations disagree about their relative power—something they're more likely to do when they are closely matched—that conflict often erupts, with war itself serving as the instrument of measurement for deciding which side really was more powerful. That peace has prevailed for so long in the Taiwan Strait owes much to the fact that China was militarily weak through the end of the twentieth century, while the United States enjoyed disproportionate strength in the Western Pacific.

Signs abound now that the People's Republic of China and the United States are more closely matched than ever before. Tabletop exercises that, fifteen years ago, produced overwhelming US victories over Chinese forces now display results that are more ambiguous. The path to shoring up deterrence in the Taiwan Strait, then, would be for the United States and its partners to *reclaim* decisive means to prevail in war, and to advertise those means to Beijing.

This is the recipe Washington employed to keep the peace during the Cold War. When the conventional forces of the Soviet Union achieved numerical superiority over NATO in the 1950s, Washington doubled down on its advantage in nuclear weapons to "offset" Soviet strength in Europe. In the 1970s, when Soviet nuclear capabilities achieved parity with the United States, Washington embarked on what became known as the "second offset strategy"—this time striving for dominance in conventional arms by leveraging superior technology. The capabilities that resulted—from precision-guided bombs and stealth aircraft to advanced sensors and "Star Wars" antiballistic-missile programs—gave the US military an unambiguous advantage over the Soviets despite NATO's numerical inferiority.

Geography affords Taiwan and its defenders an advantage that precludes the need to match the People's Liberation Army ship for ship, warplane for warplane, and rocket for rocket. Taiwan's relative lack of suitable landing beaches, its mountainous coastline, and the hundred-mile-wide Taiwan Strait (something Ukrainians can only envy) are favorable ingredients for cooking up another Cold War–style "offset." Provided that Taiwan and the United States—together with its allies—have the means to turn the Taiwan Strait into a "boiling moat," deterrence can prevail. The chapters that follow explain how.

NOTES

1. Chris Buckley and Steven Lee Myers, "'Starting a Fire': U.S. and China Enter Dangerous Territory over Taiwan," *New York Times*, updated November 10, 2021.
2. Antony J. Blinken, "The Administration's Approach to the People's Republic of China" (speech, Washington, DC, May 26, 2022), US Department of State.
3. Geoffrey Blainey, *The Causes of War*, 3rd ed. (New York: Free Press, 1988), 141.
4. Franklin Foer, *The Last Politician* (New York: Penguin Press, 2023), 72.

5. A former senior US Department of Defense official, private conversation with Matt Pottinger, January 2024. The US secretary of defense was—appropriately, in the view of the authors of this chapter—seeking to have as his formal counterpart one (or both) of the generals serving as vice chairmen of the CCP Central Military Commission. Those men, like the secretary of defense, report directly to the commander in chief in their respective systems, whereas the position of Chinese minister of defense is junior to those generals.

6. Betty Woodruff Swan and Paul McLeary, "White House Freezes Military Package That Includes Lethal Weapons," *Politico*, June 18, 2021.

7. Blainey, *Causes of War*, 143.

8. Blainey, *Causes of War*, 144.

9. Blainey, *Causes of War*, 35–51.

10. Karl Kautsky, ed., *Outbreak of the World War: German Documents Collected by Karl Kautsky* (New York: Oxford University Press, 1924), 439–41 (as cited by Blainey, *Causes of War*).

11. Blainey, *Causes of War*, 37.

12. Blainey, *Causes of War*, 37.

13. Nadège Mougel, "World War I Casualties," Centre Virtuel de la Connaissance sur l'Europe, REPERES Project, 2011.

14. Bill Bostock, "Kremlin Staff Didn't Expect Putin to Invade Ukraine and Were Shocked by the Severity of Western Sanctions, Report Says," *Business Insider*, March 4, 2022; Seth G. Jones, "Russia's Ill-Fated Invasion of Ukraine: Lessons in Modern Warfare," Center for International and Strategic Studies, June 1, 2022.

15. Blainey, *Causes of War*, 53.

16. Blainey, *Causes of War*, 291.

17. Jeff Mason and Trevor Hunnicutt, "Xi Told Biden Taiwan Is Biggest, Most Dangerous Issue in Bilateral Ties," Reuters, November 15, 2023.

18. Office of the Secretary of Defense, *Military and Security Developments Involving the People's Republic of China 2023: Annual Report to Congress*, US Department of Defense, October 19, 2023, viii.

19. See Ian Easton, *The Final Struggle: Inside China's Global Strategy* (Manchester, UK: Eastbridge Books, 2022).

20. Xi Jinping, "以史为鉴、开创未来　埋头苦干、勇毅前行," *Qiushi*, January 1, 2022, https://archive.ph/3kxGX.

21. Hal Brands and Michael Beckley, "The Coming War over Taiwan," *Wall Street Journal*, August 4, 2022.

22. Joseph Trevithick, "Alarming Navy Intel Slide Warns of China's 200 Times Greater Shipbuilding Capacity," *War Zone*, July 11, 2023.

23. Elbridge A. Colby and Alexander B. Gray, "America's Industrial Base Isn't Ready for War with China," *Wall Street Journal*, August 18, 2022.

24. John Pomfret and Matt Pottinger, "Xi Jinping Says He Is Preparing China for War," *Foreign Affairs*, March 29, 2023.

PART II
Taiwan's Job Now

CHAPTER 4

A New Military Culture for Taiwan

MICHAEL A. HUNZEKER, ENOCH WU, AND KOBI MAROM

Discipline is the soul of an army. It makes small numbers formidable; procures success to the weak, and esteem to all.

—GEORGE WASHINGTON

Although deterrence failed against Moscow and Hamas, Taipei and Washington still have time—though perhaps not much—to dissuade Beijing from "rolling the iron dice." This chapter addresses two important vulnerabilities in Taiwan's military culture that Taipei should address urgently: its lack of preparation for a *protracted* war and lack of readiness to *mobilize quickly*. (In different ways, this is also true of Taiwan's partners, the United States, Japan, and Australia, which will be discussed in subsequent chapters.)

Two years of full-scale war in Ukraine—and the eight years of low-intensity conflict that preceded it—underscore the potential for protraction. A fight for Taiwan may not be short. It could drag on for months or even years if it spills over to the wider region. Nor will Taiwan benefit from two factors that have helped keep Ukraine in the fight: strategic depth and a land border with a US ally across which Washington can surge weapons and material.

Meanwhile, Hamas's audacious assault on October 7, 2023, reminds us that Taiwan should maintain *the ability to mobilize rapidly*.

That Hamas's planning went undetected and its extensive preparations, even when visible, weren't well understood at the time proves that determined adversaries can still achieve the element of surprise, even in today's information-rich environment.

Deterring Beijing will ultimately require convincing Xi Jinping that he cannot achieve his military objectives with respect to Taiwan.[1] To this end, the more Xi thinks that Taiwan can and will resist an invasion for as long as it takes, the less likely that he will order an attack. The wars in Israel and Ukraine show us why Taiwan therefore needs a military—and a society—that is, as US officers like to say, "ready to fight tonight" and for as many days and nights as it takes thereafter.

Unfortunately, Taiwan's military is neither built nor acculturated for quick mobilization or prolonged struggle. Taiwanese military planners assume that they will be able to detect Beijing's invasion preparations weeks, if not months, in advance, providing time to arm and deploy units, scramble ships and jets, recall and train reservists, and pre-stage munitions.[2] Yet the reality is that if Beijing attacks, it seems highly unlikely that the People's Liberation Army (PLA) will allow Taiwan to mobilize unimpeded. At a minimum, Taiwan will have to deal with subterfuge, diversion, and disinformation. Realistically, Taiwan may have to mobilize its forces while under sustained cyber and missile attack. It is possible that Beijing will have infiltrated enough sleeper cells into Taiwan to knock out key symbols of national power, command-and-control nodes, and mobilization infrastructure. Thus, any realistic plan for mobilization should be designed (and rehearsed) for a worst-case scenario, not one that depends on Washington and Taipei accurately interpreting Xi's intentions ninety days in advance.

Taiwanese doctrine, training, equipment, and organization are all based on the notion that a cross-strait war will be short and decisive. Indeed, Taiwan's Ministry of National Defense (MND) downplays the risk of all-out war altogether, insisting that its posture, capabilities, and concepts should be optimized to counter China's "gray-zone" activities (discussed in chapter 6) instead of its most dangerous course of action: a large-scale invasion.[3]

To the degree that senior Taiwanese military officers and political officials contemplate full-scale war at all, such planning is based on the hope that a Chinese invasion fleet can be intercepted and destroyed before reaching Taiwan's shores. And while sinking China's fleet is indeed Taipei and Washington's best strategy (see chapters 5 and 7), we argue that training and equipping Taiwan's ground forces—and citizens—to resist Chinese incursions (such as fifth-column saboteurs, PLA paratroopers, and limited breakthroughs by Chinese amphibious assault forces) will put deterrence on an even stronger footing.

This chapter offers a set of practical and achievable steps to address these critical vulnerabilities. We call for cultivating a collective will to fight and acquiring the material, organizational, and doctrinal wherewithal to resist a Chinese military onslaught for as long as it takes. In essence, we advocate for using *social* depth to offset Taiwan's lack of geographic depth.

The chapter starts by reviewing Taiwan's long-standing approach to organizing and training its active, conscript, reserve, and civil defense forces, as well as the Tsai administration's reforms. It will discuss some lessons learned about rapid mobilization from the Israel Defense Forces (IDF), which has more experience quickly recalling and fielding a highly capable reserve force in wartime than any other military in the world. It concludes by addressing the impediments to defense reform and offering both an overarching blueprint for change and a set of practical policy recommendations for getting from here to there.

The Military Taiwan Has

Taiwan's military looks imposing, at least on paper. It consists of an all-volunteer, full-time (active) force augmented by short-service conscripts and a reserve force divided into an army, navy, air force, and marine corps.[4] Although the active force has an authorized end strength of 175,000 uniformed personnel, the MND has consistently struggled to reach this goal.[5] As of 2023, the active force had 169,000 service members, approximately 160,000 of whom were full-time volunteers and the remainder of whom were four-month conscripts.[6] The reserve force can, at least in theory, recall up to two million former troops.[7]

Although national service is mandated under Taiwan's constitution, most conscripts currently serve for just four months. Over the past two decades and across successive Democratic Progressive Party (DPP) and Kuomintang (KMT) administrations, the length of mandatory military service was reduced from over two years to its current length.[8] This requirement, as we discuss at length below, is once again shifting. Starting in January 2024, Taiwanese men born after January 1, 2005, can be called to serve for one year. The transition to yearlong conscription for a majority of young men should be complete by 2027.[9] It is also worth noting that as early as 2000, the government began to allow those potential conscripts to apply for substitute service by performing civilian tasks in lieu of military service.

The Taiwanese military likewise seems to boast a formidable arsenal of weaponry.[10] The army has 650 main battle tanks (to which it will soon add 108 modern US M1A2 Abrams), nearly 200 infantry fighting vehicles, 1,500 armored personnel carriers, nearly 100 attack helicopters, and at least 2,000 artillery pieces. The navy has 4 destroyers, 22 frigates, 44 patrol boats, 2 landing ships (with at least 3 new ones under contract), 44 landing craft, and 4 submarines (with 8 indigenously produced diesel submarines on the way). And the air force has nearly 500 combat aircraft. Taiwan's armed forces are also bristling with an ever-growing array of antiair, antiship, and long-range strike missiles.

In light of the foregoing, why should Washington worry about Taiwan's ability to defend itself against invasion? After all, China must project power across the Taiwan Strait to seize, subdue, and occupy Taiwan. Amphibious operations are extraordinarily complex to plan and execute under the best of circumstances, and the PLA might lack the amphibious shipping and combat experience to launch one.[11] Moreover, conquering Taiwan—whose main island is naturally defensible—would require the largest and most complex amphibious assault in history.[12]

It is nevertheless our considered view that if Beijing were to launch an all-out invasion tomorrow, Taiwan's military would struggle to hold out long enough for the United States and its allies to intervene with

TAIWAN STRAIT MILITARY BALANCE, GROUND FORCES

	CHINA		TAIWAN
	Total	Tawain Straight Area*	Total
Total Ground Force Personnel	1,050,000	420,000	89,000
Group Armies/Army Corps	13	5	3
Combined Arms Brigades	82	31 (6 Amphibious)	7
Artillery Brigades	15	5	3
Army Aviation Brigades	13	4	2
Air Assault Brigades	3	1	0
Airborne Brigades	7	7	0
Marine Brigades	8	5	2
Tanks	4,200	1,100	900
Artillery Pieces**	7,600	2,300	1,300

*For the purposes of this document, the "Taiwan Strait Area" includes the PLA's Eastern and Southern Theaters.
**For the purposes of this document, "Artillery Pieces" refers to systems 100mm and larger, are either towed or self-propelled, and includes Multiple Rocket Launchers (MRLs).

This chart compares the ground force personnel of China and Taiwan. *Office of the Secretary of Defense*, Military and Security Developments Involving the People's Republic of China 2023: Annual Report to Congress, *US Department of Defense, October 19, 2023, 185.*

decisive force. In particular, Taiwanese doctrine, training, equipment, stockpiles, and morale are not well suited for either a protracted struggle or a major attack that catches the island off guard.

First, Taiwan's recruiting and retention challenges mean that it does not have enough well-trained troops to wage a long fight. The sheer disparity between the Chinese and Taiwanese populations of course means that the PLA will always dwarf the Taiwanese military. Yet Taiwan has consistently struggled to get the most out of the human resources that it does have. Endemic recruiting shortfalls in the all-volunteer force played a major role in President Tsai Ing-wen's decision to extend conscription.[13]

The problem is particularly acute in frontline ground combat units. Some of these units are reportedly at 60 percent of their authorized end strength.[14] Longer terms of conscription could help address this gap—but only up to a point. As we discuss below, the existing plan for using conscripts entails training and equipping them to handle rear-area security and infrastructure protection missions, not frontline combat

roles. What is more, it will take three years before the one-year conscription scheme is fully up and running.[15] Even then, with some conscripts seeking waivers or pursuing "substitute service" in nonmilitary
roles, Taiwan's frontline combat units could still find themselves understaffed. And although these challenges are most pronounced in the
enlisted ranks, the MND also struggles to recruit officers. It has therefore also had to repeatedly lower the physical requirements and men-
tal standards for all three of its commissioning pathways: the service
academies, reserve officer training corps, and postgraduation direct-
commission programs.

Second, Taiwanese doctrine and equipment are predicated on two
potentially untenable assumptions. One, that the scale of Chinese
preparations for invasion will give ample advanced warning and therefore time for Taiwan to mobilize and posture its forces. And two, that
Taiwanese forces can go toe-to-toe with a Chinese invasion force in a
decisive fight for control over Taiwanese airspace, sea-lanes, and territory. Both assumptions are problematic. Analysts are also increasingly concerned that China will use large-scale exercises and gray-zone
activities to mask its preparations while lulling Taiwan into a false
sense of security. Moreover, as the cross-strait military balance tips
further and further in China's favor, the PLA will soon be in a position to overwhelm Taiwanese defenders both quantitatively and qualitatively.[16] Meanwhile, Taiwan has been slow to reorient its military
toward adopting the large numbers of small, mobile, lethal, and cheap
weapons discussed in chapter 5.

Third, Taiwanese military training is neither realistic nor rigorous.
Recruits spend more time listening to administrative briefs, practicing close order drill, and doing yard work than they do learning combat tactics, techniques, and procedures; first aid; logistics; and land
navigation.[17] Those responsible for leading individual and small-unit
training—noncommissioned officers (NCOs) and junior officers—are
themselves not well versed in modern training methods. Unit-level
field training among active-duty units is not much better. Exercises are
highly scripted.[18] Subordinates worry about passing "bad news" up the
chain of command. Senior officers micromanage, obsessing over tasks

that Western militaries let NCOs handle. Changing this top-heavy, highly centralized command culture will take time and dedicated effort.

Fourth, while Taiwan's reserve force will be critical to a prolonged defense of the country, few Taiwanese or American analysts think that the MND will be able to mobilize, train, and equip even a fraction of the country's eligible reservists in a crisis.[19] Indeed, only 300,000 or so of Taiwan's total pool of reservists are actually required to participate in refresher training under long-standing regulations.[20] Moreover, these reservists are obligated to do so for only five days *every other year*. And in practice most are recalled less often than that, since capacity limitations mean the military can train only around 110,000 reservists annually.[21] Worse yet, reservists waste most of this precious time attending PowerPoint briefings and filling out administrative paperwork.[22] Credible reports indicate that the army does not have enough rifles or gear to equip more than a fraction of its reservists.

Fifth, Taiwan lacks the military stockpiles it will need to wage a prolonged defense of its main island, much less outlying islands. Much attention has been paid to Taiwan's energy and food needs.[23] Yet the problem extends to the Taiwanese military. Even in peacetime Taiwan's military struggles to find parts for its many foreign-acquired weapons. As a result, less than half of the tanks, armored personnel carriers, and self-propelled artillery vehicles acquired from abroad are fully operational at any given point in time.[24] Shortages also plague Taiwan's fleet of aircraft. Less than half could be ready for immediate action in a war—a problem made worse by the heavy wear and tear caused by flying intercept missions in response to Chinese "gray-zone" provocations.[25] High-profile aviation mishaps have become increasingly common.[26] Alarmingly, the MND does not have nearly enough munitions for a high-intensity fight.[27] Such stockpiles will prove essential given that China will do everything it can to cut Taiwan off from the rest of the world in an invasion scenario. At least one open-source report suggests that Taiwan might have less than half of the munitions it will need for just two days of air combat.[28] Taiwan's ground forces may face similar shortages in terms of small arms, ammunition, individual weapons, helmets, and flak jackets.[29]

Finally, and perhaps most important, Taiwan's military has a morale problem—one that taints the way in which it is seen by society. Military service is not prestigious and does not confer the same social status in Taiwan that it does in other small nations facing difficult odds, such as Finland, Estonia, and Israel.

To understand why, it is important to remember the MND's origin as the armed forces of the nationalist government. Much in the same way that the PLA is a politicized military directly beholden to the Chinese Communist Party (CCP), for decades the Taiwanese military was under the command of, and served as the enforcement arm for, the authoritarian KMT regime. To many Taiwanese, Taiwan's MND has not modernized and fully nationalized to keep up with Taiwan's process of democratization. Taiwanese voters are also all too aware that not a single person in the entire active military has ever seen combat. It is therefore an untested organization that has not and never *had* to change. Meanwhile, high-profile hazing incidents have soured the military's image in the eyes of younger Taiwanese and the services are plagued by corruption and espionage cases. The cumulative result is a military sapped of self-confidence and estranged from the society it defends.

The aforementioned lack of rigor and realism in training could be making the morale problem worse. Many conscripts and reservists think of their service as a waste of time precisely because it is so lacking in substance. Such views may reflect—or drive—a broader skepticism about the degree to which Taiwan's military is ready to protect the island against invasion. Little wonder, then, that Taiwan is still struggling to meet its recruiting quotas even as a growing percentage of Taiwanese claim, paradoxically, that they would be willing to defend Taiwan in the event of war.

The Military Taiwan Wants

To be sure, Taiwan's political leaders know about these problems and have taken steps to address them. President Tsai unveiled the most important of such reform initiatives in a nationally televised address on December 27, 2022.[30] Her decision to extend conscription from four months to one year understandably dominated headlines. But her speech also laid out a blueprint for how Taiwan's military should reorganize itself to defend against an invasion.

President Tsai described a defense of Taiwan anchored on four mutually reinforcing elements: a main battle force, a standing garrison force, a civil defense system, and a reserve force. Serving as Taiwan's first line of defense, the main battle force will be responsible for conducting air, sea, and ground combat operations against an invading force. Because it will need to be highly motivated, well trained, well equipped, and ready to fight on short notice, President Tsai's plan is to organize the bulk of this 210,000-strong main battle force around Taiwan's 188,000 active-duty soldiers, sailors, air personnel, and marines, augmented by up to 22,000 conscripts.[31]

Meanwhile, the garrison force will handle the proverbial "home front" by protecting roads, bridges, intersections, hospitals, airfields, and other critical infrastructure; handling rear-area security tasks such as guarding command posts and resupply points; and coordinating local defensive actions against invading units that might infiltrate the front line. Historically, Taiwan's reserve forces handled these tasks. President Tsai, however, worried that reserve units might take too long to mobilize. She therefore shifted the garrison mission to the conscript force, since these troops will already be trained and on active duty.[32] Indeed, one of the reasons she extended conscription from four months to one year was to ensure that Taiwan's short-term conscripts are adequately prepared to handle this critical task.

The civil defense system will support both forces. Consisting of central and local government agencies augmented by alternative military service personnel and volunteers, civil defense units will help coordinate disaster relief, distribute essential supplies, relay critical information, oversee public safety, and conduct emergency repairs.[33]

Finally, President Tsai called for streamlining and repurposing Taiwan's massive but unwieldy reserve force.[34] Instead of mobilizing to field stand-alone units for frontline combat and garrison defense—for which there might not be enough time in an invasion scenario—reservists will now fall into one of two categories. Those with previous experience serving as full-time, active-duty service members (e.g., military retirees and those who separated from the military before qualifying for a pension) will be placed in reserve units that support and replenish the main battle force. Former conscripts, on the other hand, will be organized into units that feed into the garrison force. Here too, President Tsai said that a longer period of conscription will help reduce the amount of time it will take to prepare reservists designated to support the garrison force.

Whether President Tsai's successor, Lai Ching-te, will retain, alter, or discard this plan remains to be seen.[35]

President Tsai clearly recognized that these organizational changes were not, by themselves, sufficient. Openly acknowledging that "many citizens feel their time in the military was wasted," she sought to preempt concerns that yearlong conscription was simply going to triple the wastage by directing the National Security Council (NSC) and the MND to improve military training by studying and, where appropriate, emulating how the United States and other advanced militaries prepare for war.[36] She likewise called on the Taiwanese military to make sure conscripts and reservists spend more time handling advanced weapons (such as Javelin antitank missiles, Stinger antiair missiles, and drones), conducting live-fire exercises, practicing close combat skills, and working alongside other military and civil defense units. President Tsai also sought to reduce public skepticism—particularly among younger citizens impacted by the new mandatory service requirements—by signaling her commitment to improving morale and the quality of life among conscripts. Key changes along these lines included increasing conscript pay so that it at least comes close to minimum wage rates and ensuring that conscripts' time spent in uniform will "count" for retirement and pension purposes.

Nor should the reforms announced in December 2022 be taken in isolation. Two preceding changes to the reserve force helped set the stage. In May 2021, the Tsai administration created a new agency within the MND to coordinate reserve mobilization. Created by merging two existing, lower-level entities, the All-Out Defense Mobilization

Agency was tasked with improving reserve training, coordinating across relevant ministries (including those responsible for public health and safety), and coordinating combined exercises with US National Guard units. The Tsai administration elevated the All-Out Defense Mobilization Agency's stature within the Ministry of National Defense and increased the size of its full-time staff to 150.

The second significant change came in early 2022, when the MND unveiled a new pilot program for reserve training.[37] As highlighted above, Taiwanese reservists are typically recalled for five to seven days of training a maximum of four times over an eight-year period. Under the new system, reservists will participate in a fourteen-day training exercise, albeit only twice over an eight-year period. (As a practical matter, reservists therefore spend the same amount of time training under both schemes.) But whereas the existing annual weeklong training program mostly entails lectures and close order drill, the MND's goal is to make the fourteen-day training plan as rigorous and realistic as possible. Although the MND intends to assess this pilot program through at least 2025, the plan is to send fifteen thousand reservists a year through the fourteen-day training cycle, with priority going to reservists who have recently completed their mandatory service.

Building a Better Military

President Tsai's blueprint for defense reform is an improvement on the status quo. Even so, a military organized, trained, and equipped along these lines will, by itself, still struggle to deter—let alone defeat—a determined Chinese attack, because it does not address the fundamental challenges posed by strategic surprise and protraction. Nor are these ongoing reforms a silver bullet for solving the interconnected problems of institutional culture, public perception, and organizational morale.

To ensure that Taiwan's defense posture is built on the strongest foundation possible, we suggest that Taiwan's newly elected president, Lai Ching-te, reinforce these aforementioned military reforms in three ways.

Clean House within the MND

First, it is time to "clean house" within the MND. The main obstacles to meaningful and enduring change stem from bureaucratic resistance—not from ignorance of what needs to be done. Therefore, Taiwan's new administration should identify and promote officers—regardless of rank—who support change, are willing to explore and embrace new war-fighting concepts, and agree that national defense is a whole-of-society mission. In turn, this younger, more invigorated military leadership should prioritize or otherwise invest in professional military education as well as realistic and rigorous training methods based on the most relevant models around the world. Most challenging of all, these new military leaders must begin the painstaking, but urgent, work of building a culture of initiative, toughness, and risk acceptance at all levels of the Taiwanese military apparatus.

Look to Israel, not the United States, as the Archetype

Second, although the United States is and should continue to be the most important military training partner of Taiwan, the US military is not the best model for Taiwan. Small countries facing large foes, such as Ukraine, Estonia, Finland, Lithuania, and, perhaps most of all, Israel, are better archetypes. Taiwan should closely observe the defense concepts and cultures of these countries and rapidly adapt best practices for Taiwan.

Take Israel, which has less than half Taiwan's population and lacks the seas and mountains that protect Taiwan. Yet Israel has, by itself, won every war it has fought and—until Hamas's murderous rampage on October 7, 2023—deterred enemies from attempting an invasion for fifty years, despite facing numerically superior and technologically sophisticated foes such as Iran.

The secret ingredient that serves to catalyze all others into effective deterrence is culture.

In Israel, young men and women participate in compulsory military service—a minimum of thirty-two months for men and twenty-four months for women. They train frequently and realistically as reservists. After their active-duty service, Israelis tend to stick with, and train with, the same reserve units for many years, creating cohesive fighting teams that can mobilize quickly.

Military service is held in high esteem across Israeli society. Men and women compete to serve in the most elite units the way Americans compete to enter Ivy League schools. And soldiers acquire leadership and technical skills that enrich Israel's economy and prosperous technology sector.

Israel also maintains robust civil defense capabilities that offer a potential model for Taiwan.

We recommend that Taiwan bring over retired officers and noncommissioned officers from Israel (and perhaps from the other countries just mentioned) to engage in hands-on, long-term work to improve the organization and training of all components of Taiwan's national defense. While Israel may balk at official government exchanges given its diplomatic relations with Beijing, there is plenty that can be done in the unofficial domain. The readiness of Israel, or at least individual Israeli retired officers and defense specialists, to advise Taiwan in these ways has surely increased in light of Beijing's aggressively anti-Israeli diplomatic and propaganda posture in the wake of the Hamas terrorist attacks last October.

Establish a Territorial Defense Corps within the Ministry of the Interior

Third, Taiwan must make national defense a whole-of-society mission. This means that the MND should not be expected to shoulder the sole responsibility for Taiwan's security or receive by default most of the related budget and resources. To this end, the president should establish a local (or "territorial") defense corps within the Ministry of the Interior. While national service should continue to form the backbone of this scheme, military-aged Taiwanese citizens—regardless of gender—should have an alternative way to serve. Namely, they should be able to choose between serving as a one-year conscript in the Taiwanese army and joining a local defense force modeled on civil resistance schemes such as the Estonian Defense League. Thus, these units should be recruited from the communities in which they will train and, in the event of war, fight. Their volunteers should have access to well-stocked armories with sufficient numbers of modern weapons, ammunition, and protective gear. Local defense forces should also routinely work alongside emergency responders to be ready to respond to natural disasters, such as typhoons and earthquakes.

To be clear, although such local defense forces cannot defeat a large-scale invasion by themselves, they can make it much harder for China to achieve a quick, surprise victory by showing that the Taiwanese people have the ability to quickly resist and recover from acts of sabotage, subversion, assassination, and war. In a similar vein, a robust network of local defenses will help prepare Taiwan for prolonged conflict. Simply put, even if China manages to overwhelm Taiwan's frontline combat forces, it still needs to control the Taiwanese people. A well-organized, trained, and equipped local defense force makes doing so far harder. At best, the visible presence of such local forces in every Taiwanese community could help persuade Xi that an invasion will not succeed at a price he is willing to pay. At worst, if deterrence fails, a local defense force campaign can generate international sympathy for Taiwan's plight while buying time for the United States and its allies to respond in ways outlined in subsequent chapters of this book.

Most important of all, a robust local defense system will help convince the Taiwanese people that resistance is possible and that they have a meaningful role to play in—and a realistic way to provide for—their own defense.

Why bypass the MND by establishing this territorial defense corps within the Ministry of the Interior? One reason is that the MND has thus far resisted all attempts and recommendations to establish such a force—even those offered by Taiwan's former chief of the General Staff.[38] Another reason is that placing territorial defense under the Ministry of the Interior's aegis will allow the MND to focus its reform efforts on organizing, training, and equipping the main battle force to keep the enemy off Taiwan's beaches. As a matter of practical necessity, Taiwan's new president should allocate defense spending—and the transfer of weapons, gear, and equipment—between the MND and the Ministry of the Interior to ensure that this new territorial defense corps has what it needs to get up and running as quickly as possible. Taiwanese political leaders should be willing to let these two ministries compete with one another by investing in whichever one is most proactive about addressing Taiwan's defensive needs.[39]

To ensure that the Ministry of National Defense and the Ministry of the Interior are coordinating their efforts, the president should empower the secretary-general of the National Security Council to oversee, in close coordination with the premier, a whole-of-society national defense. At a minimum, this new local defense scheme will need enough initial funding to jump-start recruiting, organizing, equipping, and training. Thankfully, instead of needing to build such a force out of whole cloth, the Ministry of the Interior can build on—or even integrate—existing grassroots organizations such as the Forward Alliance.[40]

Obstacles and the Way Forward

Change is hard.[41] While Taiwan is already taking important steps in the right direction, we are hopeful that President Lai will consider some of the ideas we offer above. If he does, he will invariably run into a number of obstacles. We conclude by suggesting solutions to three of the most significant ones.

Critics will point to material constraints as a reason to settle for Taiwan's suboptimal readiness for war. No question about it: training space is limited. So, too, are critical facilities such as barracks, ammunition supply points, armories, and firing ranges. Munitions, parts, weapons, and protective gear to equip its entire active-duty force, let alone anything more than a fraction of its reservists, are also in short supply. Acquiring more training space, building more military infrastructure, and buying more essential gear should therefore be among a new administration's most urgent priorities.

Critics will also argue that budgetary realities will impede the pursuit of these essential items (a point we address below). Yet the fact is that Taiwan and the MND continue to spend Taiwan's scarce defense dollars on flashy and expensive weapons platforms that are unlikely to survive a surprise attack or a protracted war.[42] Diverting funds from costly, doctrinally unsound programs like the indigenous diesel submarine and Yushan-class amphibious assault ship would free up resources to build, buy, and stockpile lower-cost, highly lethal things that will allow Taiwan to fight tonight—and for as long as it takes thereafter.

Of course, pursuing the types of reforms we suggest above will require more money than cutting a few big-ticket items will save. The hard political fact is that while the Tsai administration did an admirable job of increasing defense-spending levels from US$11 billion in 2018 to US$19 billion in 2023 (special defense budgets included), Taiwan will need to spend even more to get its defenses where they need to be. That Taiwan already spends 22 percent of its national budget on defense means its elected leaders must be prepared to make difficult changes to existing fiscal and tax policies.[43]

Increased reliance on conscripts should help reduce some of the costs associated with fielding a larger and more capable ground defense, especially since a plurality of Taiwan's defense budget goes to cover personnel costs and benefits (both of which have gone up significantly in recent years in an attempt to attract more recruits). Nevertheless, President Lai will need to explain to Taiwanese voters why taxes must go up and/or why social welfare spending must go down. Although such moves are a hard sell in any democracy, we think the Taiwanese people will be far more amenable to such sacrifices if they can see that their tax dollars are being spent in ways that tangibly and meaningfully improve their nation's defenses while also reducing the risk of an even costlier war.

This is yet another benefit of creating a local defense force. By training in the communities they will defend, they will stand as tangible proof that Taiwan can protect itself and that taxpayer money is being put to use in ways that can help Taiwan in times of war and peace. Moreover, depending on how a local defense corps is ultimately structured, they could meaningfully enhance Taiwanese defenses for pennies on the proverbial dollar. This has been the experience of the Estonian Defense League. With sixteen thousand members, it is larger than Estonia's entire active-duty military. Yet because every member is an unpaid volunteer, the Estonian government has to spend money only on training and gear.[44]

But to reiterate: the single biggest obstacle to rapid transformation emanates from within the MND itself. Under President Tsai, the MND resisted, slow-rolled, or watered down virtually every meaningful reform initiative.[45] True, this problem is not unique to Taiwan. Military bureaucracies are notoriously resistant to change.[46] Ukraine had to clean house within the ranks of its own military after 2014.[47] Senior US officers, as discussed elsewhere in this book, have declined to manufacture precisely the antiship munitions needed to deter or defeat a PLA invasion of Taiwan. But the fact remains that any path toward meaningful defense reform will need to deal with the MND's entrenched bureaucratic interests and its institutional culture.

If Taiwan's new president is serious about deterring a catastrophic war, he will have no choice but to expend significant political capital to make the necessary changes, up to and including relieving any senior general or admiral who inhibits reform. Washington can and should help. And not simply by deploying a few dozen mobile teams prepared to conduct only small-unit training. Transformation, as we highlighted above, must be holistic.[48] Washington should be prepared to support top-down, bottom-up, and inside-out reform through bilateral training in both Taiwan and the United States. Washington should also facilitate robust interaction between Taiwan's military (and, hopefully, its local defense corps) and Ukrainian, Estonian, and Israeli training teams. Perhaps most important of all, Congress and the US president should be willing to play the "bad guy" by insisting on reform, even if it requires imposing clear conditions on Taipei. Doing so could prove invaluable in terms of letting Taiwan's next president honestly claim that his hands are tied.

Regardless of how Lai Ching-te decides to pursue change, national defense reform must be his top priority. He must build a culture that will strengthen deterrence and ensure that Taiwan remains a guardian, rather than a victim, at the frontier of liberty and democracy. Simply put, Taiwan is not ready to go to war with the army it has. And it may have only limited time to build the army it needs.

NOTES

1. Scholars refer to this as deterrence by denial. See Glenn H. Snyder, "Deterrence and Power," *Journal of Conflict Resolution* 4, no. 2 (June 1960): 163. See also chapters 6, 7, and 12 of this book. To be sure, some analysts and officials want Taiwan to pursue deterrence by punishment—to threaten to inflict intolerable pain on the Chinese mainland in retaliation for an attack. But in our estimation, short of acquiring nuclear weapons, there is no realistic way Taiwan can amass sufficient conventional firepower to credibly exceed Xi's pain threshold, especially if he is already willing to stomach a war with the United States.

2. Ian Easton, *The Chinese Invasion Threat: Taiwan's Defense and American Strategy in Asia* (Arlington, VA: Project 2049 Institute, 2017), 67–93; John Culver, "How We Would Know When China Is Preparing to Invade Taiwan," *Commentary*, Carnegie Endowment for International Peace, October 3, 2022.

3. Ministry of National Defense, *ROC National Defense Report 2023*, 26–59. See also Ethan Kessler, *Taiwan's Security Future: How Domestic Politics Impact Taipei's Defense* (Chicago, IL: Chicago Council on Global Affairs, 2023), 5.

4. Taiwan also has a volunteer civil defense organization made up of approximately 420,000 part-time volunteers. Although we discuss this organization in more detail below, it is worth highlighting at the outset that there are serious questions about how many of these volunteers are actually trained, able, and willing to support civil defense operations in a conflict. Focus Taiwan, "Civil Defense Reforms Needed to Meet Taiwan's Defense Goals: Experts," CNA English News, January 24, 2023.

5. The Ministry of National Defense is supported by an additional twenty-seven thousand civilian employees.

6. Ninety-four thousand of these service members are in the army, forty thousand are in the navy, thirty thousand are in the air force, and ten thousand are in the marine corps.

7. The reserve force consists of service members who have completed their voluntary or mandatory military services, provided they have not aged out (at thirty-six years old for most conscripts and fifty years old for noncommissioned officers).

8. Focus Taiwan, "Military to Present Report This Year on Extending Military Service," CNA English News, March 23, 2022.

9. Focus Taiwan, "Taiwan's Military Says Capacity Sufficient to Train One-Year Conscripts," CNA English News, January 5, 2023.

10. The figures that follow are from *The Military Balance 2023: The Annual Assessment of Global Military Capabilities and Defence Economics* (London, UK: International Institute for Strategic Studies, 2023), 291–93.

11. Office of the Secretary of Defense, *Military and Security Developments Involving the People's Republic of China 2020: Annual Report to Congress*, US Department of Defense, September 9, 2020, 114; US-China Economic and Security Review Commission (USCC), *2020 Annual Report to Congress of the US-China Economic and Security Review Commission*, "Chapter 4. Taiwan," December 2020.

12. Mike Pietrucha, "Amateur Hour Part I: The Chinese Invasion of Taiwan," *War on the Rocks*, May 18, 2022; Tanner Greer, "Why I Fear for Taiwan," *Scholars Stage* (blog), September 11, 2020.

13. As of 2018, Taiwan's armed forces were at 80 percent of their authorized end-strength of 188,000 active-duty billets. Paul Huang, "Taiwan's Military Is a Hollow Shell," *Foreign Policy*, February 15, 2020; President Tsai was in office as this book was going to press. Elections in Taiwan in early 2024 indicated Lai Ching-te of the Democratic Progressive Party as her successor, with an inauguration date of May 20. Tsai was ineligible to seek reelection because of term limits.

14. Huang, "Taiwan's Military Is a Hollow Shell."

15. For example, only 9,100 Taiwanese men will be inducted for one-year service in 2024. That number will not hit the expected maximum of 53,600 per year until 2029. "MND Shares 2029 Conscript Target," *Taipei Times*, March 6, 2023.

16. Michael A. Hunzeker and Alexander Lanoszka, *A Question of Time: Enhancing Taiwan's Conventional Deterrence Posture* (Arlington, VA: Center for Security Policy Studies, 2018), 20.

17. Greer, "Why I Fear for Taiwan"; Panel, "Is Taiwan Ready for War? Views from Taipei, Beijing, and Washington," George Mason University, YouTube video, October 11, 2022, https://www.youtube.com/watch?v=2b05yO7EfWM; off-the-record interviews conducted by the authors with Taiwanese military officers and policymakers in February 2019 and February 2021.

18. This and what follows are from off-the-record interviews conducted by the authors with Taiwanese and American military officers, elected officials, think tank scholars, policymakers, and diplomats in February 2019, January 2021, February 2021, and June 2023.

19. Michael Mazza, "Time to Harden the Last Line of Defense: Taiwan's Reserve Force," *Global Taiwan Brief* 5, no. 8 (April 22, 2020).

20. Mike Stokes, Yang kuang-shu, and Eric Lee, *Preparing for the Nightmare: Readiness and Ad Hoc Coalition Operations in the Taiwan Strait* (Arlington, VA: Project 49 Institute, 2020), 22.

21. "Military Mulls Requiring Female Veterans to Join Reservist Training," *Taiwan Newswire*, March 8, 2022.

22. Wendell Minnick, "How to Save Taiwan from Itself," *National Interest*, March 19, 2019.

23. "Taiwan to Boost Energy Inventories Amid China Threat," Reuters, October 23, 2022; Gustavo F. Ferreira and Jamie A. Critelli, "Taiwan's Food Resiliency—or Not—in a Conflict with China," *US Army War College Quarterly: Parameters* 53, no. 2 (Summer 2023): 39–60; Jude Blanchette and Bonnie Glaser, "Taiwan's Most Pressing Challenge Is Strangulation, Not Invasion," *War on the Rocks*, November 9, 2023.

24. Paul Huang, "Taiwan's Military Has Flashy American Weapons but No Ammo," *Foreign Policy*, August 20, 2020.

25. Stokes, Yang, and Lee, *Preparing for the Nightmare*, 37, 39.

26. Vincent Ni, "Taiwan Suspends F-16 Fleet Combat Training After Jet Crashes into Sea," *The Guardian*, January 11, 2022; "Taiwan Air Force Suspends Training After Second Fatal Accident in 2022," Reuters, May 30, 2022; Cindy Wang, "Taiwan Pilot Dies in Third Military Jet Crash This Year," Bloomberg, May 30, 2022.

27. David Axe, "What Good Is an Attack Submarine with No Torpedoes? Taiwan Wants to Know," *Forbes*, November 16, 2021.

28. Minnick, "How to Save Taiwan."

29. Off-the-record interviews with Taiwanese military officers conducted by the authors, February 2019 and June 2023.

30. Office of the President of the Republic of China (Taiwan), "President Tsai Announces Military Force Realignment Plan," December 17, 2022.

31. President Tsai's speech did not clarify the specific number of conscripts needed to augment the active-duty force to bring the main battle force to its full strength of 210,000. The MND has subsequently indicated that it plans to use one-year conscripts to bring the main battle force up to full strength. Qiu Caiwei, "Conscription Service Extended by One Year, Conscripts Assigned to High Mountain Military Posts for Defense Duty," *United Daily News*, November 23, 2023. For reference, the MND reports an end strength of approximately 215,000 full-time personnel, 27,000 of whom are either civilian employees of the ministry or trainees, cadets, students, or absentee personnel, yielding 188,000 uniformed servicemen and women. Luo Tianbin, "國防部: 108年要募兵2.1萬人 110年以後每年減為1萬人," *Liberty Times Net*, October 21, 2018.

32. President Tsai's plan calls for conscript units to be built around an active-duty cadre.

33. In theory, Taiwan has more than 420,000 such volunteers. However, the degree to which these volunteers are trained, physically capable, and mentally willing to serve in a conflict is unclear given the historically low levels of funding for civil defense training and the fact that the average age of a civil

defense volunteer is sixty. Focus Taiwan, "Civil Defense Reforms Needed to Meet Taiwan's Defense Goals: Experts," *Central News Agency English News*, January 24, 2023.

34. Taiwan has approximately 1.7 million reservists, according to the International Institute for Strategic Studies, *The Military Balance 2023*, 291.

35. There is also the question of whether the Ministry of National Defense and the Armed Forces will make a good-faith effort to adopt these reforms.

36. Office of the President of the Republic of China (Taiwan), "President Tsai Announces Military Force Realignment Plan."

37. Aaron Tu and Jake Chung, "Military Revamps Reservist Training," *Taipei Times*, December 10, 2021.

38. Admiral Lee Hsi-min and Michael A. Hunzeker, "The View of Ukraine from Taiwan: Get Real about Territorial Defense," *War on the Rocks*, March 15, 2022.

39. There is a robust scholarly literature supporting the idea that political leaders can harness bureaucratic competition to increase civilian control and foster innovative behavior. See Harvey M. Sapolsky, *The Polaris System Development: Bureaucratic and Programmatic Success in Government* (Cambridge, MA: Harvard University Press, 1972); Deborah D. Avant, "The Institutional Sources of Military Doctrine: Hegemons in Peripheral Wars," *International Studies Quarterly* 37, no. 4 (December 1993): 409–30; Owen Reid Cote, "The Politics of Innovative Military Doctrine: The United States Navy and Fleet Ballistic Missiles" (PhD diss., Massachusetts Institute of Technology, 1996); Harvey M. Sapolsky, Eugene Gholz, and Caitlin Talmadge, *US Defense Politics: The Origins of Security Policy* (London, UK: Routledge, 2014), 32–54.

40. One of the coauthors, Enoch Wu, founded Forward Alliance.

41. There is an extensive academic literature documenting the numerous challenges and obstacles that military organizations face when attempting to change. See, for example, Barry R. Posen, *The Sources of Military Doctrine: France, Britain, and Germany between the World Wars* (Ithaca, NY: Cornell University Press, 1986); Stephen P. Rosen, *Winning the Next War: Innovation and the Modern Military* (Ithaca, NY: Cornell University Press, 1991); Austin Long, *The Soul of Armies: Counterinsurgency Doctrine and Military Culture in the US and UK* (Ithaca, NY: Cornell University Press, 2016); Michael A. Hunzeker, *Dying to Learn: Wartime Lessons from the Western Front* (Ithaca, NY: Cornell University Press, 2021).

42. Kessler, *Taiwan's Security Future.*

43. Keoni Everington, "Taiwan Increases Defense Budget by 13.9% for 2023, Rising to 2.4% of GDP," *Taiwan News*, August 25, 2022.

44. Alexander Lanoska and Michael A. Hunzeker, *Conventional Deterrence and Landpower in Northeastern Europe* (Carlisle, PA: Strategic Studies Institute, 2019), 34.

45. Michael A. Hunzeker, "Taiwan's Defense Plans Are Going Off the Rails," *War on the Rocks*, November 18, 2021.

46. James Q. Wilson, *Bureaucracy, Bureaucracy: What Government Agencies Do and Why They Do It* (New York: Basic Books, 1989); Rosen, *Winning the Next War*.

47. Valeriy Akimenko, "Ukraine's Toughest Fight: The Challenge of Military Reform," Carnegie Endowment, February 22, 2018.

48. Jerad I. Harper and Michael A. Hunzeker, "Learning to Train: What Washington and Taipei Can Learn from Security Cooperation in Ukraine and the Baltic States," *War on the Rocks,* January 20, 2023.

CHAPTER 5

Countering China's Use of Force

IVAN KANAPATHY

In war the chief incalculable is the human will,
which manifests itself in resistance.

—B. H. LIDDELL HART

This chapter looks at China's kinetic options for subjugating Taiwan, up to and including a full-spectrum invasion. It argues that although there are several ways that Beijing might try to coerce Taiwan, *the Taiwanese military must focus overwhelmingly on the invasion threat.* Taiwan must be prepared to endure a full-scale embargo and bombardment for at least two months, while resisting invasion. The chapter outlines a strategy for Taiwan to deny a conventional People's Liberation Army (PLA) landing while eliciting support from the United States and allies, including operational concepts to maximize survivability and lethality while facilitating intervention by a US-led coalition. It concludes with a list of recommended changes to Taiwan's military force structure that would enable such a defense strategy.

When "Gray Zone" Turns Black

In recent years, China's gray-zone activities against Taiwan have included everything from luring away Taiwan's diplomatic partners and imposing targeted economic sanctions to blackmailing Taiwanese political candidates and pumping biased or false information into Taiwan's public discourse. They have also involved nonlethal actions by China's navy, air force, rocket forces, and coast guard designed to cultivate a sense of futility within Taiwan's population.

China's gray-zone activities are formidable, and we will examine them—and approaches Taiwan can take to counter them—in detail in chapter 6. But it is important to recognize up front that Beijing's gray-zone actions have so far failed to reverse Taiwan's widespread and growing disenchantment with the idea of a political union with the People's Republic of China (PRC). Beijing's activities have also failed to produce the electoral outcomes that Beijing would have preferred in each of Taiwan's last three presidential elections. To put it bluntly: Beijing's strategy to "win without fighting" is still fighting for a win.

There remains significantly more powerful approaches Beijing may yet try, such as a quarantine or blockade, that would still qualify as "gray zone" so long as they didn't escalate to lethal military force. But given the real possibility that the Taiwanese people, like the Ukrainian people, will endure such hardships to preserve their democratic freedoms and de facto sovereignty, it seems unlikely that Beijing would pursue such options without a plan and expectation that it would need to escalate to the use of force. And if Taipei, like Kyiv, still chooses to resist outside coercion, Beijing may feel compelled to move forward with a full-blown invasion. Indeed, a lesson that even casual observers of Vladimir Putin's costly ten-year war in Ukraine have drawn is that Moscow may have had more success from the start by moving rapidly with overwhelming force and presenting a fait accompli rather than easing into its conflict in stages, which gave Kyiv and its Western partners time to shore up Ukraine's defenses. Xi may have drawn a similar conclusion, judging by the concern he has evidently expressed on occasion about Putin's prosecution of his war.[1]

Coping with Close Encounters in the Sea and Air

In the military domain, Beijing has responded to perceived political slights by launching missiles and aircraft, as it did in 1995–96 to protest the Taiwanese president's trip to the United States and in 2020 and 2022 when senior US officials visited Taipei. None of these constituted kinetic attacks on Taiwanese forces or territory, however. Since 1958, PLA and Taiwanese forces have not exchanged fire, or even collided as US and PRC aircraft did in April 2001 and their ships very nearly did in 2018.

In recent years, the PRC has become increasingly risk tolerant in air and maritime encounters with US and allied forces, including ramming Philippines supply vessels in late 2023. China always shifts the blame for its dangerous actions, including when its own forces employ water cannons, deploy flares, take aggressive maneuvers, or even intentionally collide with allied vessels and aircraft. Since Beijing's propaganda machinery will perpetuate its preferred narrative, Taiwan must avoid potentially escalatory interactions with the PLA in international sea and airspace. As explained in chapter 3, the problem isn't that such actions would cause an accidental conflict, but rather that they could hand Beijing a useful pretext upon which to pursue preplanned escalation. To support this approach, Taipei can borrow the PRC strategy of employing maritime law enforcement instead of military power.

Taiwan already stations its coast guard on the two South China Sea (SCS) features it holds, with only minimal military support personnel. Rather than naval forces, Taiwan should use its coast guard and National Airborne Service Corps (Taiwan's civil aviation search and rescue agency) for routine resupply to the South China Sea islands and maritime patrols in international waters. Like military transports, coast guard vessels can be armed with twenty-millimeter cannons, including Phalanx close-in weapons systems for self-defense. Military and civil transport aircraft are likewise interchangeable. If challenged in international sea and airspace, Taiwan should attempt to disengage, capturing the incidents on video, just as the Philippines has done since late 2023. Acknowledging that the PLA enjoys strategic overmatch on the high seas, Taiwan can help set its narrative by employing more "white hull" ships, such as coast guard cutters, instead of military "gray hulls."

However, if PRC vessels approach Taiwan's twenty-four-nautical-mile (nm) contiguous zone (measured out from its territorial baselines), Taipei must be resourced and prepared to respond militarily.[2] Considering its behavior in the South and East China Seas, the PRC may lead with unarmed maritime militia. Or it could use drones to test Taiwan's defenses. In all cases, Taiwan should respond first with law enforcement, when possible, as it has done with PRC dredgers and fishers.[3] The Taiwan Coast Guard should issue warnings approaching 24 nm and judge the target's nature and intent. Inside of 12 nm, military forces should respond if Taiwan witnesses actions that go beyond innocent passage, as defined by international law. If circumstances permit, Taiwan could deliver warning fire across the bow of the interloper. But if there are too many vessels or they are moving too fast, Taipei would be within its rights to employ lethal weapons against uncooperative targets operating inside its territorial waters. If Beijing intentionally provokes in Taiwan's sovereign seas, Taipei cannot afford to back down.

The same is true for interlopers in the air, with the caveat that Taiwan may need to scramble fighters when approaching aircraft reach 40 nm, depending on the flight profile and type of aircraft. Forty nautical miles is roughly the closest distance from Taiwan's main island to the centerline of the Taiwan Strait. Taiwanese fighters should aim to intercept and determine armaments and intent before PRC aircraft reach 12 nm from Taiwan's baselines. Here, too, if the offenders are uncooperative inside territorial airspace, Taiwan should prosecute the targets rather than allow erosion of its sovereignty. This could provide pretext for retaliation by China, so Taiwan must rapidly and proactively publicize incidents in the context of homeland defense, with accompanying video evidence, to counter ensuing PRC propaganda.

If the PRC interlopers are drones, Taiwan could employ twenty-millimeter or similar light cannons (from the air or sea) to disable them. In the case of maritime militia or dredgers, the Taiwan Coast Guard should detain them if they cannot claim innocent passage. Taiwan's fighter jets can respond to air or naval threats and should establish continuous alerts with ordnance for both contingencies. Similarly, Taiwan's coast guard and navy should be on hand in various ports, prepared to scramble. Fast-attack missile boats (Taiwan has 180-ton and 650-ton missile patrol craft) are best suited for the mission—functioning as the maritime equivalent of fighter jets. Land-based coastal defense cruise missile and medium-range air defense batteries should be stationed around Taiwan's coast to provide operational depth in coordination with the fighter aircraft and missile boat alert missions.

Taiwan must also take care to avoid overreacting. In the days leading up to the January 2024 election, the PRC likely attempted to bait Taiwan by releasing balloons into the jet stream and allowing tugboats to traverse Taiwan's territorial waters under an innocent passage profile.[4] In both cases, Taipei made appropriate judgments and responses.[5]

For the offshore islands (Taiwan-held islands along the coast of mainland China), Taiwan's territorial rights do not extend 12 nm. Instead, Taiwanese forces should target direct overflight of the territory itself, as they eventually did with small drones in the summer of 2022. More critically, all Taiwan's outer island defense forces, which occupy its offshore and SCS features, should primarily prepare to resist PLA takeover.

Outer Island Seizures

If the political objective of the Chinese Communist Party (CCP) is to show measurable progress toward unification, provoking an altercation on or over the high seas may not suffice. Beijing could instead choose to take over Taiwan-held territory by seizing one or more of the outer islands along the mainland coast or in the SCS. The United States would likely be unwilling and unable to intervene on Taipei's behalf in such a scenario. Washington's Taiwan Relations Act does not cover the outer islands, and a PLA operation to seize one would probably be over in a matter of days, if not hours, given the PLA's capability overmatch. Pratas Reef, with no native population or other claimants, is a top candidate. China could also seize one or more of the offshore islands. Doing so might prove strategically obtuse, since the offshore islands tie Taiwan historically to the mainland and serve as political counterweights to independence-leaning Taiwanese. Nevertheless, because Beijing does miscalculate and overreach at times, Taipei must have a plan for responding.

To deter and, if necessary, resist such a seizure, Taipei should deploy scores of short-range defensive munitions, like Stingers and Javelins, on each of its Outer Islands. Taiwan must avoid a Crimea-like uncontested takeover at all costs, both to demonstrate its resolve and to oblige China to use lethal force. Actively resisting an island grab will send an unambiguous signal to the rest of the world: China is a violent revisionist power and Taiwan is willing to fight for itself.

In every scenario, Taiwanese crews and defenders should record or transmit their interactions with PRC forces. If China is clearly the aggressor in a limited kinetic scenario, such as an island seizure, a collision at sea, or weapons employed against transport vessels or aircraft, allies would take umbrage and the Taiwanese people would stiffen their spines, making Beijing's chances of eventually realizing "peaceful reunification" even more remote.

Blockade with Firepower Strikes

The PRC's August 2022 live-fire exercise following Speaker Nancy Pelosi's visit to Taiwan was a scripted political protest designed to avoid further escalation. With a global audience in mind, these drills were preannounced, time bound, and geographically circumscribed. PLA vessels patrolled the designated impact zones to clear stray vessels. PRC state media said the exercises included "joint blockade, sea target assault, strike on ground targets, and airspace control operations."[6] The ballistic missiles launched over Taipei were therefore intended to signal the PLA's ability to hit Taiwan with precision.

However, even thousands of guided missiles are unlikely to compel capitulation. Short of using atomic weapons, virtually no bombing campaign in history has compelled a population to concede. They typically stiffen public resolve instead. That said, because Beijing might still try to blast the Taiwanese people into submission from afar, Taiwan needs to be mentally and logistically prepared to endure large-scale missile strikes against military and critical infrastructure targets. China is unlikely to intentionally target civilians with such a campaign, because it would further turn popular sentiment against Beijing, both in

Taiwan and abroad. As with the limited kinetic operations mentioned above, Taipei's ability to communicate with the outside world will be critical to rallying and coordinating external intervention. In the meantime, Taiwan's thousands of fishing vessels could serve as stents for maintaining access to critical supplies. If the Taiwanese people demonstrate resilience and resolve to sustain themselves, global public outrage and the acute shock to global electronics supply chains will motivate the United States and others to intervene, arguably more urgently than with a non-kinetic blockade, as discussed in the next chapter.

The abiding condition of a PRC bombardment and blockade, while certainly disastrous for Taiwan, would be more bearable than what many Ukrainians and Israelis endured over the past two years, including rape and torture at the hands of the enemy. All the while, Beijing would find itself at an increasing disadvantage vis-à-vis Washington, as China would suffer more economically and expend more militarily to sustain the blockade.[7] Politically, the developed world would condemn and isolate the CCP, adding to the regime's challenges.

Moreover, not only would Taiwan remain effectively independent from China under this scenario, but Taipei may even move to formally separate with the support of the United States and key allies. Such an outcome would be analogous to, if not worse than, Putin's ill-advised reinvasion of Ukraine in 2022, which triggered the very thing he sought to avoid: a stronger and expanded NATO. If Taiwan can successfully communicate while countering a PRC embargo for several weeks, Beijing will be forced to back down as it did in 1958, settle for a limited victory like a small-island seizure, or invade to take Taiwan itself.

Given the inadequacies of all other options (including those discussed in the next chapter), the PRC's most likely path to victory may therefore be a full-scale invasion to rapidly assume control of Taiwan by force. It is, after all, the scenario for which the PLA has been preparing for decades. Russia expected to achieve a similar fait accompli in Ukraine in February 2022. But the Ukrainians repelled the main effort and endured other initial attacks, forcing the operation into a years-long siege. The Taiwanese people must be willing and prepared to do the same.

Taiwanese soldiers on Kinmen Island during the 823 Artillery Battle. *John Dominis/The LIFE Picture Collection/Shutterstock*

The 823 Artillery Battle

A PLA blockade coupled with lethal territorial bombardment of Taiwan is most likely a precursor to an amphibious operation. Taiwan experienced an analogous attack during the 823 Artillery Battle, a more than three-month battle named for its starting date of August 23, 1958 (the event is also known as the Second Taiwan Strait Crisis). An artillery barrage attack of Kinmen, two offshore islands occupied by the Taiwan-based Republic of China (ROC) forces, was not followed by a PLA takeover because of timely American intervention. The ROC Army retreated to defilade while the PLA's continuous artillery fires effectively blockaded Kinmen, wearing down the defenders. Two weeks later, the US Navy began escorting resupply convoys to Kinmen. China dared not fire on the US-led formations, creating an opening for deliveries of critical supplies and munitions.

The United States also sent fighter jets, weapons, and even amphibious ships to Taiwan. Most of the ROC's eighty-five thousand ground troops in Kinmen remained in bunkers while its aircraft operated from Taiwanese bases more than a hundred miles away. US and ROC naval convoys also remained outside the range of PLA artillery fire. Only ROC landing vessels traversed the last miles onto Kinmen's beaches, delivering shells and supplies to continue resisting China's offensive.[8]

Facing replenished resistance and a diminishing ammunition stockpile, PRC forces conceded the stalemate after a few weeks. With timely assistance from the United States, Taiwan's forces had successfully defended Kinmen, preventing the PRC from taking territory.

Taiwan should apply three relevant lessons from its own historical experience in the 823 Artillery War to deter a future PLA amphibious assault:

1. *Forces within range of enemy surface fires must be survivable and protected.* In 1958, the PLA killed or destroyed some of Taiwan's forces on Kinmen, including some senior officers, that were not protected in underground bunkers. Today, the PLA's precise ballistic and cruise missiles can range anywhere in Taiwan, not just the offshore islands. Moreover, Taiwan does not have enough ballistic or cruise missile defense capacity to offset the large number of incoming munitions. With limited and costly interceptors, Taiwan must prioritize protecting its leadership, major cities, and critical infrastructure.

2. *Forces within range of enemy surface fires must have enough supplies and munitions to outlast the enemy.* If China attacks, Taiwan should deploy its fishing vessels to transport rations and supplies as needed from staging ports in nearby friendly territories, like Japan and the Philippines. But if China also attacks allied territory, Taiwan may have to survive much longer without resupply. Either way, it will be very difficult to transport weapons into Taiwan after hostilities begin. Instead, Taiwan should accumulate and maintain adequate stockpiles of wartime rations, munitions, and equipment.

3. *Naval and air forces must originate from outside the range of enemy surface fires.* Taiwan's military ports and docked

vessels will be early targets of a missile bombardment. Similarly, to neutralize Taiwan's air force, the PLA need only attack nodal vulnerabilities, like airfield fuel depots and electricity hubs, or taxiways and runways. Capabilities and concepts like rapid runway repair or landing on highways are not responsive enough to outpace the PLA's kill chain, which can identify and prosecute fixed targets on Taiwan in a matter of minutes.

The Principal Mission: Counterinvasion

The PRC is deterred by the specter of US intervention, not by Taiwan's defenses alone. As with Ukraine, Taiwan cannot resist a far larger enemy indefinitely without assistance. Therefore, Taiwan's principal defense strategy should be based on two symbiotic objectives: deny a conventional PLA landing and elicit maximum assistance from a US-led coalition. Just as Ukraine repelled the assault on Kyiv and continued to fight, Taiwan must keep PRC forces at bay while ensuring that China is viewed as the militant aggressor and the Taiwanese people as innocent victims. As with the gray-zone contingencies, continued connectivity with the outside world will be critical and necessary to mobilize an international coalition to assist.

Regardless of whether the United States is formally committed to defending Taiwan in the event of a PRC attack, the Taiwanese military's task remains the same.[9] The mission is to protect Taiwan's core territory and its inhabitants from a PRC takeover—and to do it alone until external help arrives or China quits. If the PRC manages to successfully establish a lodgment (such as an operational seaport or airport) in Taiwan, the likelihood of international acceptance and restraint would increase significantly. In contrast to Ukraine, without a friendly bordering nation, allies would be challenged to provide security assistance for a ground campaign in Taiwan. Taiwan's international isolation and undetermined status, along with China's economic and military heft, accentuate this reluctance to intervene. For these reasons, the Taiwanese military must prioritize denying a PLA lodgment above all else.

Taiwan should be prepared to endure missile and bomb strikes, an enforced embargo, cyberattacks on critical infrastructure, disinformation campaigns, and other associated threats for up to *two months* while denying a landing operation. This would allow one month for allied political decision making, including countering disinformation, building coalitions, and mobilizing forces. Taipei should anticipate an additional month for US-led military operations to "peel back the layers" of the PRC's anti-access, area denial (A2AD) forces designed to keep coalition forces away from the vicinity of Taiwan. In other words, the United States and its allies will have to fight their way in from hundreds of miles away. These operations could vary in character and duration depending on how the political situation unfolds. For example, US forces might initially limit themselves to semi-deniable capabilities like cyber, electronic warfare, long-range expendable drones, or even undersea warfare to control escalation and avoid risk to US personnel.

The primary threats in a PLA landing operation are the amphibious ships, landing craft, air assault helicopters, and airborne delivery planes. These platforms will transport first echelon troops to seize and hold a lodgment, allowing follow-on PLA forces to flow unimpeded into Taiwan. The immediate enabling threats are the thousands of (mostly land-based) ballistic and cruise missiles, rockets, drones, and strike aircraft capable of hitting Taiwan and the Penghu Islands in support of landing operations. These are the threats that Taiwan must counter, by attacking the former and avoiding the latter.

Although counterintuitive, the threats from PLA Navy submarines, surface combatants, and aircraft carriers are largely inconsequential to the primary mission of denying a lodgment. In an operation to invade Taiwan, the core assault force would be the PLA Army's amphibious combined arms brigades, supported primarily by other elements of the army.[10] While certain naval units would participate in landing operations, the blue-water vessels will mostly be tasked to block the United States and allies from the Taiwan area as part of China's A2AD campaign. Taiwan should deprioritize blue-water naval targets, especially since associated costs and risks are high, and instead let the US military prosecute them using its qualitative advantages, including long-range precision strike weapons and advanced submarines.

Some defense analysts in Taiwan believe that striking Shanghai or a PLA aircraft carrier should be among Taiwan's primary objectives—to deliver a psychological blow and weaken the enemy's will. Here again, Ukraine's experience is instructive. On the strategic level, these attacks have not deterred Putin, lessened his popularity in Russia, or undermined his grip on power. Similarly, a Taiwanese countervalue strike on a symbolic target would only serve to escalate the stakes and reduce the chances of a PLA stand-down. Taiwan should target its mainland strikes against military targets that most directly support PLA landing operations.

On the operational level, Ukraine can conduct deep strikes only because it is seventeen times the size of Taiwan and has a secure rear area from which to operate. Taiwan is more comparable to Crimea in landmass (Crimea is three-fourths the area of Taiwan). In this era of modern weapon systems, Taiwan is essentially a single battle space. To maintain a secure rear area, Taiwanese forces must hold all of Taiwan and the Penghus by decisively repelling PLA landing forces.

Asymmetric Defense Strategies

For several years, the United States recommended that Taiwan adopt an "asymmetric" defense strategy, but with no agreed definition or capabilities. The United States generally pressed Taiwan to acquire greater numbers of resilient and cost-effective platforms, like coastal defense cruise missiles (i.e., antiship missiles launched from trucks), more munitions to sustain operations, and greater investment in training and maintenance. Taiwan instead prioritized replacing its aging marquee platforms with newer versions: advanced fighter jets and helicopters, ships with phased array radars and vertical missile launchers, modern tanks and tracked artillery, and so on.

Washington argued that China would not be deterred by a handful of exhibition weapon systems that represent lucrative targets in conflict, especially as the PLA has modernized to specifically counter the US platform-centric style of power projection warfare. For many years, Taiwanese military leadership denied that the PRC would attack Taiwan and was dismissive of US warnings. For example, a Taiwanese army general told US interlocutors that mainlanders and Taiwanese were "cousins" so they would never actually fight each other, as if their civil war had not occurred.[11] An admiral, when asked why Taiwan trained for amphibious assault operations, argued that Taiwan might need to take on Vietnam in the SCS. And an air force general, when confronted with the assessment that airfields could not survive a PLA missile barrage, responded curtly that the backbone of any self-respecting air force simply had to be fighter jets, bar none. Taiwan's general officers were settled into a worldview whereby Taiwan's military should prepare to assume control of the mainland if and when the communist regime collapses. Hence Taiwan's reluctance to divest from power projection capabilities like tanks, attack helicopters, paratroopers, amphibious assault, and airborne early warning.

Around 2019, however, the Tsai administration finally began moving Taiwan's defense establishment toward a force development strategy more aligned with the US vision. Taiwan announced its intent to purchase Stinger man-portable air defense systems, Harpoon antiship missiles and vehicular launchers, HIMARS (High Mobility Artillery Rocket System) launchers, and MQ-9 Reaper uncrewed intelligence, surveillance, and reconnaissance (ISR) aircraft. Since 2022, the Ukraine war has validated the wisdom of this shift. Washington and Taipei now largely agree on the capabilities Taiwan must grow to enhance deterrence, although implementation remains alarmingly slow.

At a basic level, exploiting asymmetry means pitting one's strengths against the opponent's weaknesses and avoiding the opposite, like David against Goliath. Taiwan is engaged in a long-term military competition against an increasingly better-resourced and more technologically advanced rival. Only thirty years ago, Taiwan's GDP was more than half that of China's. Now it is less than one-twentieth the size. This asymmetry of economic power is reflected in military power and necessitates a correspondingly asymmetric Taiwanese defense strategy.

On a related note, Taiwan's 2022 defense spending amounted to only 1.6 percent of GDP while China's more opaque spending added up to 3.8 percent of its much larger economy, according to US government assessments.[12] Taiwan did increase defense spending to more than 2 percent for 2023 and 2024, but Taipei should spend proportionally at least as much as the United States (3.5 percent of GDP). The burden of defending Taiwan cannot fall more heavily on Americans than Taiwanese. Increasing defense purchases from the United States would not only show resolve and enhance deterrence, provided the right capabilities are procured, but could also bring about a more balanced trading relationship (in 2022, Taiwan enjoyed a $51 billion trade surplus with the United States).

Exploiting Asymmetries

Taiwan needs to maximize the efficiency of its defense resources over time. To do this, Taiwan's political leadership must clearly articulate its priorities and focus the defense establishment on the core, critical mission of defending Taiwan from a PLA invasion. This chapter argued earlier that Taiwan's offshore islands should be minimally equipped to credibly resist a PRC military seizure, acknowledging that the PLA can succeed in such an operation with its overwhelming firepower. The next chapter will show that Taiwan's gray-zone defense should consist of long-endurance, uncrewed ISR platforms embracing the concept of deterrence by detection.[13] These are important yet relatively low-cost, low-manpower military requirements.

The Taiwanese military also has diplomatic and disaster response support missions, but it should not allocate force development (i.e., acquisitions and training) resources specifically for midshipman cruises to the Caribbean or typhoon relief operations. These collateral missions should be accomplished using ready forces as available.

Therefore, the overwhelming preponderance of the Taiwanese military should be purpose-built for fending off a PLA assault. Meanwhile,

Taiwan should use its civilian talent to create a whole-of-society home-land defense establishment. This should include part-time adjuncts in areas such as cybersecurity (IT workers), healthcare (trauma medicine practitioners), aviation (pilots), logistics (truckers), and homeland de-fense (local community residents).

If resources permit, Taipei should also consider maintaining a counterforce strike capability. If the PLA does not employ lethal force against allied territory, the United States may restrain from striking PRC territory to limit nuclear escalation risks. But Taiwan would be justified responding to kinetic attacks by targeting, for example, the PLA's coastal command-and-control facilities and amphibious vessels in port.

To suit this purpose, Taiwan already has hundreds of Hsiung Feng IIE (HF-2E) land-attack cruise missiles paired with relocatable launch vehicles. Taiwan is also acquiring Army Tactical Missile System (ATACMS) ballistic missiles and should procure larger quantities of its replacement, the Precision Strike Missile (PrSM). Anticipating the denial of airfield operations in Taiwan, the military could also pre-emptively redeploy its US and Taiwan-based fighters to the Second Island Chain to prepare for a standoff air campaign, where perhaps Taiwanese aircraft would be the only ones authorized to strike main-land targets. To support such an option, Taiwan should acquire and pre-position large quantities of Joint Air-to-Surface Standoff Missiles (JASSMs) (and Long Range Anti-Ship Missiles [LRASMs]) on US bases in Guam. If circumstances prevent Taiwanese aircraft from redeploy-ing, US forces could employ these missiles in defense of Taiwan.

In the undersea domain, China has invested in building underwater sensor networks in the waters surrounding Taiwan.[14] Meanwhile, Taiwan's submarine technology is decades behind the times. Japan has air-independent propulsion submarines. The United States, and now China, added pump-jet propulsion technology to theirs. Taiwan's new-est submarine has neither of these improvements, making it the noisiest and most vulnerable modern boat in the region, despite its exorbitant cost.[15] Taking a page from Ukraine, Taiwan should develop uncrewed sea drones, particularly lethal expendable ones (i.e., smart torpedoes), instead of building more manned submarines.

Modern antiship and antiair missile systems match up against manned power projection platforms at a fraction of the cost. In modern warfare, the cost curve favors the territorial defender, as seen in Ukraine. The most prominent Pacific example is China's A2AD network, designed to protect against US military intervention. As one would expect, the shorter the effective range, the cheaper the projectiles and more mobile (and thus survivable) the launchers. Taiwan must develop its own A2AD network with enough mobile short- and medium-range air and coastal defense systems to deny a PLA landing for two months.

Additionally, active missile defense and extensive hardening are more expensive than corresponding offensive ballistic and cruise missile capabilities. As an example, a single counter-ballistic Patriot missile costs $4 million, which is more than the projectile it is tasked to intercept. Therefore, Taiwan should pursue a missile defense strategy that relies chiefly on mobility—fixed, high-value targets are unlikely to survive PLA strikes. The same is true of larger platforms such as manned aircraft and vessels. And if not destroyed at home base, they would be vulnerable to the PLA's dense A2AD weapons in the seas and skies around Taiwan.

To mitigate numerical disadvantages, the Taiwanese military must utilize resilient sensors and weapons platforms and target efficiently to maximize lethality. China's embargo operations and firepower strikes will likely be coupled with cyberattacks and possibly direct action and fifth column (sleeper cell) sabotage to accomplish the three doctrinal prerequisites for PLA landing operations: information, air, and maritime superiority. Taiwanese forces must avoid or minimize the effects of these operations against Taiwan while maneuvering and attacking to deny the three superiorities.

PLA information superiority involves attempts to blind the enemy and disrupt communications. Taiwan can minimize the effects of these operations by decentralizing command and control. If tactical-level operators have organic ISR, fires, and engagement authority, they can

identify and attrit at close range enemy forces that meet certain prede-
termined profiles (e.g., landing forces). To better exploit asymmetries,
Taiwan should not attempt to attain air or maritime superiority, even
for limited durations, as the costs and risks are exponentially higher
than to simply deny the PLA the freedom to maneuver in those domains. Large quantities of lethal, distributed, and survivable antiair
and antiship missiles are the backbone of an effective extended denial
campaign.

Taiwanese war planners should also concede that the "force protection phase" of its defense plan will not conclude until the conflict ends.
For example, aircraft parked in east coast tunnel complexes will be un-
available for the duration of the fight. Instead, the Taiwanese military
should expect to be suppressed by PLA fires whenever exposed and
embrace its role as a "stand-in" force. US forces in southwest Japan
and the northern Philippines will also assume a stand-in role if the war
expands to those regions. The remaining US and allied forces, operating initially from farther distances, will approach the conflict from
standoff (as covered in later chapters).

Accordingly, Taiwan's training regimen should pursue interoperability with US Marines and special forces, either of which might pre-
deploy stand-in or advisory forces to Taiwan. Taiwan's F-16s are already largely interoperable with the United States through daily training
and exercises in Arizona and could participate in standoff operations
during a contingency. The rest of Taiwan's military, as a homeland defense stand-in force, need only de-conflict from US and allied forces to
avoid friendly fire incidents. Taiwan should concentrate its fires in the
near littorals and avoid targeting the open seas. The United States will
not coordinate sensitive submarine operations with Taipei, so Taiwan
should avoid the undersea domain outside its coastal waters. As stated
above, Taiwan's principal mission does not require targeting the PLA's
blue-water naval assets. As an example, Taiwan could keep its manned
platforms within its 12-nm territorial space and its fires within 40 nm,
plus attacks on targets in PRC territorial space. Allied forces could then
de-conflict accordingly.

Our Recommended Military Force Structure Changes

Taiwan's defense establishment should accelerate acquisitions to attain the following operational capabilities in the next two years (in order of importance):

1. 4,000+ man-portable air defense missiles (e.g., Stinger)
2. 200+ mobile short-range air defense vehicles, with 3x missile reloads (e.g., MADIS, Avenger/Stinger, Antelope/TC-1)
3. 40+ counter-UAS, counter-rocket, artillery, mortar systems, with 10x missile reloads (e.g., MRIC/SkyHunter, Iron Dome/Tamir)
4. 200+ mobile medium-range antiair missile vehicles, with 5x missile reloads (e.g., NASAMS High-Mobility Launcher/AMRAAM, mobile TC-2)
5. 2,000+ man-portable antiarmor missiles, suitable for employment against landing craft (e.g., Javelin)
6. 200+ mobile coastal defense cruise missile vehicles, with 3x missile reloads (e.g., HCDS, NMESIS, HF-2)
7. 2,000+ small, expendable, intelligent autonomous UAS to assist in finding and identifying priority naval troop transport targets
8. 1,000+ small, expendable, autonomous surface/undersea drones for targeting amphibious shipping, both in PRC ports and in transit
9. Enough rifles, pistols, and ammunition such that each member of the military, reserves, and civil defense force has emergency access to a personal weapon that is routinely function-checked and fired
10. 50+ mobile rocket launchers (e.g., HIMARS, RT-2000) with 1,000+ rounds of precision munitions for beach defense (e.g., GMLRS) and 1,000+ rounds of precision munitions for mainland counterforce targeting (e.g., ATACMS, PrSM)
11. Up to 200 fighter aircraft with antiship and antiair identification and targeting capabilities (e.g., F-16 Viper)
12. 90+ 200-ton class fast-attack missile craft (e.g., Kuanghua FACG)
13. 36+ 600-ton class guided-missile patrol craft (e.g., Tuojiang, Anping PGG)
14. 25+ medium-altitude long-endurance maritime surveillance UAS (e.g., MQ-9 Reaper)
15. Aerostat radar systems for low-altitude air surveillance
16. Satellite surveillance data subscriptions
17. LEO internet communications subscriptions
18. 300+ long-range air-to-surface cruise missiles held by US forces outside the First Island Chain, for use by redeployed Taiwanese fighters (e.g., JASSM stored in Guam)
19. 100+ long-range antiship cruise missiles held by US forces outside the First Island Chain, for use by redeployed Taiwanese fighters (e.g., LRASM stored in Guam)

Conclusion

To maximize survivability, lethality, and sustainability, Taiwan should have hundreds of weapons platforms and thousands of munitions. Ideally, these platforms are land (or perhaps coastal) based and highly mobile. Launch platforms should operate in complex background terrain (avoid open fields and waters) and move into defilade within minutes of firing (i.e., "shoot-n-scoot" tactics). Sensors should also move regularly, especially when emitting. Rugged wheeled platforms provide versatility in Taiwan's urban and mountainous terrain, rather than heavily armored tracked vehicles.

The Taiwanese military's tactical employment of its limited weapons must be coldly efficient, prioritizing PLA manned aircraft and seaborne troop transport. Hundreds of fuel depots, weapons armories, and ammunition stockpiles should be distributed across the island in protected bunkers, caves, and buildings. Taiwan's air defense units should have permissive engagement authority—yet another reason friendly manned air operations over Taiwan are ill-advised. Antiship missile teams should employ tactical drones to assist with locating and identifying priority naval targets. If the PLA attempts landing operations, hundreds of infantrymen should be ready to target landing craft with antiarmor rounds (e.g., Javelins) and shoot transport planes and helicopters with antiair missiles (e.g., Stingers) as they approach the beach.

For deterrence to be effective, the PRC must believe that Taiwan's relevant capability can and will be deployed in a contingency. Beijing, with its impressive intelligence capabilities, likely has very accurate assessments of Taiwan's military capabilities and capacity. Prestige platforms and performative statements will not suffice. Deterrence can be achieved only through realized capabilities, including all readiness factors like personnel, training, maintenance, parts, ammunition, logistics, and so on. To prevent conflict, Taiwan must be both willing and able to fight effectively in a sustained fashion.

For decades in Taiwan, the army has centered itself around armored maneuver brigades, the navy has operated in surface action groups, and the air force has revolved around fighter aircraft. But none of these capabilities is relevant to the task of defending against a proximate and determined attacker with qualitative and quantitative overmatch. All credible analyses of a cross-strait conflict assess that the PLA will destroy or neutralize the bulk of Taiwan's marquee platforms within days. If Taiwanese leaders continue to present these platforms as the backbone of their defense force, then the rapid loss of them in an attack will sap the morale of the troops and the people, all but guaranteeing failure. Alternatively, the new Taiwanese administration should promote an entirely new military culture as described in the previous chapter, adopt a credible wartime defense strategy as described in this chapter, and adjust its gray-zone defense strategy as proposed in the next chapter.

NOTES

1. Matthew Johnson, John Pomfret, and Matt Pottinger, "'No Limits': Xi's Support for Putin Is Unwavering," Foundation for Defense of Democracies, October 11, 2022.
2. A nautical mile and a regular, or "statute," mile differ in length. Nautical miles are about 15 percent longer than statute miles and are used for navigation. The unit is based on the circumference of the earth, with one nautical mile equal to one minute of latitude.
3. Lawrence Chung, "Taiwan to Seize Intruding Sand Dredgers from Mainland China to Fight Illegal Mining and 'Grey Zone Warfare,'" *South China Morning Post*, December 18, 2023.
4. Guermantes Lailari, "China Tries Influencing Taiwan Elections with Balloons and Ships," *Taiwan News*, January 9, 2024.
5. "Coast Guard Drives Chinese Tugboats from Southern Coast," *Taipei Times*, January 2, 2024.
6. John Dotson, "An Overview of Chinese Military Activity Near Taiwan in Early August 2022, Part 2: Aviation Activity, and Naval and Ground Force Exercises," *Global Taiwan Brief* 7, no. 18 (2022).
7. Charlie Vest, Agatha Kratz, and Reva Goujon, "The Global Economic Disruptions from a Taiwan Conflict," Rhodium Group, December 14, 2022.
8. Morton H. Halperin, "The 1958 Taiwan Straits Crisis: A Documented History (U)," memorandum to the Office of the Assistant Secretary of Defense (International Security Affairs), RAND Corporation, March 18, 1975.

9. Ivan Kanapathy, "Taiwan Doesn't Need a Formal U.S. Security Guarantee," *Foreign Policy*, April 26, 2022.

10. Dennis J. Blasko, "China Maritime Report No. 20: The PLA Army Amphibious Force," *CMSI China Maritime Reports* 20 (2022).

11. This and the other examples in the paragraph were gleaned from the author's personal conversations with Taiwan military officers over the years.

12. Nan Tian, Diego Lopes da Silva, Xiao Liang, Lorenzo Scarazzato, Lucie Béraud-Sudreau, and Ana Carolina de Oliveira Assis, "Trends in World Military Expenditure, 2022," Stockholm International Peace Research Institute, April 2023; Editorial Board, "What Does China Really Spend on Defense?," *Wall Street Journal*, June 9, 2023.

13. Travis Sharp, Thomas G. Mahnken, and Tim Sadov, "Extending Deterrence by Detection: The Case for Integrating Unmanned Aircraft Systems into the Indo-Pacific Partnership for Maritime Domain Awareness," Center for Strategic and Budgetary Assessments, July 13, 2023.

14. Alastair Gale, "The Era of Total U.S. Submarine Dominance over China Is Ending," *Wall Street Journal*, updated November 20, 2023.

15. Thompson Chau, "Taiwan's Presidential Candidates at Loggerheads over Submarines," *Nikkei Asia*, December 15, 2023.

CHAPTER 6

Countering China's Gray-Zone Activities

IVAN KANAPATHY

When a snake wants to eat his victims,
he first covers them with saliva.

—WINSTON CHURCHILL, 1936

Almost exactly two years after Beijing decided it would draft and enact the national security law that would snuff out the "high degree of autonomy" Beijing had promised Hong Kong, a senior Chinese diplomat penned an op-ed in Hong Kong's main English-language newspaper. The audience that Qin Gang, a future foreign minister, was addressing in his May 2022 missive in the *South China Morning Post* wasn't the former British colony: it was Taiwan.

Qin told his readers that while Beijing would do its "utmost for a peaceful reunification," it was "not renouncing the use of force" to deter "separatists and external interference."[1]

He diluted that shot of vinegar with a spoonful of honey, telling an anecdote about a Taiwanese physical fitness trainer who had made a splash as a social media influencer by attracting tens of millions of followers in China. Digital unification, Qin seemed to be saying, needn't wait for political union. "The mainland's social media applications are widely loved and used by the people of Taiwan."

"Promoting peaceful reunification while not giving up on the use of force are like two sides of the same coin," Qin wrote. Though Qin was mysteriously purged by supreme leader Xi Jinping in the summer of 2023 and hasn't been heard from since, Qin's quote still stands as an apt encapsulation of Beijing's approach.

While the previous chapter addressed China's potential use of force, this chapter discusses the other side of Qin's proverbial coin: China's non-kinetic options for seducing, intimidating, and subjugating Taiwan. It looks at steps ranging from information warfare and economic inducements to the use of a prolonged air and naval blockade. It also recommends a strategy for countering efforts of the Chinese Communist Party (CCP) along this entire spectrum, one organized around the principles of patience and perspective. Specifically, Taiwan should focus on acquiring the latest tools for blocking cyber intrusions and countering mis- and disinformation; adjusting the way it talks about air and naval intrusions carried out by the People's Republic of China (PRC); acquiring persistent intelligence, surveillance, and reconnaissance (ISR) capabilities; and improving its ability to communicate and endure in the face of a sustained blockade.

Of course, it is important to note that China's vigorous efforts in the gray zone have not yet succeeded in persuading the Taiwanese people that they would be better off with a political union with the PRC. This fact should not induce complacency, as Beijing is constantly finding new approaches to "win without fighting." But it also highlights an unfortunate paradox: Taiwan must continue to resist China's non-kinetic efforts. Yet the more the CCP loses faith that it can succeed in the gray zone, the more it will be compelled to choose force instead. The steps Taiwan should take urgently to deter or defeat a PRC military invasion were covered in the previous chapter.

Information Operations

The CCP is waging a multifaceted cyber and information campaign against Taiwan. It relies upon a combination of virtual and in-person networks along with witting and unwitting Taiwanese surrogates to flood Taiwan with disinformation and amplify misinformation.[2] To be sure, Taiwanese media and netizens have become more discerning, but disturbing narratives still slip through. For example, in July 2023, a major Taiwanese newspaper published a series of stories falsely alleging that the United States had asked the Taiwanese government to help develop biological weapons.[3]

China also exploits Taiwan's commitment to free speech. Outlets indirectly funded by China—that is, Taiwanese enterprises that receive favorable treatment in China owing to their pro-China positions—continue to have prominent voices across Taiwanese media.[4] Opposition-leaning ("pan-blue") media, especially, often amplify content that is critical of the United States or supports Beijing's preferred narratives. In one rare case, Taiwan's broadcast regulatory agency denied pro-China outlet CTi News' application for license renewal in 2020.[5] Yet this episode was an exception that proved the rule that free speech reigns in Taiwan: the public backlash over the government shuttering a TV channel ultimately helped torpedo a draft bill that would have imposed greater accountability on social media platforms and websites for accuracy of their content.[6]

At the same time, it is important not to overstate the impact of China's information campaigns, which are often diluted by Beijing's self-inflicted setbacks. For example, Xi Jinping's remarks on cross-strait relations in January 2019—during which he insisted that the discredited "one country, two systems" formula must be applied to Taiwan—garnered near-universal disapproval in Taiwan. When Beijing cracked down on peaceful pro-democracy protesters in Hong Kong later that summer, Taiwanese polls regarding unification and independence confirmed sharp increases favoring the latter at the expense of the former.[7] A generational evolution in attitudes toward Taiwanese national identity compounds the challenge for Beijing.

Indeed, China's propaganda and influence operations have not arrested, much less reversed, this trajectory.[8] As a result, most Taiwanese don't advocate for formal independence to avoid provoking Beijing, but they increasingly regard Taiwan as a nation separate from China.[9] Alarmed, Beijing is turning to more sticks and fewer carrots. For example, in October 2023, PRC provincial tax and land-use authorities audited two of Taiwanese electronics manufacturer Foxconn's mainland facilities in an apparent attempt to drive Foxconn founder Terry Gou to quit Taiwan's crowded presidential race.

Still, Taiwan must remain vigilant against Chinese information warfare. The PRC will likely expand its influence operations in 2024 and beyond. It is also possible that Xi Jinping's ham-fisted overreach may have more to do with the ineffectiveness of China's political warfare efforts than Taiwan's inherent resilience. In any case, CCP-sponsored-and-aligned disinformation is worryingly gaining traction in Taiwan. Taiwan should therefore continue collaborating with other open societies to share threat vectors and best practices to counter CCP political warfare in the ever-changing information environment, especially as artificial intelligence–powered deep fakes and algorithms mature and proliferate (as Taiwan has already seen).[10]

To this end, in 2022, Taiwan launched the Ministry of Digital Affairs (MODA) to coordinate government and nongovernmental efforts to combat disinformation. In its first year of operation, MODA engaged with many democratic governments and pro-democracy organizations, including in the United States, the United Kingdom, the European Union, Israel, and several multilateral institutions.[11] Taiwan should enact bans on PRC-based cloud infrastructure and social media providers, as it did with Huawei and ZTE telecommunications infrastructure a decade ago. Although not a panacea, such restrictions will provide Taipei with greater trust in the data and algorithms that are generating the content consumed by the Taiwanese people. Taiwan should also work closely with non-PRC private-sector platforms to flag and demote divisive and incendiary false narratives promoted by the CCP.

Cyberattacks

MODA also coordinates Taiwan's resistance and response to cyber intrusions. It has implemented several measures to defend against cyberattacks like the relatively benign ones following then US House

Speaker Nancy Pelosi's August 2022 visit to Taiwan.[12] To further resist China's efforts, Taiwan must invest in maintaining the highest standards of cyber hygiene across all government and critical infrastructure systems. Anything less would be gross negligence.

As the 2022 attacks highlighted, China possesses cyber capabilities that could severely disrupt or damage Taiwan's critical infrastructure and military facilities. But for now, Beijing has demurred from regularly employing its most potent cyber capabilities in the gray zone. After all, high-profile cyberattacks would reveal Chinese capabilities and jeopardize access points for a future contingency. The Taiwanese government would also attribute such attacks to the PRC, increasing domestic and international public opposition to China—as it did after the military demonstrations and cyberattacks following the Pelosi visit.[13] Beijing is therefore biding its time in the cyber domain by collecting information and positioning itself for future disruptions.

Taiwan should nevertheless actively defend against gray-zone probing operations precisely because China will likely use information gained from these intrusions to support a future assault. To this end, Taiwan's digital ministry should sponsor the establishment of a volunteer group like Ukraine's IT Army, which can assist with critical network defense while identifying a pool of expert volunteers to assist in offensive operations when the need arises.[14] In addition, Taiwan should invite the US Cyber National Mission Force to conduct defensive "Hunt Forward" operations across all of Taiwan's government, critical infrastructure, and industry networks.[15] This type of operation requires Taiwanese government and military officials to trust their US counterparts, effectively handing over keys to the house. The sophistication of China's cyber forces calls for urgent and exceptional measures to improve Taiwan's resilience.

Economic Inducements and Coercion

The PRC complements its information warfare with economic warfare, and the two are often intertwined. China pressures multinational companies not to veer from its preferred political positions, as Marriott,

Delta, and the National Basketball Association have learned in recent years. Taiwanese companies face even more pressure. The CCP threatens and fines China-based subsidiaries of Taiwanese businesses suspected of supporting the incumbent Democratic Progressive Party (DPP) while doling out profits to those that mimic China's party line.[16]

PRC representatives also support local Taiwanese officials willing to echo Beijing's talking points by favoring their constituencies for investment and business deals. Conversely, Beijing targets DPP strongholds with selective inspections on products and producers. For example, after learning of Pelosi's Taiwan visit, Beijing suspended the import of more than two thousand Taiwanese food products.

Of course, economic coercion can also prove counterproductive. Despite causing immediate pain, sustained economic punishment incentivizes Taiwanese producers to reduce their dependencies on China. Nor is there evidence that Chinese economic coercion makes Taiwanese voters want to mollify Beijing. Instead, societal trends in the opposite direction continue apace.

A decade ago, the then ruling Nationalist Party, or Kuomintang (KMT), quietly negotiated a services trade agreement with Beijing. The agreement would have opened large sectors of Taiwan's economy to the PRC. The KMT government, knowing the agreement would prove unpopular, attempted to push it through the legislature without public review. This incited the Sunflower Movement, when student protesters occupied the legislative building for twenty-four days, delivering knockout blows to both the mooted agreement and the KMT's popular support.

Since 2016, Taiwan has pursued a different path. Under the New Southbound Policy (NSP), Taiwan's government has enacted policies to economically diversify away from China by incentivizing Taiwanese investment in South and Southeast Asia while putting curbs on business with the mainland, especially in the prized semiconductor industry. These successful policies were boosted by the pandemic and broader geopolitical trends, resulting in reductions in PRC-Taiwan bilateral trade and investment today.[17]

Taipei could reinforce its economic diversification efforts while also better aligning itself with maritime Southeast Asian states, the concept of a free and open Indo-Pacific, and international law by debunking and refuting maritime claims stemming from China's infamous South China Sea (SCS) "nine-dash line" (now ten dashes). Such claims stem from Republic of China (ROC) maps that predate the founding of the PRC. Taiwan holds these maps in its archives. It could cite them while clarifying its maritime claims to accord with a ruling from the Permanent Court of Arbitration in 2016, which determined that there is no legal basis for China's claims to historic rights and resources within the nine-dash line. Taipei should also publicly accept the ruling that the Taiwan-administered SCS feature Itu Aba does not generate an exclusive economic zone. In doing so, Taiwan would align itself with international law and further weaken China's illegal maritime claims. Finally, Taiwan might even consider renouncing its SCS territorial claims on features occupied by Southeast Asian states.

Air and Naval Provocations

Many of the air and naval activities that the People's Liberation Army (PLA) carries out are best understood as political signaling. Beijing seeks to demonstrate resolve, often in response to US forces operating in the East and South China seas. Such signals are of course also directed at Japan, Taiwan, the Philippines, and other claimants of disputed maritime territories. By executing these operations outside Taiwan's territorial space, which extends 12 nm from its baselines, the PRC is conducting acts of gray-zone political warfare that have little to do with a kinetic attack on Taiwan.

It is therefore important for Taiwan to keep the PLA's air and naval patrols and exercises in their proper context. Such activities are not a physical threat to Taiwan, especially not when compared to Beijing's standoff strike capabilities. Take, for example, the PLA Rocket Force, which maintains thousands of ballistic missiles with precision strike capability that can range anywhere in Taiwan. The PLA Army also has countless low-cost, guided, short-range rocket artillery rounds (i.e., close-range ballistic missiles). Given the short distances involved, Taiwan has no less indication and warning of these land-based weapons than from deployed PLA ships and aircraft. Moreover, in a surprise attack profile, PLA Air Force bombers and PLA Navy vessels would launch cruise missiles from hundreds of miles away to avoid Taiwan's defenses.

The media's obsession with Chinese intrusions into Taiwan's Air Defense Identification Zone (ADIZ), and over the so-called centerline, is also misleading and unhelpful. Both control measures were designed for a bygone era and never elicited PRC buy-in in any case. Taiwan's Cold War–era ADIZ encompasses roughly four hundred nautical miles of China's coastline, nearly half the distance from the Shandong peninsula to Hainan Island. Moreover, Taiwan still depicts its ADIZ with half of it sitting over PRC territory, underscoring the zone's anachronistic nature. Taipei argues that Beijing should honor Taiwan's ADIZ even as Taipei ignores China's ADIZ, which overlaps Taiwan's.

In September 2019, Taiwan's Ministry of National Defense (MND) began publishing instances of the PLA's so-called air incursions, primarily into the southwest corner of Taiwan's ADIZ. The Taiwanese military likely deemed these operations as threatening to its forces on Pratas Reef, which sits farther to the southwest. Pratas and the southwest corner of the ADIZ are closer to China than Taiwan, making it difficult to argue that these PLA operations are "incursions." Moreover, the area is outside the combat-operating range of Taiwan's fighters, which would have only minutes of loiter time if scrambled to defend Pratas. PLA fighters, on the other hand, operate from closer locations and can refuel in the air.

Taipei's unofficial strait centerline is similarly rooted in the Cold War. It served as a western limit to the operations of US military aircraft, which were not treaty-bound to defend Taiwan's offshore islands. It wasn't until 2004, as the PLA acquired more modern combat aircraft, that Taipei explicitly defined the centerline as a no-go area for the PRC.[18] Taipei's declared centerline includes similar unhelpful distortions: the northeast end sits squarely within the PLA's ADIZ and the southwest end is more than twice the distance from Taiwan as from China.[19] PLA aircraft routinely cross these extreme portions of the centerline, often in response to US and other foreign naval forces operating in the Philippine Sea.

Our Recommended Divestments and Transfers

To avail force structure and resources without sacrificing capabilities needed across the full spectrum of competition and conflict.

1. *Divest amphibious assault.* Taiwan does not have a requirement to attack a beach in any realistic contingency scenario. Taiwan Navy should retire all its older US-made amphibious ships and cancel procurement of additional indigenous Yushan-class LPD vessels, keeping only a single new Yushan LPD.
2. *Divest armor.* Armor is optimized for offense across open terrain. Taiwan Army should retire all old armor, keeping only its 108 new M1A2 tanks. Taiwan Marine Corps should retire all old armor, keeping only its 90 new AAV-P7 vehicles.
3. *Transfer and divest naval surface combatants.* Taiwan Navy should transfer its Lafayette class frigates to the coast guard, replacing them and its recently decommissioned Knox class frigates with additional CDCM units and more 200-ton and 600-ton class missile craft.
4. *Divest manned aircraft.* Taiwan's fighters should be used for point defense of Taiwan. Taiwan Air Force should retire its Mirage 2000 fighters and E-2 early-warning surveillance aircraft to free up force structure for additional uncrewed, mobile antiair, and tethered aerostat surveillance units.
5. *Divest ASW helicopters.* Taiwan Navy should retire its S-70C naval helicopters in favor of its P-3s and additional MQ-9s for maritime patrol and surveillance.
6. *Divest submarines.* Taiwan Navy should retire its four Guppy and Zwaardvis submarines and cancel all new submarine procurement, keeping only a single new Narwhal class indigenous submarine. Taiwan Navy should instead invest in uncrewed undersea vehicles and expendable sea drones, drawing on lessons from Ukraine.
7. *Transfer transport aircraft.* Taiwan Air Force should transfer ten or more C-130 transports to the National Airborne Service Corps to conduct, among other missions, routine resupply of the coast guard units on Taiwan's two South China Sea features: Itu Aba and Pratas Reef.

The middle portion of the centerline, however, is less than 40 nm from key strategic nodes such as Taipei Port and Taiwan's largest airport. In 2020, China crossed the middle portions of the centerline twice—both timed to coincide with Taipei meetings between high-level US officials and the Taiwanese president—to send unmistakable political signals. Unfortunately, these infrequent higher-threat center-line crossings are buried among the larger count of nonthreatening activities, like PRC observation balloons floating near China's coast more than a hundred miles from Taiwan.[20]

Overall, the PRC's military gray-zone strategy is not bearing fruit. Compared with a decade ago, Taiwanese society is arguably further from being enticed or coerced into political union with China.[21] Accordingly, the key to a more effective response strategy can be summed up in two words: patience and perspective. Specifically, Taipei should focus on deterring through information operations, improving surveillance, and preparing for potential blockade or quarantine scenarios.

Deterring through Information Operations

Taiwan cannot prevail in the gray zone by countering China symmetrically. Claims that Taiwan can deter PLA air and naval "incursions" with ever more fighter intercepts and surface combatant patrols strain credulity and misunderstand the purpose of the PLA provocations. The gross military imbalance is such that the PLA can keep adding sorties and, if challenged, escalate with confidence. Taiwan, on the other hand, will remain disadvantaged and resource constrained. Any direct engagement between Taiwanese and PLA forces on or over open seas will almost certainly end in a PRC "victory" in which Taiwan either backs down or is defeated in a skirmish, having been "taught a lesson" by China. There is no scenario where the military or political leadership in Beijing would accept anything less.

If Taiwan responds with force to PRC bullying at sea, the PLA will simply continue up the escalation ladder. Beijing could even decide to seize Pratas Reef or an offshore island. Such an operation would likely be over in a matter of hours and result in permanent loss of Taiwan's territory. Worse yet, as the PLA continues to modernize, PRC leadership is likely to become more tactically aggressive. Concurrently, Xi may grow increasingly willing to escalate strategically by authorizing a full invasion. No Taiwanese leader can afford to give Xi a pretext for attacking by taking the first swing, which Beijing would accuse Taipei of doing regardless of the facts.

Trying to symmetrically match Beijing ton-for-ton or qualitatively in the open seas and skies is thus a misuse of Taiwan's limited resources that would also prove counterproductive. Beijing is more than content to hear Taiwan's military leaders call for more fighters and more frigates to "deter" and "defend against" the PLA's gray-zone operations, as this diverts Taiwan's limited resources away from the coming real fight. Keeping things in perspective, Taiwan's defense planners should remember that the PLA's land-based missile threat can visit more death and destruction on Taiwan than all the PLA's fighters, bombers, and surface combatants combined.

Those who argue that Taiwan's population needs to see additional new advanced platforms to feel confident in their military underestimate the intellect and sophistication of the Taiwanese people. Polls consistently show that the people have little confidence in their own military's prospects for going toe-to-toe against the PLA. As the popularity of former Taiwanese chief of General Staff Lee Hsi-min and his pathbreaking ideas on asymmetric warfare indicate, many Taiwanese would instead respond positively to a realistic and cost-effective strategy to defend their homeland.[22]

Therefore, instead of confronting the PLA in the global commons, the Taiwanese government should counter gray-zone political warfare with its own version of the same. The military should continue to publish PLA activity, but as mentioned above, not in relation to the ADIZ and centerline. Taiwan has astutely reduced its range criteria for fighter scrambles to conserve resources, but it should also align its messaging to blunt the PLA's political warfare aims. Just as intercepts have failed to deter growing PLA activity around Taiwan, alarmist reports about PLA exercises only enhance the adversary's messaging and support the CCP's narrative that resistance is futile.

Furthermore, challenging China's offshore military activities is neither legally nor normatively justifiable, especially when considering US and allied operations across the global commons. Taipei should not protest the PLA's geographically and militarily nonthreatening "incursions."[23] Highlighting these instances only serves to distract audiences and numb them to the true threat. Instead, the Ministry of National Defense (MND) should use Taiwan's official maritime boundaries map when depicting PLA activity. This map does not depict either the ADIZ or the centerline. It does, however, demarcate Taipei's territorial baselines and territorial seas. This is the critical, realistic, and legitimate area that Taiwan must defend—it also matches the territories covered by the Taiwan Relations Act. This central area includes the inner islands, such as the Penghu Islands to the west, Pengjia Islet to the north, and Orchid Island to the south, but excludes the outer islands along China's coast and in the SCS.[24] By depicting PLA activity in this context, the MND could provide a more useful public inventory of how and when the PLA is threatening Taiwan's sovereign territory, including trends over time.

Taipei can also reference policies and messaging from friendly countries, including the United States, Japan, and South Korea. The US military does not notify China or Taiwan when crossing their ADIZs. Nor does the United States require transiting foreign military aircraft to comply with US ADIZ procedures. Japan shows even more restraint than the United States. With the high frequency of PLA flights into Japan's ADIZ, Japan does not advertise these incursions.[25] (It is worth noting that US, Japanese, and other allied military aircraft routinely operate in China's ADIZ—the PRC does not amplify these "incursions" either.) Instead, Tokyo publicizes select incidents of PRC government transits into the contiguous zone and territorial seas around the Senkaku Islands, which Japan administers.[26] And while South Korea has also experienced the steady erosion of its "centerline" with China in recent years, Seoul has chosen not to publicize this normative change, perhaps because it calculates that protesting would appear feckless.

Deterring through Surveillance

PLA exercises and patrols in international waters do not themselves endanger Taiwan's military, people, territory, or prosperity. However, the presence of Taiwanese forces in proximity to Chinese ships and jets does increase the chance of inadvertent escalation and the opportunity for intentional escalation. Both risks can be reduced by minimizing intercepts and other symmetric responses while emphasizing early, accurate, and detailed intelligence collection. To this end, Taiwan should transform the preponderance of its "peacetime competition" force from periodic, expensive power-projection platforms to persistent, low-cost surveillance platforms.

The deterrence by detection concept envisions a network of overlapping areas of surveillance responsibility comprising partners persistently operating various platforms and sensors across multiple domains.[27] Taiwan should aim to become an integral part of an allied ISR network across the Western Pacific. To do this, Taiwan must acquire and deploy the surveillance capabilities of the future rather than those of a generation ago. Taipei should also consider how it procures these capabilities. When practical, Taiwan should opt for data-as-a-service subscriptions or leased hardware instead of purchasing new platforms. The former options can reduce procurement timelines, personnel training requirements, and upgrade costs while providing flexibility to the user. They could also avail Taiwan of sensitive advanced technology that partners may not be willing to directly transfer due to counterintelligence, intellectual property, or political concerns.

For example, in addition to acquiring a handful of MQ-9 Reapers from the United States, Taiwan should lease additional aerial drones to achieve persistent maritime domain awareness, augmented by Taiwan's P-3 fleet. More platforms with longer endurance will provide greater coverage and earlier warning and thus help enhance deterrence. With appropriate sensor payloads, Reapers can perform both anti-surface and antisubmarine warfare surveillance missions, including dropping sonobuoys.[28] Taiwan should also invest in a network of long-endurance (measured in months, not hours) surface drones to provide sanitization and cueing to the airborne platforms.[29]

In both cases, purchasing data and operational control rather than hardware and training will enable Taiwan to more easily integrate its surveillance mission with the United States and allies. US contractor-owned-and-operated ISR platforms could operate from

Taiwan, Japan, the Philippines, Guam, or some combination thereof. This would inherently provide additional deterrence, as the PRC would have to consider the impacts on third parties before disrupting or attacking these assets.

In the air domain, Taipei's daily ADIZ reports show that Taiwan can readily detect, identify, and track PLA aircraft using its ground-based systems. But Taiwan must also be able to reliably screen for over-the-horizon helicopters and low observable targets, such as cruise missiles and small drones. Taiwan should acquire multiple, advanced, tethered aerostat radar systems to fill this critical surveillance gap. These would be far less expensive and more persistent than airborne early-warning platforms. For persistent space-based ISR coverage, including PLA missile warning and tracking, Taiwan should also retain data-as-a-service satellite operators.

Deterring through Preparations for a Blockade or Quarantine

Thus far, this chapter has focused on the lower end of the gray-zone spectrum. Yet China also has options at the high end of the non-kinetic continuum. A blockade is the most aggressive alternative. Beijing could try to strangle Taiwan in a number of ways. It could order a complete air and naval blockade, replete with crippling cyber and electronic warfare attacks. Or the PRC could launch a partial blockade (i.e., a quarantine) on only certain types of ships or cargo, possibly requiring inspections at sea or even diversion to Chinese ports.

Regardless of which option Beijing chooses, blockades and quarantines are extraterritorial economic sanctions, just as the United Nations has imposed on North Korea and the United States has imposed on Iran. In both cases, the military enforcement tool has never achieved anything close to full compliance.

As with the PLA military gray-zone options discussed above, there is no path for Taiwan to achieve a military "victory" against a PRC blockade or quarantine. Taiwanese attempts to run or break the blockade with naval forces could result in kinetic clashes—providing the very pretext that China seeks to justify escalation. Again, Beijing enjoys military overmatch and will not back down from a fight with Taiwan. As discussed in the previous chapter, it is unlikely that Beijing would implement a blockade unless it was fully prepared to conduct an invasion.

We also should not underestimate the challenges and trade-offs Beijing will face if it tries to strangle Taiwan. For example, a limited quarantine would bring political and economic costs on Beijing without necessarily pressuring Taiwan into submission. After all, if some civil aircraft or ships are free to move in and out of Taiwan, China will not be able to inspect or otherwise control passengers or cargo. As a result, Taiwan's semiconductor industry would be able to remain relatively solvent as aircraft shuttle between Taiwan and Southwest Japan (in a reprise of the Berlin Airlift).

Conversely, if China launches a full air and naval blockade, it will have to contend with international political backlash as it attempts to imprison and starve 23.5 million free people. Any blockade operation would also challenge the legitimacy of the global trading system, which recognizes Taiwan as a distinct member economy. And Beijing would have to answer for trapping hundreds of thousands of foreign nationals in Taiwan. The longer the restrictions continue, the more international pressure Beijing would face over family separations, medical attention, and other humanitarian concerns.

A full naval and air blockade of Taiwan will also deprive global supply chains of one of their most fundamental inputs: silicon chips. Given the dearth of semiconductor stockpiles worldwide, China would face a rising tide of international opprobrium because of Taiwan's unique criticality to the global economy. Therefore, although Taiwan's world-leading semiconductor manufacturing industry will not deter invasion—a CCP political decision that would already plan for China's rapid economic decoupling from the free world—Taiwan's "silicon shield" does deter a lengthier but less aggressive PLA operation like a blockade or quarantine.

Militarily, enforcing a blockade will tax the PLA and the China Coast Guard (CCG). A naval blockade or quarantine, enforced outside

Taiwan's territorial seas against multiple ports and approaches, would require a large continuous PRC maritime presence. An air blockade would be virtually impossible to enforce since fighters must intercept traffic arriving from the east. The PLA would have to commit scores of aircraft, including tankers, across long distances to maintain an airborne fighter presence around the clock—commanding tremendous resources and rapidly wearing down readiness. Without an airborne presence, allied transport aircraft could easily make the flight from Okinawa to Taipei unmolested. China's aircraft carrier capabilities are also years away from being able to handle this challenge.

Given the increasing difficulty of sustaining a blockade or quarantine politically, economically, and militarily over time, China would enact such a decree only if it were convinced of two things: that Taiwan is unlikely to challenge the blockade and that it is likely to yield in a matter of weeks, if not days. Therefore, to deter a PRC blockade, Taiwan should leave no doubt about its capabilities and intentions to resist and endure.

Responding to a Blockade

Although a blockade is unlikely for the reasons just mentioned, Taiwan must nevertheless prepare for such a contingency. Thankfully, these preparations will also be useful for countering a full invasion, since an all-out attack will include a maximalist blockade. Taiwan's primary objectives under a blockade or quarantine are to survive and communicate. To ensure connectivity, Taiwan should invest in large bands of access within multiple US and allied low earth orbit (LEO) satellite internet systems. To increase survivability, Taiwan must stockpile additional energy stores and prepare to ration food, energy, and internet bandwidth.

The longer Taiwan can resist a blockade, the more such an operation will impact foreign nationals, global supply chains, and the world economy. In the short term, the more resolve Taiwan's people can demonstrate, the more sympathy they will gain from the free world. In the event of a blockade, Taiwan therefore should lobby the international community to levy political pressure and economic sanctions against China, as Ukraine's president Volodymyr Zelenskyy did following Russia's 2022 invasion. PRC strategists acknowledge China's own vulnerability to blockades, known as the Malacca Dilemma.[30] The credible prospect of an allied counterblockade provides an added measure of deterrence and, if implemented, could further stretch the PRC's naval assets.

In the longer term, experts predict that first-order effects of a Taiwan blockade would reduce global production value more than two trillion US dollars per annum, threatening to plunge the world into economic depression.[31] The world's major economies will quickly see a vital interest in ending the blockade, especially if Taiwanese semiconductor supply chains are severed. Therefore, Taiwan should be prepared to weaponize its semiconductor industry against China in response to the full range of blockade scenarios.

Partial Blockade or Quarantine

The PRC may choose not to restrict air traffic in an effort to reduce international pushback. In this scenario, foreign nationals and Taiwanese citizens would be able to leave Taiwan, potentially reducing international resistance to China's efforts to absorb the island. China's leaders may choose this option because they are convinced that the Taiwanese people would accept a union with the mainland if freed from the influence of foreign agitators and diehard separatists, both of whom might escape under duress. Alternatively, Beijing could declare a partial blockade by sector, whereby China would restrict only certain goods, such as the import of weapons, for example.

In normal circumstances, Taiwan's semiconductor-manufacturing industry operates nearly at capacity, with many customers on back order. Depending on the options that Beijing exercises, Taiwan's chip fabs could find themselves producing below normal capacity because of cyberattacks, sabotage, lack of parts and consumables, energy shortages, workforce departures, and so on. In any case, faced with an elevated national threat, the Taiwanese government should compel its domestic industry to make strategic choices among its customers.

Taiwan cannot accept Beijing's terms for even a limited quarantine, as Taipei will have ceded its sovereignty and would be effectively on its way to "peaceful reunification." Instead, the Taiwanese government should respond in kind to a partial blockade by restricting exports of technology to or for China. A strict export control regime should allow transfer of chips (which travel by air) to approved third countries with reexport restrictions, such that only friendly supply chains and end users would continue to receive Taiwanese inputs. As friendly nations begin condemning and sanctioning China, most likely led by the United States, Taipei should prioritize countries' access to Taiwan's chip supply accordingly. This strategy depends heavily on sustaining a significant portion of Taiwan's semiconductor industry. Thus, in addition to investing heavily in critical infrastructure cyber resilience as noted above, Taiwan should also pursue early adoption of advanced small modular reactor nuclear power generators for its semiconductor fabrication facilities, as a matter of national security.

Full Blockade

Under a more robust or full blockade that restricts air transport in and out of Taiwan, the government should nationalize and assume control of its commercial airline fleet. While this option exists on paper within Taiwan's national mobilization plans, Taipei should routinely rehearse the transfer of control of civil aircraft to enhance readiness and deterrence. Since the PLA likely cannot sustain a continuous combat air patrol east of Taiwan, Taipei could begin airlift operations, exchanging semiconductors for humanitarian and other supplies in places like Luzon (Philippines), the Ryukyus (Japan), or the Marianas (United States). Without fighters, the burden would fall on China to escalate by engaging unarmed civil aircraft with naval surface-to-air missiles. While it is impossible to predict what orders might be handed down, Taiwan should consider that the PLA has not enforced China's East China Sea ADIZ since its declaration more than a decade ago. Taiwan could also ask the US military to participate in the airlift operation, citing the precedent of a C-17 landing there as recently as 2021.

An emergency airlift operation in Taiwan would resemble the 1948–49 Berlin Airlift, which provided supplies to West Berlin, blockaded by the Soviet Union from road and railway access to the West. *Bettmann via Getty Images*

The Taiwanese government should likewise prepare to take operational control of several large container ships and oil tankers. These could be Taiwan owned and operated but should be foreign flagged under friendly nations to present more dilemmas to China. If Taipei decides to challenge the naval blockade to import energy or other necessities, these vessels should do so without military escort. Based on the law of gross tonnage (or Newtonian physics), a CCG cutter or PLA warship would sustain disabling damage in an attempt to block or ram a commercial vessel many times its size. The PRC would have to board or shoot missiles, again placing the burden of escalation on China against unarmed civil vessels operating in international waters. Boarding operations would increase already high resource requirements, adding naval helicopters and special operators, to effectively guard Taiwan's ports around the clock. When practical, Taiwan's transport vessels should be equipped with satellite transceivers so crews can livestream their encounters.

Finally, Taiwan should prepare to mobilize a volunteer fishing fleet militia. These fishing vessels operate from dozens of fishing harbors dotting Taiwan's coastline. The fishing fleet militia would be primarily tasked with transporting food, fuel, medicine, and other necessities from friendly logistics hubs in nearby islands. The PLA and the CCG, even with the help of China's own maritime militia, would be unable to intercept and board hundreds, if not thousands, of Taiwanese fishing vessels on the high seas. If PRC vessels or aircraft venture into Taiwan's territorial seas, Taiwan must intercept and prosecute, with lethal force if appropriate, as described in chapter 5.

As with commercial aircraft and large merchant ships, the Taiwanese government already has the relevant authorities to mobilize fishing vessels but should rehearse them at the operational level, which would demonstrate both capability and intent and thus enhance deterrence. For all three capabilities, the Ministry of Transportation and Communications should be the lead agency contesting a non-kinetic blockade or quarantine. As mentioned above, a blockade is inherently a form of economic warfare and Taiwan should avoid responding militarily, as that would likely enhance Beijing's narrative, reduce international support, and hand the PLA a pretext to escalate. Taiwan's legislature should review relevant laws and regulations and make changes and clarifications where necessary to ensure that elected civilian leadership retains ultimate authority throughout all levels of national mobilization.

Conclusion

Taiwan already has many tools and initiatives that it will need to deny PRC success in the gray zone. In the information space, in addition to blocking China's access to Taiwan's digital infrastructure, the Taiwanese people must have the latest tools to identify, interpret, and filter mis- and disinformation. In many ways, Taiwan has been a leader in economically and technologically de-risking and diversifying away from China. Taiwan should expand and accelerate these efforts while firmly aligning itself with partners against China's unlawful maritime claims. Taiwan must also make deep investments in cyber resilience and energy reliance.

To blunt PRC military gray-zone provocations, which are a form of political warfare, Taiwan should adjust its messaging strategy to focus on the PRC's most threatening operations instead of all exercises along China's coastline. To achieve the earliest, most detailed information on PLA activities, Taiwan should subscribe to persistent ISR data-gathering capabilities, including coverage of subsurface and low-altitude platforms and munitions, and land-based rocket launches. Deployed effectively, these tools could deter further gray-zone escalations or worse.

In the unlikely event that Beijing announces a blockade or quarantine, Taipei should view it as a precursor to a kinetic operation, possibly an invasion. Until its territory is violated or attacked, however, Taiwan cannot afford to be portrayed as the provocateur and should avoid employing military assets outside its territorial waters and airspace. Taiwan should prioritize enabling an international response against China, in part by staying connected to the world and sustaining itself through rationing. Taipei could weaponize semiconductor exports against China and nationalize civil transportation assets to frustrate or break the blockade operation.

China is pursuing two parallel tracks to accomplish its goal of absorbing Taiwan. This chapter addressed the CCP's efforts toward "peaceful reunification." As China's policies toward Taiwan turn more coercive, they increasingly rely on a credible threat from the other track of violent, forceful unification. And as the former becomes less viable, Beijing will increasingly favor attempting the latter. Unlike his predecessor, Xi Jinping can claim no progress on the Taiwan issue during his tenure and has ordered his military to be prepared to invade as early as 2027. Unfortunately, the CCP's revanchist instincts will be only reinforced by Taiwan's effective gray-zone defenses, as recommended in this chapter. Therefore, the Taiwanese military's most urgent mission is to better prepare for China's eventual escalation to a full-scale invasion, as recommended in the previous chapter.

NOTES

1. Ministry of Foreign Affairs of the People's Republic of China, "Ambassador Qin Gang Publishes an Article on the South China Morning Post," press release, May 26, 2022.
2. Erin Hale, "China Spinning a 'Web' of Influence Campaigns to Win over Taiwan," Al Jazeera, June 13, 2023.
3. Chen Yun and Jonathan Chin, "Officials Links Biological Weapons Story to China," *Taipei Times*, July 13, 2023.
4. For further discussion about these outlets, see Chris Horton, "'The Plan to Destroy Taiwan,'" *The Wire China*, March 26, 2023; for further discussion about these enterprises, see Brian Hioe, "US Bioweapons Story Reignites Concerns About Disinformation in Taiwan," *The Diplomat*, July 14, 2023.
5. Nick Aspinwall, "Taiwan Learned You Can't Fight Fake News by Making It Illegal," *Foreign Policy*, January 16, 2024.
6. Chia-Shuo Tang and Sam Robbins, "Taiwan's Failed Social Media Regulation Bill," *News Lens*, October 3, 2022.
7. Election Study Center, "Taiwan Independence vs. Unification with the Mainland (1994/12~2023/06)," National Chengchi University, July 12, 2023.
8. Ivan Kanapathy, "The Collapse of One China," Center for Strategic and International Studies, June 17, 2022.
9. Taiwan National Security Studies, "TNSS Survey Data (2002–2022)," Duke University, last modified December 2022.
10. Dylan Welch, "Taiwan's Election: 2024's Canary in the Coal Mine for Disinformation against Democracy," Alliance for Securing Democracy, German Marshall Fund, December 19, 2023.
11. Huang Tzu-ti, "Taiwan's Digital Ministry Slammed for Splurging on Overseas Trips," *Taiwan News*, August 24, 2023.
12. "Digital Minister Tang Shares Taiwan's Experience at Israel Cyber Week," *Taiwan Today*, June 29, 2023.
13. Chen Yu-fu and Jake Chung, "Half of Taiwanese Back Independence," *Taipei Times*, August 17, 2022.
14. Aiden Render-Katolik, "The IT Army of Ukraine," blog, Center for Strategic and International Studies, August 15, 2023.
15. Joseph Gedeon, "Taiwan Is Bracing for Chinese Cyberattacks, White House Official Says," *Politico*, September 27, 2023; Gordon Corera, "Inside a US Military Cyber Team's Defence of Ukraine," BBC, October 29, 2022.
16. Lawrence Chung, "Fines on Taiwan's Far Eastern Group Fan Fears of More Retaliation by Beijing over Political Donations," *South China Morning Post*, November 24, 2021; Horton, "'The Plan to Destroy Taiwan.'"

17. Joyu Wang and Nathaniel Taplin, "China Tried Using Economic Ties to Bring Taiwan Closer: It Isn't Working," *Wall Street Journal*, November 23, 2023.

18. GlobalSecurity.org, "Taiwan Strait Middle Line," last modified September 7, 2011.

19. Yimou Lee and Liz Lee, "Taiwan Says It Convinced China to Rein In No-Fly Zone Plan," Reuters, April 13, 2023.

20. AP News, "Taiwan Reports 2 Chinese Balloons near Its Territory as China Steps Up Pressure ahead of Elections," updated December 18, 2023.

21. Kanapathy, "Collapse."

22. Thompson Chau, "Taiwan's Ex-Defense Chief Calls for Sweeping Military Reforms," *Nikkei Asia*, July 20, 2022.

23. Global Taiwan Institute, "An Assessment of the Recent Chinese Incursion over the Taiwan Strait's Median Line," *Global Taiwan Brief* 7, no. 11 (2022).

24. CIGeography (@CIGeography), "PLA live fire areas published by Xinhua overlaps Taiwanese Internal and Territorial waters," h/t @StuartKLau @PolGeoNow @fravel @samsonellis #pelosi," Twitter, August 2, 2022, 12:09 p.m., https://twitter.com/CIGeography/status/1554499596155494400.

25. Mercedes Trent, "Number of Chinese Unauthorized ADIZ Intrusions by Year & Country," in *Over the Line: The Implications of China's ADIZ Intrusions in Northeast Asia* (Washington, DC: Federation of American Scientists, 2020), 15–16.

26. Ministry of Foreign Affairs of Japan, "Confirmation of Chinese Government Vessels in Japan's Maritime Areas Surrounding the Senkaku Islands," press release, August 17, 2016.

27. Thomas G. Mahnken, Travis Sharp, Chris Bassler, and Bryan W. Durkee, *Implementing Deterrence by Detection: Innovative Capabilities, Processes, and Organizations for Situational Awareness in the Indo-Pacific Region*, Center for Strategic and Budgetary Assessments, July 14, 2021.

28. Usman Haider, "The MQ-9B Sea Guardian and the Revolution in Anti-Submarine Warfare," Wavell Room, November 3, 2023.

29. ThayerMahan, "Sector: Defense & Intelligence," online, last accessed November 30, 2023.

30. Lucas Myers, "China's Economic Security Challenge: Difficulties Overcoming the Malacca Dilemma," *Georgetown Journal of International Affairs*, March 22, 2023.

31. Charlie Vest, Agatha Kratz, and Reva Goujon, "The Global Economic Disruptions from a Taiwan Conflict," Rhodium Group, December 14, 2022.

PART III
America's Job Now

CHAPTER 7

Sink China's Navy

**ROBERT HADDICK, MARK MONTGOMERY,
AND ISAAC "IKE" HARRIS**

*The first task, then, in planning for a war is to identify the
enemy's center of gravity, and if possible trace it back to a
single point. The second task is to ensure that the forces to be
used against that point are concentrated for a main offensive.*

—CARL VON CLAUSEWITZ, *VOM KRIEGE (ON WAR)*

A war for the control of Taiwan would be bloody for all combatants.
But that prospect may not dissuade Xi Jinping and the leaders of the
Communist Party of China (CCP) if the result was China's control of
Taiwan. From the CCP's perspective, the short-term costs and risks of a
People's Liberation Army (PLA) lunge for Taiwan may fade to nothing
compared with the achievement of the CCP's millenarian dreams.

The United States and its allies therefore need, and need to display, the military capacities to directly defeat any Chinese course of
action aimed at seizing Taiwan by force and pacifying its surviving
population. This is "deterrence by denial"—getting the adversary to
understand that its military strategies have little chance of success, thus
discouraging it from aggression.

The focus of chapters 7–9 is the military balance pertaining to
Taiwan scenarios. The reason for this focus is that hard military power
determines the outcome of high-stakes geopolitical contests, such as
the future of Taiwan. When the stakes are the highest and one side has

convincing military options for achieving its goals, that side will have a strong incentive to escalate to decisive military options to resolve the conflict in its favor. The purpose of deterrence by denial is to convince the opponent that it does not have that option available. Chapters 7–9 will discuss how the United States and its allies can achieve deterrence by denial for Taiwan and prevent a war over the island's fate.

Today's PLA can mass enormous combat power over and around Taiwan. China's military buildup constitutes the most rapid expansion of military power by a major country in peacetime since the 1930s.[1] The PLA now has more warships than any navy in the world, the largest array of airpower in Asia, and the greatest inventory of missile power in the Indo-Pacific region. In addition, the PLA has put in place the command and reconnaissance capabilities required for modern, high-tech, and high-intensity military operations. The result is a region-spanning battle network, combining sensors and long-range missiles, that is specifically designed to destroy US naval forces underway out to Guam and the Second Island Chain and to devastate the US military's air and naval bases in the Western Pacific.[2]

Even so, the United States and its allies can fashion a strategy and military capabilities that focus their competitive advantages against China's weakness and, importantly, that do not provide an opportunity for the PLA to do the same in return. If the United States and its allies swiftly implement the reforms described below, they can defeat a PLA amphibious assault against Taiwan or an extended air and maritime blockade. The US-led coalition needs to make some urgent investments to ensure that its battle network in the Western Pacific can strike the PLA's vulnerabilities and thus close the window of opportunity that might now be open for the PLA.

The Imperative of Deterrence by Denial

"Deterrence by denial" differs from "deterrence by punishment" and is the stronger and preferred form of deterrence in great power competition. Having the capability to directly defeat, or "deny," the adversary's military strategy and forces will leave the adversary with no further useful military options or a path to success.[3] When both sides agree that this state exists, deterrence by denial will exist.

If a defender cannot defeat or "deny" the aggressor's military strategy, the defender will instead have to resort to inflicting pain to dissuade the aggressor. The aggressor gets to decide how much pain it is willing to suffer, which, as numerous combatants throughout history have displayed, can be very high indeed. Those pursuing a punishment strategy cede the initiative to the target of the punishment and then must hope for the best. Unfortunately, hope is not a good strategy. It is much better to possess the capabilities to directly defeat the adversary's strategy and forces, denying it good choices or the initiative.[4]

What a Military Strategy to Thwart a PLA Lunge for Taiwan Should, and Should Not, Do

US and allied military planners should thus fashion an operational concept and acquire the supporting military forces designed to directly defeat the strategy and military forces the PLA will require for a military invasion of Taiwan. Although seemingly self-evident, this concept becomes more complex under deeper analysis. The PLA's carefully designed buildup over the past three decades reveals Chinese commanders and planners who understand the tasks they must accomplish and who have a deep understanding of the opportunities created by rapid advances in military technology.

The sheer size of the military force the PLA could aim at Taiwan is frightening. For example, under conservative assumptions the PLA's airpower can launch more than 1,400 precision-guided antiship and land-attack cruise missiles per day, day after day, at allied bases and warships out to the Second Island Chain, three thousand kilometers from China's coast.[5] The number of these PLA air-to-surface cruise missiles is not publicly known, but given the PLA's extraordinary buildup and China's military-industrial capacity, many thousands are likely available to the PLA's strike aircraft units.

In addition, in October 2023 the US Department of Defense identified 2,800 PLA land-based surface-to-surface ballistic and cruise missiles (a 70 percent increase according to the Pentagon's 2022 report), some capable of precision attacks out to Guam and against surface warships underway.[6] The PLA Navy's surface ships and submarines are armed with an equally large number of long-range land-attack and antiship cruise missiles. Some analysts suspect that China has developed the capability to launch cruise missiles hidden inside standard shipping containers, useful for surprise attacks on targets anywhere in the world.[7] US and allied commanders and planners face a steep challenge defending Taiwan from an assault with this quantity of precision-guided firepower.

How can US and allied military planners prepare for this challenge? The US Defense Department's *Joint Publication 5-0, Joint Planning* is the Pentagon's official doctrine for planning military operations. *JP 5-0* advises military planners to identify and attack the adversary's "center of gravity," which the publication defines as "the source of power or strength that enables a military force to achieve its objective and is what an opposing force can orient its actions against that will lead to enemy failure."[8]

Loss of a center-of-gravity asset can mean defeat when the center of gravity is an essential military capability a combatant requires for its campaign. The loss of political-military icons, like aircraft carriers and their embarked aircraft and crews, could demoralize policymakers and the public and similarly lead to defeat. The PLA specifically designed its "counter-intervention" force structure, its long-range battle network, to find, attack, and destroy US air and naval bases and carrier strike groups in the Western Pacific that would be used to intervene and counter a PLA assault on Taiwan. JP 5-0 advises US military planners to attack the adversary's center of gravity while avoiding the exposure of US and allied centers of gravity as they do so. Accomplishing this against the PLA in the Western Pacific will not be easy.

The PLA Navy Is the Center of Gravity

Designing a military strategy under *JP 5-0*'s center-of-gravity guidance implies that it won't be necessary to defeat the entirety of the PLA, or even all its invasion force, to deny a Chinese conquest of Taiwan. US and allied planners need only to find and destroy the PLA invasion force's center of gravity, the essential capability the PLA requires for a successful assault of Taiwan. The PLA Navy is that essential center-of-gravity target.[9] China needs its navy intact and free to operate if it is to land the hundreds of thousands of soldiers and millions of tons of equipment and supplies it will need for the conquest and long-term pacification of Taiwan. Airlift alone cannot provide the needed haulage capacity. Defeating China's navy will deny China military success.

How can US and allied military forces get to the PLA Navy in the Taiwan Strait when the PLA's region-spanning battle network is in place protecting the PLA Navy from US and allied intervention? In August 2022, a research team from the Center for Strategic and International Studies (CSIS) conducted twenty-four iterations of a war game that simulated a PLA amphibious assault against Taiwan. The team and game participants used the iterations to vary assumptions and parameters of the simulation to reveal interesting findings. The research team published those findings in January 2023, one of very few rigorous and unclassified studies of the Taiwan assault scenario released to the public.[10]

The good news from the perspective of Taiwan, the United States, and its allies is that the US-led coalition almost always defeated the PLA assault attempt, by annihilating the PLA Navy. The bad news is that US losses of warships, fighter aircraft, bases, and personnel in the Western Pacific were severe. Intense and continuous PLA antiship and land-attack missile strikes on air and naval bases and warship groups underway took a steep toll. Losses typically included two complete US aircraft carrier strike groups attempting to sail to Taiwan's aid; destruction of amphibious groups attempting to bring US troops to Taiwan; many hundreds of US Air Force and Marine Corps fighter aircraft destroyed on the ground at their Western Pacific bases; and more than ten thousand US personnel killed in action after three weeks of missile combat.[11]

This could be the butcher's bill for saving Taiwan. The United States and its allies would have struck China's vulnerable center of gravity, its navy. But in doing so, the allies would have exposed their own center of gravity to the PLA's firepower. The intensity of such losses, compressed into just a few weeks, would be shocking to the US public and could put at risk the will to continue the war should China choose to do so. US military planners should provide policymakers with an operational concept that can defeat the PLA Navy without risking such high casualties to do so.

Assembling a Broad Team to Defeat the PLA Navy

As this chapter will explain, all branches of the US military can contribute to defeating a prospective PLA amphibious assault against Taiwan. When all services contribute to the effort, PLA commanders and planners will face increasing operational dilemmas that will add complexity to the challenge of successfully crossing the Taiwan Strait with an invasion force. Fortunately, all branches of the US military are now preparing for the PLA threat. Even so, there remain shortcomings and missed opportunities within these preparations, which policymakers and planners in Washington and elsewhere must address.

The US Space Force, along with other government and private-sector space-based intelligence-gathering resources, will make the first contribution to thwarting a PLA attack on Taiwan. Imaging and signal intelligence satellites will detect Chinese war preparations potentially many months in advance. Such indications would include a surge in the production of the missiles and munitions the PLA would need for its assault on Taiwan; the construction of new bases, warehouses, and infrastructure needed for transporting and positioning military equipment, supplies, and personnel; changes in the pattern of training and maintenance cycles for military personnel and equipment; repositioning military forces at coastal bases and embarkation areas; repositioning command posts to wartime sites; the diversion of normally civilian ferries, cargo ships, trucks, rail equipment, and aircraft for military use; the diversion and stockpiling of fuel, food, and other supplies near embarkation areas; and the call-up and deployment of reserve forces.[12]

USS *Springfield,* a Los Angeles–class attack submarine, docks at its home port at Polaris Point, Guam. The USS *Springfield* is a part of the US forward-deployed submarine force in the Pacific. *Mark Pavely/US Navy*

Space-based intelligence-gathering resources would detect these and many other signs of impending military action. Such advanced warning would allow US and allied political leaders to make their own diplomatic, economic, and informational preparations. And of course, US and allied military commanders could use this interval to prepare and reposition their forces.

Should Chinese leaders proceed with their assault on Taiwan, the US Navy's attack submarine force would likely be the first to engage in the kinetic phase of the war. The US Navy has assigned twenty-four of its forty-nine attack submarines to the Pacific Ocean, each of which carries more than twenty Mk-48 heavy torpedoes.[13] The US Navy's attack submarines are thought to be the best in the world and are the foundation of US dominance in undersea warfare.[14] As such, they are well matched for countering a PLA Navy amphibious force attempting to cross the Taiwan Strait.

The US Air Force's bomber force—141 aircraft capable of large payloads and global range with aerial refueling—is also an excellent matchup against the PLA Navy.[15] US bombers are based outside the PLA's reach, can refuel beyond the PLA's interception range, can raid the PLA Navy in the Taiwan Strait or at China's ports with long-range missiles, and can then withdraw to secure bases to prepare for more missions. With each aircraft able to carry and launch sixteen to twenty-four long-range precision-guided land-attack and antiship missiles, the US bomber force, flying about one-third of the force's aircraft each day, could launch about eight hundred of these missiles against the PLA assault forces per day.[16] The latest US aircraft adapted to fire the Long Range Anti-Ship Missile (LRASM) is the US Navy's P-8 Poseidon maritime patrol aircraft. These modified, in-flight refuelable Boeing 737 aircraft, of which there are more than one hundred in inventory, will significantly increase the attack vectors the PLA Navy will need to consider.

PLA commanders and planners will also have to account for the US Navy's guided missile destroyers, dozens of which are based in the Pacific. The US Navy's destroyers will soon be able to launch a maritime strike variant of the long-range Tomahawk cruise missile. In addition, the navy has adapted its destroyer-launched Standard Missile 6 (SM-6) long-range air defense missile for use against surface targets.[17]

US ground forces are also building their own shore-based antiship capabilities. The US Army is acquiring the Precision Strike Missile, future versions of which will be capable of attacking surface ships underway.[18] The US Marine Corps is reorganizing itself for missile combat against the PLA from outposts along the First Island Chain. The service is acquiring the Naval Strike Missile for its shore-based antiship forces.[19]

The Challenge of Missile Combat in the Western Pacific

The development of these capabilities across the services demonstrates the Department of Defense's growing focus on countering possible Chinese military aggression. Even so, the massive volume and range of potential PLA missile firepower, the large number of targets the United States and its coalition partners will have to attack, the vast distances in the Western Pacific, and the relatively tiny amount of island terrain available for basing US military forces combine to limit the effectiveness of much of what the US military services are attempting to build.

As mentioned, the August 2022 CSIS Taiwan war-game series described the devastation that PLA missiles would inflict on US and allied forces attempting to operate from the Second Island Chain westward. This devastation occurs for three reasons. First, as mentioned, PLA airpower can launch over 1,400 antiship and land-attack cruise missiles per day, with the PLA's 2,800 land-based missiles and numerous ship-based missiles adding to this total.

Second, the PLA's electro-optical, synthetic aperture radar and nearly three hundred electronic intelligence satellites in orbit will provide continuous, all-weather, day-and-night, and finely detailed observation of US and allied military units operating within the PLA's missile engagement zone, which extends more than three thousand kilometers from China's coast (space-based synthetic aperture radar is now capable of image resolution of fifty centimeters or less, detailed enough to distinguish individual ship types and vehicles through any weather). The PLA possesses a comprehensive and redundant command and communication system, supported by over sixty communication and forty-nine navigation satellites, through which PLA commanders will control their theater-wide missile-based campaign.[20]

Third, US and allied forces have few places to hide: the surface of the ocean provides no concealment and the PLA's overhead reconnaissance system can continuously surveil the small islands in the Western Pacific.

Thus, the task of countering a PLA amphibious assault on Taiwan will fall most heavily on US and allied attack submarines plus the US Air Force's long-range bombers based outside the range of the PLA's missiles. The US Army and Marine Corps antiship missile programs will serve to complicate PLA planning. But these units on the First Island Chain may struggle to survive and aren't currently in a position to make more than a minor contribution, a conclusion the CSIS research team also reached.[21] Short-range tactical aircraft and surface naval forces will similarly be at great risk. The CSIS war-game series revealed that the more the US commander built up his naval and tactical air forces close to Taiwan, the worse the outcome for the United States since this exposed more targets for the PLA's missiles to destroy.[22]

US commanders will have to weigh the contribution these forces could make to the battle versus the likely rapid destruction they would suffer.

Requirements for Success and Capability Gaps

US and allied campaign planners may have to reckon with over a thousand ship targets, consisting of over three hundred PLA Navy "gray hull" warships, supported by hundreds more from China's paramilitary coast guard, its "maritime militia," and large and advanced ferries and civilian cargo ships that were designed to transport military vehicles and supplies across the Taiwan Strait.[23] Thwarting a PLA amphibious assault may also require attacks on the ports, piers, and warehouses the PLA would use to embark its Taiwan-bound landing force. US and allied forces may also need to suppress PLA airbases and air defense systems. The result is a long list of targets, amounting to perhaps thousands of individual weapon aimpoints.

For the United States, its Pacific Fleet attack submarines will likely be the first to attack the PLA warships and elements of the amphibious assault armada. The stealthy and sophisticated submarines will inflict a high toll on PLA warships that block entry into the Taiwan Strait or that attempt to move east of Taiwan to establish air and sea control positions. The submarines' Tomahawk cruise missiles could also attack shore-based air defense targets, a task the submarines have performed numerous times since the 1991 Persian Gulf War.

Unfortunately, maintenance problems are limiting the submarines' availability; one-third of the navy's attack submarines are idle at depot maintenance shipyards.[24] Applying this factor to submarines assigned to the Pacific leaves just fifteen submarines available for all missions, which include responding to Russian and North Korean contingencies. Policymakers could transfer attack submarines based outside the Pacific, taking risks with possible opportunistic aggression elsewhere in the world.

Fifteen US attack submarines responding to the Taiwan crisis would carry with them about 375 torpedoes, enough to potentially destroy scores of PLA Navy and auxiliary ships. After expending their torpedoes, surviving submarines would have to return to a functioning naval base to reload. Accounting for PLA missile strikes, the nearest such US base would be Hawaii or, if also damaged, the West Coast of the United States. There are closer naval bases in allied countries, but these would likely be damaged if those countries entered the war or closed for US military operations if they had not. The result would be a two- or three-week interval before the reloaded US submarines returned to the Taiwan battle.

The US bomber force would have to assume responsibility for most of the remaining campaign against the PLA armada. Like the submarine fleet, maintenance problems limit the bomber force's availability. In 2022, 41 percent of the B-1Bs, 59 percent of the B-2As, and 59 percent of the B-52Hs were designated "mission capable."[25] Applying these percentages to the current bomber force yields seventy-three potentially available bombers for all missions, including strategic nuclear deterrence and other contingencies. Under a conservative assumption of forty bombers ready and assigned each day to the Taiwan war, the bomber force could launch about eight hundred long-range land-attack and antiship missiles per day.

Munitions Are the Problem

A shortage of appropriate munitions for the bombers' counter-maritime campaign remains the most serious, but fixable, problem. The best US missile for attacking PLA warships is the air-launched LRASM. The LRASM is stealthy and designed to identify and attack a particular ship in a formation of ships underway. Its 375-mile range allows the launching aircraft to remain outside the range of most PLA air defenses. The LRASM is a variant of the Joint Air-to-Surface Standoff Missile-Extended Range (JASSM-ER), a precision long-range missile for attacking fixed targets on land. Lockheed Martin assembles both missiles at the same production facility. Both the JASSM-ER and the LRASM are fully tested and in production.[26]

Unfortunately, the US Air Force plans to acquire only a negligible quantity of LRASMs even as it plans for a large stockpile of the land-attack JASSM variant. The air force's fiscal year 2024 budget proposal requests the purchase of only twenty-seven LRASMs during the fiscal year, compared with 550 JASSM-ERs. For the missiles' entire acquisition programs ending later this decade, the air force envisions acquiring only 488 antiship LRASMs, compared with an eventual stockpile of 12,323 land-attack JASSMs.[27] The US Air Force's B-1B bombers could expend the entire planned inventory of LRASMs with just twenty aircraft sorties—only one or two days of combat over the Taiwan Strait.

The US Navy and Air Force acquisition plans for LRASMs are insufficient to counter a prospective PLA amphibious assault against Taiwan. During such a scenario, the US bomber force is the only tool capable of launching the large volume of antiship missiles needed to cope with the PLA invasion fleet, potentially numbering over a thousand vessels.[28]

Are there other suitable air-launched antiship munitions that could add to the slim inventory of LRASMs? The US bomber force needs munitions with at least moderate range (up to three hundred miles) that airmen can fit with different sensors depending on the target (fixed or moving targets on land or ships at sea underway), that suppliers can assemble in large numbers at a steady rate, and that the US Air Force and Navy can purchase in large numbers at reasonable prices. The JASSM and the LRASM do not meet these requirements; although long range and highly effective, these missiles are expensive ($3.25 million for one LRASM) and too difficult to assemble in large numbers.

To remedy this problem, the Boeing Company has developed the Powered Joint Direct Attack Munition (PJDAM). The PJDAM is a kit that includes a small jet engine, fold-out wings, fuel, a small electrical generator, and precision-guidance sensors that attach to a standard five-hundred-pound bomb. The PJDAM has a range of three hundred miles from its launch point and is capable of precision attacks on moving targets including ships underway.[29]

Although not as sophisticated as the JASSM-ER or the LRASM, the PJDAM is an example of an "affordable mass" munition that the US bomber force could employ for a long, sustained campaign.

Forty bomber sorties per day, with each aircraft armed with thirty of the smaller PJDAMs, would deliver strikes against 1,200 aimpoints per day and at ranges that greatly reduce the risks to the bombers from China's air defenses.

US and allied attack submarines could assist the bombers' counter-maritime campaign by focusing their torpedo attacks on the PLA Navy's air defense cruisers, destroyers, and frigates, beginning with those warships operating east of Taiwan. About one hundred PLA warships are on this list.[30] The submarines could also assist the bombers with Tomahawk land-attack missile strikes on PLA air defense targets.[31]

Reconnaissance and Command from Space

In addition to providing early warning of a PLA military operation against Taiwan, US and allied space forces would provide overhead optical, infrared, synthetic aperture radar, and electronic surveillance and reconnaissance of the battle zone around Taiwan, identifying targets for the bombers and submarines. Space forces will also provide critical communication pathways for imagery data and commands to and from commanders and the "shooters," the bombers and submarines.[32] US space forces will also require the capability to defend themselves against PLA counter-space operations and should possess the capability to hold at-risk PLA space assets to deter Chinese escalation into the space domain.[33]

Given the PLA's formidable counter-space capabilities, success in the space domain will require accelerating the buildout of the new generation of satellite constellations composed of scores or hundreds of satellites. With space now militarily contested "terrain," the United States and its allies also require space assets that monitor the space domain for adversary activity and defend US and allied space assets.

The US Space Force is currently deploying its Proliferated Warfighter Space Architecture (PWSA), which will eventually comprise an integrated network of up to five hundred communication and missile-warning satellites in low earth orbit. The PWSA will provide global coverage, securely and reliably transporting targeting data and commands to individual air, naval, and ground units in combat.[34] It will be difficult for the PLA to defeat the widely distributed and self-healing PWSA network.

As it builds out its own proprietary distributed communication and reconnaissance satellite constellations, the US Space Force and other US government agencies have supporting relationships with numerous private-sector space service providers. For example, under the Starshield program, Space Exploration Technologies (SpaceX) provides secure communications, earth observation, and specialized launch services to the US Space Force.[35] Other private-sector space companies also provide the US Defense Department and other government agencies with electro-optical and synthetic aperture radar images, electronic intelligence, and specialized space domain awareness and adversary tracking capabilities. Although necessary under current circumstances, the US Defense Department and intelligence agency officials should assess how reliable these private vendors will be during the stress of combat and what risk mitigation they should consider while the government completes its own proprietary constellations.

The US Space Force and other agencies are in a transition from legacy constellations composed of a few expensive and highly vulnerable satellites to new resilient constellations composed of hundreds of networked assets. There is a race to establish these new capabilities in the face of the PLA's counter-space capabilities and a looming showdown in the Western Pacific.

Preparing for War

US military commanders in the Western Pacific will require guidance from policymakers on the scope of their latitude to employ military force. These rules of engagement will govern the amount and types of US military forces allocated to the battle, the weapon systems they are permitted to employ, the types of targets they can attack, and the geographic boundaries for these operations.

Policymakers and military commanders should expect a PLA amphibious assault attempt against Taiwan to be incredibly intense and rapid. For the commanders tasked with repelling the assault, there will be little time for contemplating alternative parameters to the rules of engagement. The CSIS war-game series revealed that delaying the US decision to enter the battle greatly increased the probability of a PLA victory and increased the losses of US forces that entered the war.[36]

Therefore, the US president and his advisors should determine well in advance of a crisis the authorities and rules of engagement under which US military commanders will operate given various scenarios. These authorities will have to consider permitting attacks on China's port, piers, embarkation facilities, and air defenses. In war games, people playing the role of American decision makers have often been loath to strike the Chinese mainland out of concern it would lead to an escalatory spiral. This is another reason why the air force's tiny stockpile of antiship missiles is so problematic. It constrains a US president's options and may force him to confront a dilemma he wouldn't otherwise face, either using more plentiful land-attack missiles to repel a PLA invasion or accepting a colossal US defeat.

In any case, delaying this analysis and crucial decisions about rules of engagement until after the war begins will benefit the PLA and increase US and allied losses. Policymakers may believe that strategic warning (discussed earlier) will allow them time for contemplation, but it will be dangerous to assume that there will always be adequate warning. Beijing should be kept guessing, of course, about how far the US president would be willing to go in war. Announcing in advance what the US president would *not* be willing to do is a cardinal sin when trying to maximize deterrence.

The US Eighth Air Force, responsible for all US bomber units, should regularly practice operating from a wide variety of dispersed and expeditionary locations around the United States and the Pacific region. Commanders should prepare to disperse the bomber force into small units and prepare systems to support and maintain these distributed units under wartime conditions. The US Air Force's aerial refueling force should similarly prepare to support the prospective bomber campaign spanning the Pacific Ocean. Commanders should ensure that a resilient command system is in place to coordinate the elements of this campaign. This should all be integrated into the US Air Force's "Agile Combat Employment" concept, a plan to rapidly distribute US aircraft to numerous temporary airfields that have Deployable Air Base Sets (DABS) with fuel bladders, runway repair kits, temporary air control, and unique maintenance and weapons-handling gear.

Military forces and relevant defense industries inside the US homeland should also prepare for war. The PLA's ability to strike the continental United States is limited, but it is not zero. Without preparation, critical targets could be vulnerable to damage from cruise missiles launched from submarines and shipping containers or from infiltrators prepositioned inside the US homeland. Potentially vulnerable sites might include aircraft and missile production facilities, naval bases, and air bases. These facilities are also dependent on the utilities that supply them with electrical power, which could also be vulnerable. PLA-linked infiltrators could target bomber crews and their families, as well as critical defense industry workers, living in unprotected areas. Commanders and managers inside the United States should prepare for worst-case scenarios.

To assault Taiwan, the PLA would have to expose its amphibious fleet to a US and allied battle network. US commanders and planners can fashion and organize the tools to hold this vulnerable Chinese center-of-gravity target at risk and do so without also risking large-scale US casualties. However, gaps in US capabilities and preparations remain. US policymakers and military planners should immediately focus their attention on ensuring that their team is ready for the amphibious assault scenario.

Two-Year Action Plan

What actions in the near term should US policymakers and planners take to ensure the readiness of their forces to defeat a PLA amphibious assault against Taiwan?

1. The US Department of Defense and Congress should urgently appropriate supplemental funding to reform and improve the US submarine industrial base, to reduce the backlog of attack

submarines currently idle while awaiting maintenance. Congress should also increase funding for bomber maintenance, to increase bomber mission readiness.

2. Policymakers should direct the commanders of US bomber and air-refueling forces to make the counter-maritime mission in the Indo-Pacific theater their top conventional military priority. Bomber and refueling force commanders, planners, air crews, and support personnel should focus their training and logistic preparations on Indo-Pacific contingencies, especially those related to Taiwan. Bomber force commanders and support units should practice operating from a wide variety of dispersed and expeditionary bases.

3. US Air Force and Navy acquisition officials should urgently acquire the largest feasible stockpiles of "affordable mass" precision-guided air-to-surface munitions, such as the Powered Joint Direct Attack Munition. Engineering and testing teams should rapidly certify these munitions with a variety of sensor and precision-guidance options to reliably strike maritime targets in all weather, illumination, and electronic warfare conditions. Executing this action is feasible using already proven technology employed in other weapon systems.

4. The US Navy and Air Force program offices responsible for JASSM and LRASM procurement should work with the supplier to dramatically and rapidly increase the production of the LRASM variant, even though it will mean fewer JASSMs, of which the air force already has thousands in stock.

5. US Air Force policymakers should recall ten B-1B Lancer bombers the service retired in 2021 and request Congress to appropriate the approximately $300 million it would take to restore these aircraft to flight operations.[37] This action would add the capacity to launch 240 JASSM and LRASM missiles to the total bomber launch capacity and more than 300 PJDAMs or similar munitions.

6. US policymakers and defense planners should consider plans to pre-position US Army and Marine Corps antiship munitions

and combat supplies in Taiwan to facilitate the option of deploying these US forces to Taiwan before or during a contingency.

7. Acquisition officials in the US Space Force should accelerate the deployment of the service's Proliferated Warfighter Space Architecture satellite constellation, to provide US and allied combined and joint forces with a resilient and reliable global communication network impervious to PLA counter-space capabilities.

8. Leaders of the US Space Force and the US intelligence community should review their relationships with private-sector space-based imagery and satellite communication companies that currently provide detailed electro-optical, synthetic aperture radar, infrared, and electronic intelligence imagery and communication services, to ensure that these relationships will be reliable during wartime and that these vendors integrate effectively with combat intelligence products and war plans.[38]

9. The US Space Force should acquire, and the US Space Command should employ, maneuvering and potentially armed space assets. These systems should be capable of closely inspecting adversary space assets and providing prospective offensive military capabilities in space, with the goal of deterring aggressive adversary actions against US and allied space-based capabilities.

10. US policymakers should direct US Indo-Pacific Command and US Air Force Global Strike Command commanders to periodically conduct large- and short-notice "show of force" training exercises in and over the Western Pacific, to display to Chinese and allied leaders the ability of US forces to quickly mobilize large-scale battle networks and firepower for prospective Taiwan military contingencies. Such exercises are good training opportunities, and they also display capabilities and will to potential adversaries and partners, essential for sustaining deterrence and reassuring allies.

11. Commanders of military facilities in the US homeland, along with managers of critical defense industrial sites and the private-sector owners and operators of US critical infrastructure, should prepare their facilities and personnel for potential cyberattacks,

long-range missiles strikes, and infiltrators in the event of a crisis over Taiwan. Special attention should be paid to the critical infrastructure that support military mobility—rail, air, and port systems and the power grids and utilities that support them.

12. The US Navy should expedite operational certification and delivery of Maritime Strike Tomahawks to the fleet. This would provide more than one hundred additional long-range strike platforms for US commanders.

13. US planners must plan and exercise with Taiwan counterparts to understand the capability and capacity of Taiwanese surface ships, submarines, aircraft, and ground-based units to sink PLA vessels. Taiwan has a large number of missiles, but these will be heavily attacked by the PLA. This planning effort would allow for maximum coordination among forces in a kinetic conflict and help prevent friendly-fire incidents.

Summing up, the United States and its allies in the region could have the tools in place to defeat a prospective PLA amphibious assault against Taiwan and do so without exposing large and vulnerable formations of its forces to the PLA's firepower, as happened during most iterations of the 2022 CSIS Taiwan war-game series. These tools would include the US Navy's attack submarines; the US Air Force's bombers and air-refueling tankers; cheap, easy-to-build, precision-guided munitions, like the PJDAM; and overhead reconnaissance, targeting, and communications support from the US Space Force and other stealthy strategic reconnaissance capabilities.

Policymakers should urgently turn their attention to completing the actions described above. Doing so will strengthen deterrence against the amphibious assault scenario, a looming danger to US, Taiwanese, and allied interests over the remainder of this decade.

NOTES

1. Jacqueline Deal, "China Could Soon Outgun the U.S.," *Politico* China Watcher, May 27, 2021.

2. Office of the Secretary of Defense, *Military and Security Developments Involving the People's Republic of China 2023: Annual Report to Congress*, US Department of Defense, October 19, 2023, v–vii.
3. Lawrence Freedman, *Deterrence* (Cambridge, UK: Polity Press, 2004), 37–39.
4. Freedman, *Deterrence*, 37–40.
5. Robert Haddick, "Defeat China's Navy, Defeat China's War Plan," *War on the Rocks*, September 21, 2022.
6. Office of the Secretary of Defense, *Military and Security Developments Involving the People's Republic of China 2022: Annual Report to Congress*, US Department of Defense, November 29, 2022, 167; Office of the Secretary of Defense, *Military and Security Developments Involving the People's Republic of China 2023*, 186.
7. Ronald O'Rourke, *China Naval Modernization: Implications for U.S. Navy Capabilities—Background and Issues for Congress*, Congressional Research Service (RL33153), October 19, 2023, 15–18.
8. US Department of Defense, *Joint Publication 5-0: Joint Planning*, December 1, 2020, iv–22.
9. Mark F. Cancian, Matthew Cancian, and Eric Heginbotham, *The First Battle of the Next War: Wargaming a Chinese Invasion of Taiwan*, Center for Strategic and International Studies, January 2023, 111.
10. Cancian, Cancian, and Heginbotham, *First Battle of the Next War*.
11. Cancian, Cancian, and Heginbotham, *First Battle of the Next War*, 106–15.
12. John Culver, "How We Would Know When China Is Preparing to Invade Taiwan," Carnegie Endowment for International Peace, October 3, 2022.
13. US Department of the Navy, "Attack Submarines—SSN," Fact File, March 13, 2023.
14. Ronald O'Rourke, *Navy Virginia-Class Submarine Program and AUKUS Submarine Proposal: Background and Issues for Congress*, Congressional Research Service (RL32418), November 13, 2023.
15. US Department of the Air Force, *FY 2024 Department of the Air Force Budget Overview*, March 2023, 43.
16. Haddick, "Defeat China's Navy."
17. US Department of the Navy, "Destroyers (DDG 51)," US Navy Fact File, December 13, 2022.
18. Gabe Camarillo, *U.S. Army Fiscal Year Budget Overview 2024*, Department of the Army, 22.
19. US Department of the Navy, *Highlights of the Department of the Navy FY 2023 Budget*, Department of the Navy, 2–10.
20. Office of the Secretary of Defense, *Military and Security Developments Involving the People's Republic of China 2023*, 98–101.
21. Cancian, Cancian, and Heginbotham, *First Battle of the Next War*, 129–31.

22. Cancian, Cancian, and Heginbotham, *First Battle of the Next War*, 131–32.

23. US Department of the Navy, US Marine Corps, and US Coast Guard, *Advantage at Sea: Prevailing with Integrated All-Domain Naval Power*, December 2020, 4.

24. O'Rourke, *Navy Virginia-Class Submarine Program*, 5.

25. Rachel S. Cohen and Stephen Losey, "US Air Force Fleet's Mission-Capable Rates Are Stagnating: Here's the Plan to Change That," *Air Force Times*, February 14, 2022.

26. David B. Larter, "The US Military Has Put Scores More Ship-Killer Missiles under Contract as Pacific Tension Continue," *Defense News*, March 11, 2021.

27. US Department of the Air Force, *Fiscal Year (FY) 2024 Air Force Justification Book, Missile Procurement*, March 2023, 31, 53.

28. Cancian, Cancian, and Heginbotham, *First Battle of the Next War*, 111.

29. Boeing Corporation, "Powered Joint Direct Attack Munition: Affordable Standoff," fact sheet, 2022.

30. Office of the Secretary of Defense, *Military and Security Developments Involving the People's Republic of China 2023*, 186.

31. Cancian, Cancian, and Heginbotham, *First Battle of the Next War*, 112–13.

32. US Space Force, Space Development Agency, home page, July 2023.

33. Charles S. Galbreath, *Building U.S. Space Force Counterspace Capabilities: An Imperative for America's Defense*, Mitchell Institute for Aerospace Studies Policy Paper, vol. 42, June 2023.

34. US Space Force Space Development Agency, "Space Development Agency—Transport," November 2023.

35. Brett Tingley, "SpaceX Wins $70 Million Space Force Contract for Starshield Military Satellites," Space.com, October 2, 2023.

36. Cancian, Cancian, and Heginbotham, *First Battle of the Next War*, 92, 100.

37. John A. Tirpak, "First of 17 B-1Bs Heads to the Boneyard," *Air & Space Forces Magazine*, February 17, 2021.

38. Mitchell Institute for Aerospace Power, "Spacepower and the Commercial Realm: Insider Perspective," *Aerospace Advantage* podcast no. 133, June 17, 2023.

CHAPTER 8

Quarantines and Blockades

**ROBERT HADDICK, ELAINE LURIA,
AND MARK MONTGOMERY**

*A defensive campaign can be fought with offensive battles. . . . The
defensive form of war is not a simple shield, but a shield made up of
well-directed blows.*

—CARL VON CLAUSEWITZ, *VOM KRIEGE (ON WAR)*

Do Chinese Communist Party (CCP) leaders have other military options to coerce Taiwan into subjugation? A blockade of Taiwan by the
People's Liberation Army (PLA) that attempted to deny the island not
just weapons but also food, fuel, and other commerce would be an
alternative course of action. Indeed, as this chapter will explain, a PLA
blockade of Taiwan would be difficult for Taiwan, the United States,
and its allies to counter, since it emphasizes Chinese military "home
court" advantages that cannot be offset by many of the US capabilities
discussed in chapter 7 that would be useful in repelling an amphibious
assault.

As an island, Taiwan is particularly vulnerable to a blockade.
Summing the island's consumption of crude oil, liquid fuels, coal, and
liquefied natural gas, Taiwan imports 93 percent of its total energy requirement.[1] Taiwan also imports about 65 percent of its daily food calorie consumption (though it also exports a significant amount of food
and has large and well-diversified fishing and agriculture industries).[2]

Taiwan can certainly improve its national security by building stockpiles of essential commodities such as fuel and food. But stockpiles, however large, will only buy Taiwan some time. The island's long-term survival will require breaking a prospective PLA blockade.

A blockade is not merely a "lesser and included case" within the amphibious assault scenario for US and allied military planners. The blockade scenario has separate characteristics and thus separate challenges for military planners and political decision makers. Deterring a blockade will require distinct military capabilities not essential for countering a PLA amphibious assault of Taiwan. These capability requirements are more sophisticated and more difficult to develop and produce, leaving US and allied forces with greater capability gaps compared with those revealed for the amphibious assault scenario.

For these reasons, the blockade scenario is dangerous for Taiwan and the US-led coalition—one that negates many US asymmetric military advantages while still carrying a high risk of escalating to a full war. Chinese policymakers and planners appear to understand this, as their air, sea, and missile exercises around Taiwan in August 2022 suggest.

Why China's Leaders Could Prefer a Blockade

For China's leaders, initiating a military campaign for Taiwan with a blockade has several attractive features.

First, China's leaders would present a blockade against Taiwan as a legitimate exercise of sovereignty. China's leaders would argue that Taiwan is Chinese territory (a condition few have yet to formally dispute) and that China, like all sovereign countries, has a legal right to extend its authority over all its territory.[3] China's government could begin the blockade as a customs and regulatory inspection quarantine, explained to prevent contraband and illegal goods, such as weapons, from arriving on the island. Should Taiwan resist its disarmament, China could then escalate the blockade to include more and more commerce, culminating with a complete siege, including food and fuel. The world had a hard time rallying behind Ukraine after Russia's military

Taiwan president Tsai Ing-wen (left) meets with US Speaker of the House Kevin McCarthy (right) in the spring of 2023. The PRC had just announced that it would board and inspect cross-strait merchant and construction vessels for three days. Although the Fujian Maritime Safety Administration did not act on its retaliatory threat, the pronouncement serves as an example of what a prelude to a blockade might look like. *Mario Tama via Getty Images*

encroachments began in 2014, despite Ukraine being recognized worldwide as a sovereign state with a United Nations seat. Imagine how much more difficult it could be to rally support for Taiwan, which only a handful of small countries officially recognize with formal diplomatic ties.[4] In contrast to the amphibious assault scenario discussed in chapter 7, a Chinese inspection quarantine could begin with little warning, causing US and allied policymakers who had not prepared for the scenario to scramble for effective options and responses.

Second, China could begin the initial inspection quarantine without kinetic military action. It would then be up to policymakers in Taiwan and elsewhere, not to mention the companies that underwrite insurance policies for commercial ships and airplanes, to "run" the blockade. If Beijing were effective at enforcing the blockade without using kinetic force—an assumption that is widely debated (more on this in a moment)—the onus would fall on Taiwan or its partners to escalate to violent military action. China's leaders would portray this as Taiwan or its partners "taking the first shot" in a war to resist China's sovereignty claims.[5]

Third, if China were willing to use force, it could impose a complete blockade against Taiwan without exposing a critical center-of-gravity target, namely the PLA Navy, to US and allied firepower beyond China's territory, as it would have to with the amphibious assault scenario. This is because China could use airpower and missile forces based on the Chinese mainland, as well as coast guard cutters and PLA Navy submarines, to impose the blockade on merchant shipping and air traffic in and out of Taiwan. The PLA would not have to deploy the bulk of its navy or air force assets.

Antiship missiles on aircraft and transporter-erector-launchers (TELs) in southeast China are presently capable of holding at-risk merchant ships bound to or from Taiwan's ports (see chapter 7 for a description of these capabilities). Similarly, the PLA's fighter aircraft and mobile surface-to-air missiles batteries based in southeast China could threaten air cargo attempting to fly in or out of Taiwan. The PLA can strangle Taiwan without having to bombard Taiwan or attack US or allied military forces in the region.

Fourth, CCP and PLA leaders could view a blockade strategy as a form of slow-boiling irregular warfare, the type of war that has repeatedly flummoxed US policymakers and military strategists and tested the resolve of the US public. The blockade might be much less shocking than the "sneak attacks," such as Pearl Harbor in December 1941 and the al-Qaeda terror assault in September 2001, that enraged and galvanized Americans. Without this dramatic beginning, the US public might not respond to the situation and US policymakers would have to explain the case for intervention, which they may struggle to do. In recent decades, US policymakers and the public have struggled with how to respond to limited wars. Fears about uncontrolled escalation and resource constraints have undermined the formulation of effective strategy. China's leaders will have a strong motivation to exploit this syndrome.

Fifth, a blockade would potentially create an opportunity for the PLA to threaten to employ its battle network, a PLA competitive advantage, against vulnerable US and allied maritime targets. Should the PLA impose a total blockade of Taiwan, saving Taiwan would require the arrival of relief convoys that would have to run through and survive the PLA's land-based blockade forces.

As discussed in chapter 7, the PLA has specifically designed its battle network to overwhelm and defeat naval task forces that would attempt to protect a convoy of merchant ships trying to make it to Taiwan's ports. The PLA has long prepared for this scenario, which presents a difficult challenge for the forces that would attempt to bring food, fuel, and other products to Taiwan.

A Blockade's Road to War

A PLA blockade would eventually compel US policymakers to decide between reneging on their informal security commitment to the island, likely resulting in Taiwan's defeat, and risking a large-scale missile war against the PLA.

As mentioned, a PLA blockade would likely begin with the announcement of a customs and regulatory inspection quarantine, focusing on the seizure of weapons bound for Taiwan's defense forces. China's coast guard would attempt to stop and board merchant ships, while the PLA Air Force would attempt to divert selected aircraft bound for Taiwan to Chinese airports for inspection.

Taiwan's government would have to decide how to respond. It would do so based not only on its own will to resist at that time, but also on what indications of support it would receive from the US government and the international community. CCP and PLA leaders would observe while also visibly preparing additional military forces for action.

If Taiwan resists the quarantine through increasingly aggressive action against China's coast guard cutters and fighter aircraft imposing the quarantine, it courts the likelihood of missile attacks on cutters and warships, air battles over and around Taiwan, and the PLA imposing a complete maritime and air blockade of Taiwan.

With that, Taiwan would face a rapidly growing humanitarian crisis as it consumed its fuel and food reserves. Within weeks, Taiwan would require relief convoys to keep supplies flowing and the economy functioning at a basic level. The US military would be the only force capable of challenging the PLA's blockade. US policymakers would have to decide whether to risk doing so. If they did not, Taiwan and its population of twenty-four million would eventually have to surrender.

Should the US government intervene, it would do so by organizing a relief convoy escorted by US Navy warships and military aircraft, hopefully supported with similar military assets from allies in the region.

As the convoy approached Taiwan, China's leaders would then face the choice of letting the convoy dock and offload in Taiwan, or attacking and destroying it. Allowing the convoy to pass would reveal the attempted blockade to be a Chinese bluff. That could end the crisis around Taiwan only to invite one inside China, where Xi Jinping could be weakened in the eyes of rival elites and the general population after having lost face so dramatically to the US Navy.

US and allied leaders should instead expect that CCP and PLA leaders would not begin the quarantine gambit without having thought its sequence and consequences all the way through. Since the Third Taiwan Strait Crisis in the mid-1990s, the PLA has designed and built its "counter-intervention" battle network for this scenario. China's leaders would begin an inspection quarantine of Taiwan when they are confident that the PLA could defeat a US-led maritime relief operation of Taiwan. US and allied leaders should not assume that China's leaders are bluffing. Instead, they should expect a relief convoy to trigger missile combat and high casualties imposed on US and allied personnel in the convoy.

Why Breaking a PLA Blockade of Taiwan Is So Challenging

Historically, countries imposed blockades on adversaries by positioning some of their midsized warships, such as coast guard cutters, cruisers, and destroyers, on the approaches to the adversary's ports, to prevent cargo ships from arriving or departing. Today, the PLA's long-range battle networks, deployed in the Taiwan scenario on bases and mobile missile launchers in southeast China, are now sufficient to thwart the travel of cargo ships to and from Taiwan's piers. The PLA's battle network, spanning the Western Pacific Ocean, will continuously track, with redundant overhead imagery assets, the positions and movements of convoys, merchant ships, and their warship escorts. The PLA's sensors and command networks are linked to a variety of long-range precision-guided antiship weapons, such as China's land-based antiship ballistic missiles and air-launched antiship cruise missiles.

Defeating a blockade of Taiwan would thus require much more than sinking Chinese coast guard cutters, cruisers, and destroyers lurking off Taiwan's ports. Breaking the blockade would require suppressing the PLA's extensive battle network deployed and dispersed across southeast China.[6]

This means that top US policymakers must first have the will to authorize a wide-ranging and prolonged bombing campaign of the Chinese mainland. During the 2022 CSIS war-game series discussed in chapter 7, US force commanders decided against such a bombing campaign. According to the war-game report, these commanders thought such a campaign was unnecessary for thwarting the PLA's amphibious assault attempt against Taiwan. In addition, US commanders thought the risks of aircraft losses and possible uncontrolled escalation outweighed possible benefits for the task they were assigned, defeating the PLA's invasion of Taiwan.[7]

But the CSIS war-game series specifically did not examine the blockade scenario.[8] As discussed above, the characteristics of the blockade scenario differ from those of the amphibious assault scenario, and the progress of a war-game modeling a blockade would reflect that. US and allied policymakers would face the threshold question of whether to authorize widespread attacks on the Chinese mainland to suppress the PLA's land-based counter-maritime forces. Without that approval, there are no effective military options for directly breaking a PLA blockade of Taiwan. If US policymakers are unwilling to approve such a military operation, the PLA will starve Taiwan into submission.

Assuming China launched attacks on the US military and that US and allied policymakers approved counterattacks on the Chinese mainland, what would US and allied forces then attack to suppress the PLA's anti-maritime force and reopen shipping to and from Taiwan? The list of targets is long and would be challenging to reach. Essential targets would include the PLA's integrated air defense systems protecting southeast China. These systems consist of air bases for the PLA's fighter-interceptor aircraft and the PLA's mobile surface-to-air missile units. The extensive sensor and command networks linking these forces are more priority targets.

Suppressing the PLA's air defenses would allow more freedom for US and allied airpower to then attack the PLA's land-based anti-maritime forces. These forces include PLA fighter-attack and bomber aircraft capable of launching antiship cruise missiles. The ports, piers, and support facilities for the PLA Navy's submarine forces is another priority target. The mobile TELs for the PLA's antiship ballistic and cruise missiles are on the list, as are the bases and support systems for these weapons.

These targets sum to potentially thousands of aimpoints inside China that US and allied airpower and naval long-range land-attack cruise missiles would have to strike and periodically restrike to allow relief convoys to reach Taiwan's ports. Such an effort would require US and allied leaders to commit to a major military effort against China. And it would require military forces that can find mobile targets inside China, penetrate and function inside China's air defense in a sustainable manner, and effectively deliver firepower on required aimpoints for a prolonged and possibly open-ended duration.

Deterring a Blockade

The good news is that, despite China's military advantages, the political and economic downsides to Beijing pursuing a blockade are also significant. Enforcing a blockade using nonlethal means is notoriously difficult, even for big coast guards and big navies like those China has. Taiwan could nationalize commercial vessels and aircraft to keep trade flowing to and from the island. Container ships are a lot larger than even the biggest Chinese coast guard cutters, which would not fare well in games of "chicken" on the high seas. Taiwan's position as the world's primary manufacturer of high-end semiconductors could also be leveraged to Taiwan's advantage in a blockade scenario in ways it couldn't in an invasion. Chips are normally shipped by air in any case, and Taiwan's production could be directed to friendly countries and withheld from China. The United States and its allies could simultaneously squeeze the input and output of mainland Chinese chip plants through bans and tariffs and export controls, dealing a severe economic blow to the Chinese economy. The United States, Japan, and other friendly countries could assist in running the blockade, generating sympathy from democracies and comparisons with the successful Berlin Airlift during the Cold War. Economic and financial sanctions and a heightened trade war with the West would follow at a time when China still depends heavily on external trade, despite its concerted strategy to achieve economic self-reliance.

If Beijing resorted to force against the United States, it would mean war. And although the United States and its allies may lack the military capabilities or will to directly deny a PLA blockade of Taiwan through strikes against mainland Chinese targets—and therefore lack credible "deterrence by denial" for this prospective PLA strategy—the coalition could still resort to "deterrence by punishment."

As discussed in chapter 7, deterrence by punishment is a weaker and less desirable alternative to deterrence by denial but may be the only available fallback option for preventing a PLA conquest of Taiwan through a blockade.

As the name suggests, deterrence by punishment seeks to impose pain on the aggressor's decision makers in the hope of altering their behavior toward outcomes favorable to the defender. With a punishment strategy, the aggressor retains the initiative because it gets to decide how much pain it is willing to tolerate, something the defender will not know in advance and may never find out during the conflict. Achieving success with a punishment strategy will likely require more ruthlessness than a defender might have initially presumed; leaders targeted for punishment may then view the conflict's stakes as existential, limiting the options for a negotiated end to the fighting.

Despite these drawbacks, the US-led coalition may conclude that punishment is the only available option. In that case, US and allied policymakers would have to search for vulnerable points of leverage that could coerce CCP leaders into settling a Taiwan conflict on terms acceptable to the US-led coalition.

The paramount goals for CCP leaders are to maintain control over the CCP itself and its monopoly over China's political system, the PLA, and the broader Chinese population. US and allied policy-makers and military planners would presumably value kinetic and non-kinetic actions—including economic ones like the measures just discussed—that would weaken CCP control, putting at risk that which CCP leaders value the most.

Targets under this theory could include prestigious symbols of the CCP's achievements, such as the PLA Navy's capital ships and China's space ports, which would also be legitimate military targets after China initiated hostilities. Using cyber and information warfare to degrade China's controls over information could weaken the party's control over the population. Public exposure, seizure, and destruction of the personal assets of senior CCP officials could create dissent within the party; in the 1999 Kosovo conflict, NATO employed this tactic against Serbia's leadership, helping end that war.[9] Finally, US and allied gov-ernments could employ information operations to divide the Chinese population from the CCP.

A controversial but feasible action would be a "counter-siege" di-rected at the Chinese population in response to a prospective PLA siege of Taiwan that cuts the island off from food and fuel. An at least partial counter-siege of the Chinese mainland would likely occur spontaneously in any case, as most merchant ships would avoid a missile-combat war zone in the western Pacific Ocean. US and allied military forces could deepen this spontaneous blockade by mining Chinese harbors or the approaches to them. The goal of these actions, justified in response to the PLA siege of Taiwan, would be to induce the Chinese population to resist the CCP's war policy against Taiwan.

Punishment strategies are often morally questionable, are fraught with unknowable consequences, and have frequently failed in the past. A counter-siege of China will be more porous than the PLA's siege of Taiwan since China has land borders and Taiwan does not; the CCP may be able to endure a siege longer than Taiwan.[10]

For these reasons, policymakers and military planners prefer military capabilities that are ready to directly defeat an adversary's military aggression. When these capabilities are present, displayed, and understood by decision makers on all sides, the defender will have achieved deterrence by denial.

The United States and some of its allies now have programs that could create credible military capabilities for defeating, and thus perhaps deterring, the blockade scenario. Unfortunately, most of these efforts should have begun a decade ago. The present, and urgent, challenge is for policymakers and military planners to do what they can in the short term to thwart a prospective PLA blockade of Taiwan.

Mission Requirements and Capability Gaps

So, if China were to violently enforce a Taiwan blockade, would US and allied military forces have the equipment, training, and doctrine to credibly suppress the PLA's land-based anti-maritime forces? As just described, this would be a highly challenging mission, more challenging than defeating a PLA amphibious assault. US and allied forces are lacking some critical capabilities.

The first capability US and allied forces would need are comprehensive and resilient overhead intelligence, surveillance, and reconnaissance (ISR) networks covering southeast China. These networks would ideally be based in space, given the dangers posed by the PLA's integrated air defenses. The task for the ISR networks would be to monitor the PLA's air, naval, and missile bases in near real time. More challenging would be monitoring in near real time the locations and movements of the PLA's mobile TELs used for moving and launching surface-to-surface and surface-to-air missiles. The US Space Force and the National Reconnaissance Office have plans for space-based ground-moving target indicator (GMTI) systems to track the position and movements of military vehicles, such as TELs, from space. Mature space-based GMTI capabilities are still in development.[11]

Next, the United States and its allies would need resilient regional and global command, control, and communications (C3) systems for transporting data and commands among disparate units and assets across all five war-fighting domains (space, air, naval, land, and cyber). These C3 systems should remain functioning while under physical, electronic, and cyberattacks. This implies that they should be distributed among hundreds or even thousands of nodes; be self-healing while under stress; be redundant; and resist jamming, adversary decryption, and deception. The US Space Force is currently deploying its Proliferated Warfighter Space Architecture satellite constellation, discussed in chapter 7.

To suppress the PLA's mobile land-based anti-maritime forces in southeast China, the United States and its allies would need the capability to respond rapidly to fleeting targets identified by their ISR networks. This implies stealth bombers continuously on patrol nearby, armed with hypersonic air-to-surface munitions to effectively strike targets before they disperse and hide again. The US Air Force is supplementing and eventually replacing its B-1B and B-2A forces with the new B-21 Raider stealth bomber. But that aircraft is just entering its initial test-flight phase of development and is years away from a substantial combat capability over China. Research and development continues on hypersonic air-to-surface munitions.

Various program offices inside the Pentagon have developed, at least conceptually, ideas for large numbers of low-cost and autonomous aircraft and undersea vehicles that would search for and attack specific targets the weapons' sensors would find. Engineers successfully developed some aspects of this technology more than two decades ago.[12] Such technical capabilities would be highly useful for holding at risk the PLA's land-based anti-maritime forces. However, US policymakers have imposed strict review processes (almost certainly stricter than those of the PLA) for the approval of lethal autonomous unmanned search-and-strike weapons.[13] These policies are slowing the fielding of low-cost autonomous attack weapons that would be especially useful in the scenario described in this chapter.

Finally, US and allied forces will need to defeat large numbers of PLA Navy attack submarines that would hunt merchant ships sailing to and from Taiwan. And the allies will need to continuously clear naval mines that the PLA would overtly or covertly emplace to thwart shipping in and out of Taiwan's ports. Taiwanese and allied personnel will need techniques and equipment for delivering bulk cargo to Taiwan without the benefit of piers and port infrastructure, which they should assume the PLA will destroy.

This is a daunting list of mission requirements, all which US and allied forces would need to accomplish to keep goods flowing in and out of Taiwan and thus directly deny the PLA's blockade strategy. Across the mission requirements needed to directly counter a PLA blockade of Taiwan—target acquisition, resilient communications, enough stealth bombers, rapid response weapons, and autonomous search-and-strike weapons—US and allied military forces are a decade behind where they should be to directly deter this potential PLA course of action.

A Two-Year Action Plan

What actions can US and allied policymakers take over the next two years to prepare their military forces to counter a PLA blockade of Taiwan?

1. During the current prewar period, senior US policymakers should direct military commanders and their staffs to prepare war plans that will include extensive and sustained kinetic and non-kinetic military action against the Chinese mainland should the PLA blockade Taiwan. It will be necessary to strike the Chinese mainland to counter such a blockade, and US policymakers and military planners should formulate plans for such in advance. And to deter a PLA blockade, US policymakers should inform their Chinese counterparts about their willingness and preparations for such actions.

2. US Indo-Pacific command, along with allies in the region, should periodically rehearse relief convoy operations to prepare for such a scenario regarding Taiwan. The US Department of Transportation's Maritime Security Program (MSP) maintains a fleet of commercially viable, militarily useful merchant ships active in international trade and could be the core of relief convoy rehearsals and operations.[14] Training will entail preparing MSP ships on short notice and coordinating convoy and warship escort operations across potentially hostile areas. The US government should enlist allied nations to participate in these rehearsals.

3. Senior US policymakers should promulgate policies that will accelerate the development and fielding of effective low-cost autonomous search-and-strike weapons. US and allied forces will need large quantities of these weapons to suppress the PLA's land-based anti-maritime forces in southeast China. Although the Pentagon's current policy on lethal autonomous weapons does not ban their development or require continuous human supervision of such weapons after they are launched, the current policy institutionalizes an elaborate review process that is slowing the development and fielding of needed capabilities. The urgency of the blockade threat to Taiwan now requires changes that will accelerate the fielding of these lethal autonomous weapons.

4. US and allied defense policymakers should accelerate the development and fielding of robust, redundant, and survivable target acquisition systems to support the suppression of PLA systems in southeast China. These systems should include air- and space-based sensors to identify ground- and sea-based moving targets. These target acquisition systems should include high-altitude long-endurance unmanned air systems, satellite constellations, and low-cost expendable unmanned air and undersea vehicles.

5. US and allied defense policymakers should accelerate the deployment of distributed and networked satellite communication

constellations such as the follow-on tranches of the US Space Force's Proliferated Warfighter Space Architecture, a capability that US and allied forces will need for a suppressive campaign over southeast China.

6. US defense policymakers should accelerate the development and fielding of affordable hypersonic air-to-surface munitions that US bombers will need to rapidly engage the PLA's mobile and fleeting ground-based anti-maritime forces in southeast China. Such weapons are technically feasible and will require commitments from the US Defense Department to the defense industrial base.

7. US and allied maritime forces, in coordination with Taiwan, should prepare for clearing naval mines on the approaches to Taiwan's ports; antisubmarine operations against the PLA Navy's submarines; and methods for transferring bulk cargos from ship to shore on Taiwan in the absence of functioning port infrastructure.

8. Senior US and allied policymakers and military planners should prepare in advance for a prospective campaign of punishment aimed at coercing the CCP leadership toward a favorable conflict outcome should military denial options not be available. To do so, policymakers and planners should study how to obtain coercive leverage over CCP leaders and develop supporting military and nonmilitary plans to achieve this coercive leverage during a prospective conflict.

This is a difficult list of actions to execute, especially during a compressed period. The list of military preparations, especially those directed at targets at China's mainland, are technically challenging and are at the current limits of military science and engineering. The policy challenges are equally daunting, requiring policymakers to take uncomfortable moral and escalatory risks on lethal robotic weapons, a sustained bombing campaign of mainland China, and the possible necessity to engage in the overt coercion of China's leadership.

NOTES

1. Joseph Webster, "Does Taiwan's Massive Reliance on Energy Imports Put Its Security at Risk?," Atlantic Council, July 7, 2023.
2. Effendi Andoko, Wan-Yu Liu, Hua-Jing Zeng, and Agnes Sjoblom, "Review of Taiwan's Food Security Strategy," Food and Fertilizer Technology Center for the Asia and Pacific Region, September 10, 2020.
3. Bradley Martin, Kristen Gunness, Paul DeLuca, and Melissa Shostak, *Implications of a Coercive Quarantine of Taiwan by the People's Republic of China*, RAND Corporation, 2022, 1–2.
4. Max Hastings, "America Is Headed to a Showdown over Taiwan, and China Might Win," *Bloomberg*, March 14, 2021.
5. Martin et al., *Implications of a Coercive Quarantine*, 12–13.
6. Lonnie D. Henley, *Beyond the First Battle: Overcoming a Protracted Blockade of Taiwan*, US Naval War College, China Maritime Studies Institute, China Maritime Report No. 26, March 2023.
7. Mark F. Cancian, Matthew Cancian, and Eric Heginbotham, *The First Battle of the Next War: Wargaming a Chinese Invasion of Taiwan*, Center for Strategic and International Studies, January 2023, 128–29.
8. Cancian, Cancian, and Heginbotham, *First Battle of the Next War*, 20.
9. Benjamin Lambeth, *NATO's Air War for Kosovo: A Strategic and Operational Assessment*, RAND Corporation, January 1, 2001, 68–72.
10. Martin et al., *Implications of a Coercive Quarantine*, 22–23.
11. Theresa Hitchens, "How Space Force, NRO Are Sharing the Ground-Tracking Mission, for Now," *Breaking Defense*, May 3, 2023.
12. James R. FitzSimonds, "Cultural Barriers to Implementing a Competitive Strategy," in *Competitive Strategies for the 21st Century*, ed. Thomas Mahnken (Stanford, CA: Stanford University Press, 2012), 290–92.
13. Office of the Under Secretary of Defense for Policy, *DoD Directive 3000.09: Autonomy in Weapon Systems*, January 25, 2023.
14. US Department of Transportation Maritime Administration, "Maritime Security Program (MSP)," May 31, 2023.

CHAPTER 9

Mobilizing and Equipping

ROBERT HADDICK

*The first, the supreme, the most far-reaching act of judgment that
the statesman and commander have to make is to establish . . .
the kind of war on which they are embarking.*

—CARL VON CLAUSEWITZ, *VOM KRIEGE (ON WAR)*

US and allied policymakers and military planners should assume that
a prospective war against China will be long, even open ended, and
at waxing and waning levels of intensity. These policymakers and
planners should prepare now for that outcome. Doing so will give
them the best chance of dominating the conflict should it occur. Even
more important, preparing for a long, open-ended conflict and showing China's leaders that they are doing so will be critical elements of
a stronger deterrence posture that, if successful, will prevent the war
from occurring.

That said, mobilization, or even preparing for mobilization before a
conflict, is a hazardous act. Done unwisely, mobilization can reduce a
country's readiness for conflict, the opposite of the intended outcome,
if it wastes resources on inappropriate military capabilities or expands
centers of gravity vulnerable to enemy targeting. A poorly designed
mobilization could weaken rather than strengthen a society if mobilization leads to economic inflation or social upheaval and resistance.

The United States and its allies need to do more to prepare for a
long war against China. Doing so now strengthens deterrence and sets

up the conditions for victory should deterrence fail. But policymakers and planners need to think carefully about how they prepare lest they make their strategic situation worse rather than better.

Why US Policymakers Should Assume a PLA Conflict Will Be Long

US and allied policymakers and planners should assume a war against China will be long if for no other reason than wars are difficult to end. A fundamental purpose of war is to provide new information to the combatants that they did not have prior to the war's inception, namely which side will be stronger as the war continues and which will be weaker. The war presumably began because the combatants did not agree on this assessment; if they did agree on which side was weaker, that player would have had a strong incentive to avoid the war by offering concessions instead. The war likely occurred because both sides believed they had a good chance to win or concluded that fighting was the least-worse option. Subsequent combat, and losses, should clarify which side's judgment on this matter was best.[1]

Even so, war is often an imperfect and slow-moving creator of the new information that should resolve this uncertainty and disagreement.[2] In addition, even when one leader knows he will lose, he may still be unwilling to stop the war because it could literally be fatal for him and his ruling circle to do so.

The leaders of the Chinese Communist Party (CCP) would launch a war for Taiwan because they would have the confidence, mistaken or not, that they could prevail at an acceptable price. And for them, the price they may be willing to risk could be much higher than anyone outside their circle in Beijing might expect. The capture of Taiwan is a millenarian goal for the CCP and a goal to which the CCP has committed its prestige.

Beyond that, these leaders will see the capture of Taiwan as dramatically weakening the strategic position of regional rivals such as Japan and the United States since it would lead to the PLA's domination of the western Pacific Ocean's sea and air lines of communication. This outcome would go far to establish China as the dominant power of eastern Eurasia, worth a high risk for the CCP's leaders. It would be difficult for these leaders to turn back after they openly committed to achieving this goal with war.

The type of war CCP and PLA leaders choose could also bear on the duration of the conflict. Chapter 8 discussed why the blockade option is difficult for the United States and its allies to counter and why China's leaders may prefer it to an amphibious assault. The very nature of the blockade option, with its gradual and escalating strangulation of Taiwan, would purposely be a long-run endeavor for the PLA. US and allied policymakers and planners will need a matching time horizon if they wish to counter the blockade.

China's leaders would choose an amphibious assault if they thought it would be more decisive than a blockade or because they sought to avoid a long war and calculated they could achieve a quick fait accompli with a forceful seizure.

But if the option fails, China's leaders would face difficult decisions. A likely cause of such a failure would be the widespread destruction of China's maritime power during the PLA's assault attempt (discussed in chapter 7). Having successfully defended Taiwan from a direct assault, US, allied, and Taiwanese leaders would likely prefer a quick ceasefire and de-escalation, to limit the risk of further destruction. China's leaders would then face the choice of accepting, or not, this "off-ramp."

The argument from China's perspective for accepting a quick armistice is that it would give China a largely undisturbed interval, lasting perhaps several decades, to reconstitute the PLA and put China in a position to revisit the Taiwan issue later. Reconstitution would be a straightforward technical and production task and PLA leaders could apply lessons learned from the recent combat. If Taiwan and the coalition conducted few strikes on China's homeland (as was the case during the 2022 CSIS war-game series discussed in chapter 7), China's leaders would also have an incentive to limit the risk of further destruction, to get on with reconstitution.

There is, however, a darker scenario. Internal political pressure may compel CCP and PLA leaders to continue the war, even after a failed amphibious assault. These leaders would still possess the land-based anti-maritime forces they would need for a blockade of Taiwan, as discussed in chapter 8. All the factors that make the blockade option appealing would still be present.

The risk for China's leaders would be escalation that would lead to widespread bombing of mainland China, as the US coalition either attempted to suppress the PLA's land-based blockade forces or pursued a coercive punishment campaign against the CCP leadership. China's leaders would opt for continuing the war in this manner if they concluded that US and allied leaders lacked the will to escalate to attacks on the Chinese mainland or to continue a war long enough to rescue Taiwan from the blockade's strangulation.

In any of these cases, the United States, its allies, and Taiwan will face a long-term and open-ended strategic competition against the PLA's potential military power. In one outcome, the contest would be a long struggle to counter a blockade of Taiwan, an effort that would likely wax and wane in intensity. The other outcome would see a truce followed by China rebuilding a more capable PLA, applying lessons learned from recent combat. Both paths will require the United States and its allies to fashion a wise mobilization strategy and organize industry and financial resources to execute the strategy.

Mobilization Is a Competitive Act

Mobilization means more than the call-up of reservists and National Guard soldiers. For this chapter, military mobilization is the substantial and exceptional displacement, through either conscription or bidding, of a country's labor, financial, and industrial capacities that would otherwise naturally go to civilian purposes. Combatants in a war invariably mobilize their resources for the war effort. This is a competitive act that usually benefits one combatant more than the other, and in potentially unexpected ways.

The Willow Run Creek factory produced one B-24 an hour in 1944. US prewar mobilization set the stage for later US victory in the race for military production in World War II. *Bettmann via Getty Images*

Mobilization can occur in a prewar period (and is arguably what the PLA is doing now). For example, with the international situation deteriorating, the US Congress passed several important military bills in the years before the United States entered World War II in December 1941. First was the Naval Act of 1938, which authorized a 20 percent increase in the navy's warship budget, authorized the Iowa class of 16-inch gun battleships, and greatly expanded the navy's cruiser and destroyer fleets.[3] Next was the Two-Ocean Naval Expansion Act in July 1940, which authorized an additional 7 new battleships, 18 aircraft carriers, 29 cruisers, 115 destroyers, 42 submarines, and 15,000 aircraft for the fleet.[4] And in September 1940, President Franklin Roosevelt signed the Selective Training and Service Act of 1940, which authorized the country's first peacetime conscription for military service, permitting the call-up of up to nine hundred thousand men at a time.[5]

These actions, especially the advanced procurement of slow-to-build warships, put the United States in a better position when the war arrived. And they prepared US industry for the massive wartime mobilization that would occur later and that would overwhelm the Axis adversaries. After the United States entered the war and fully mobilized, the Allies easily won the mobilization competition, a clear misjudgment by the Axis leaders who declared war on the United States.

Mobilization Is a Risky Act

The goal of mobilization is to rapidly increase a country's military strength. But mobilization can be risky, especially if policymakers do not consider the country's economic backdrop or its social context. Done unwisely, mobilization can be self-defeating.

The mobilization the US government undertook for its entry into the Vietnam War is an example. In 1965, the Johnson administration decided to fight a large ground war in South Vietnam, to fend off the North Vietnamese army and local communist guerillas. President Lyndon Johnson believed that military mobilization would create "escalation dominance" for the United States over its adversaries in Vietnam, just as mobilization for World War II had so successfully achieved dominance over the Axis powers just over two decades previously.

In March 1965, two battalions of US Marines landed in Da Nang, South Vietnam. By December, 184,300 US military personnel were in the country, a force that grew to 536,100 by 1968.[6] To support this ground war, the Pentagon expanded the US Army and Marine Corps from a combined 1,163,015 personnel in June 1964 to 1,877,595 in June 1968, a 61 percent increase.[7]

Meeting this manpower mobilization requirement required the Selective Service System to triple the number of men it conscripted, an action that proved highly unpopular and resulted in widespread civil disobedience.[8] In addition, the US labor force and overall economy were already running at or beyond full capacity in 1965. The additional demand for manpower and war production sent the economy into rapidly accelerating inflation, a condition that typically ignites political instability.[9]

In less than three years, political support for President Johnson's war policy collapsed and he declined to run for reelection. By 1968, the only politically tenable policy was withdrawal from the war and a reversal of mobilization, which Johnson's successor, Richard Nixon, carried out.

Johnson and his advisors failed to appreciate the country's macroeconomic and social backdrop. For the Vietnam War, mobilization created the conditions for defeat rather than victory, a lesson future policymakers should remember.

Mobilize What and Why?

From the perspective of the US Department of Defense's *Joint Publication 5-0, Joint Planning*, discussed in chapter 7, mobilizing half a million ground troops for the Vietnam War and placing them within the range of the enemy's firepower was a reckless strategy. Through the lens of *JP 5-0*, the United States rashly exposed a vulnerable center of gravity, conscripted foot soldiers from homes across the country, to the guns of an adversary that retained the initiative of when and how to engage on the battlefield. At the same time, the US strategy failed to identify the adversary's centers of gravity or to formulate methods to effectively attack these.

The lesson is that policymakers and planners need to first develop an effective strategy based on center-of-gravity analysis and the operational concept to execute the strategy. They should then tightly tailor the mobilization plan to support only what the strategy and operational concept require.

Chapter 7 discussed what military capabilities the United States and its allies will require to defeat a PLA amphibious assault against Taiwan while chapter 8 discussed the requirements for thwarting a PLA blockade. These two lists of requirements considered the recommendations of *JP 5-0*, to find and strike the adversary's centers of gravity while avoiding its doing the same in return. The military resources the United States and its allies mobilize before and during a war against the PLA should support these theories.

Dominant air and space power are the top requirements for countering both the amphibious assault and the blockade scenarios. The United States and its allies cannot safely conduct significant naval or ground operations for Taiwan contingencies until they have achieved dominance over the PLA in the air and space domains. Thus, mobilizing air and space resources and capabilities before and during a prospective conflict should be the coalition's top planning priority.

Fortunately, the United States and its allies possess clear dominance in global aerospace research, engineering, and industrial capacity. By itself, the United States controls half the world's aerospace industrial capacity. It is also the global leader in advanced aerospace technology development, in areas such as propulsion, electronics, space systems, and unmanned systems. Although China's aerospace engineering and production capabilities are growing, these remain far behind those of the United States; US annual aerospace output is nearly seven times that of China.[10]

The coalition's military aerospace potential is an enduring competitive advantage compared with China's. And as chapters 7 and 8 explained, aerospace power is the best available matchup against PLA centers of gravity, such as the PLA Navy and the PLA's land-based anti-maritime forces in southeast China. These chapters explained how allied aerospace power can apply the tenets of *JP 5-0* to strike the adversary's centers of gravity while avoiding having the adversary do the same.

The US and allied coalition is fortunate that the best tool for the Taiwan scenarios, long-range air and space power, is also the tool where the coalition enjoys a substantial and enduring competitive advantage over the adversary. The coalition's military strategy, war-fighting concept, and mobilization plan should exploit this advantage.

This analysis informs actions that US defense policymakers and planners can take during the current prospective prewar period to deter a conflict from occurring and to accelerate production of critical capabilities should deterrence fail. In general terms, these actions should expand and diversify assembly capacities for long-range strike platforms like the B-21 Raider bomber aircraft; long-range air-to-surface munitions like the JASSM and the LRASM; affordable mid-range munitions like the Powered Joint Direct Attack Munition; affordable hypersonic air-to-surface munitions; additional and diversified launch capacity to low earth orbit; additional small satellites for reconnaissance, communications, and space domain awareness; and affordable and expendable unmanned air and subsurface vehicles for reconnaissance and autonomous attack.

Given its already dominant position in the global aerospace industry, the United States is well positioned to expand assembly capacities in these areas. The aerospace companies, engineering expertise, management experience, and the labor force are already in place and could either expand existing military assembly capacities or divert existing civilian aerospace capacity to needed military programs when national mobilization programs call on them to do so.

This describes a mobilization program tailored to the military strategy and war-fighting concept most appropriate for attacking the PLA's centers of gravity exposed in the amphibious assault and blockade scenarios. This mobilization program would accelerate the production of the most useful weapon platforms and munitions and would take advantage of US and allied competitive advantages in aerospace power.

As important, it would avoid expending resources or taking social risks mobilizing military capacity where the United States is not competitive or that would not be relevant to the military problem. For example, the US Navy's Office of Naval Intelligence concluded that China's ship production capacity exceeds that of the United States by 232 times; the United States is not competitive with China in naval mobilization.[11] And the 2022 CSIS Taiwan war game revealed that US ground forces would have minor relevance in Taiwan scenarios and could expose a vulnerable center of gravity to the PLA's firepower; ground forces should not be a mobilization priority for Taiwan scenarios.[12]

What Mobilization Will Cost

The macroeconomic and financial situation in the United States constrains the mobilization options available to policymakers. A mass,
World War II–style mobilization, with conscription and mass purchases of military equipment, is not available to a US economy that is
already running at full capacity. In addition, the Congressional Budget
Office projects the federal government to run a fiscal deficit of 5.8 percent of national economic output in 2024, and the office projects the
government's long-term fiscal situation to dramatically worsen in the
decades ahead.[13] The additional financial burden of a mass mobilization would risk financial calamity. The United States has neither the
available labor force nor the financial resources required for a mass
mobilization. For these reasons, a narrowly tailored mobilization as
described above matches the recommended military strategy and is
more economically and financially feasible.

The Pentagon's proposed budget for fiscal year 2024 provides a
starting point for formulating a rough estimate of the cost of a tailored
prewar mobilization for prospective Taiwan scenarios.

The table below lists the Pentagon's fiscal year 2024 budget requests
for selected weapon programs that chapters 7–9 have discussed as most
relevant for the Taiwan scenarios. The column on the right displays the

PROGRAM	FY 2024 BUDGET REQUEST (US $BILLIONS)	ADDITIONAL 50%
B-21 Raider bomber	$5.3	$2.7
Joint Air-to-Surface Standoff Missile	$1.8	$0.9
Long Range Anti-Ship Missile	$1.1	$0.6
Joint Direct Attack Munition (all types)	$0.2	$0.1
Hypersonic air-to-surface research	$0.5	$0.3
Unmanned combat aircraft research	$0.1	$0.1
Unmanned underwater systems	$0.4	$0.2
Satellite communication, space defense	$5.2	$2.6
Total	**$14.6**	**$7.5**

cost of adding 50 percent to these programs to expand and diversify their production capacities (amounts are in billions of US dollars, rounded).[14]

The US Defense Department could apply the additional funding to expand assembly capacity; build redundant and geographically separate assembly facilities; hire and retain additional research, engineering, and manufacturing talent; support new business entrants into the defense industrial base; and deepen component supply chains for critical weapons and systems.

The additional annual spending on programs most useful for preparing for the Taiwan scenarios—roughly estimated at $7.5 billion—is a minimal sum in the context of either the overall US defense budget (0.9 percent of $863 billion for fiscal year 2024) or the total projected output of the US economy in 2024 (0.03 percent of $27,238 billion).[15]

The US government and taxpayers can afford this sum. Most notably, it would represent a new, precise, and focused way of mobilizing for a war that the mobilization itself would aim to deter from ever occurring.

Needed Now: A Sustainable War-Fighting Concept and Military-Industrial Policy

US and allied policymakers should prepare their wartime mobilization plans well in advance of a prospective conflict. Time will be a critical variable for all combatants, with mobilization laggards risking higher wartime costs and even defeat. Establishing a mobilization plan implies also establishing a military strategy and operational concept in advance, since the mobilization plan should support the strategy and concept.

The US mobilization experience in World War II provides a lesson. This chapter earlier described how US mobilization for the coming conflict began with the Naval Act of 1938, the Navy Expansion Act in 1940, and military conscription in 1940.

Despite these acts of foresight, Roosevelt and his top military officers did not decide on a comprehensive operational concept and supporting military production plan until late November 1942, nearly a year after the United States entered the war. Prewar mobilization plans were based on World War I and nineteenth-century concepts that called for a massive infantry-centered US military force of 215 army divisions, with air and naval forces providing minor and supporting roles, and war industries starved of labor to fill the army's ranks.[16]

But in the summer and autumn of 1942, Admiral William Leahy, Roosevelt's newly installed military chief of staff, advised Roosevelt to redirect the mobilization program to a military force centered on air and naval power, an inclination that Roosevelt already favored based on his observations of the war and his previous service as assistant secretary of the navy. Roosevelt and Leahy believed that an operational concept centered on globe-spanning and dominant air and sea power would play to US technological and industrial advantages and greatly reduce US casualties compared with the previous ground force-centered mobilization plan.[17]

By late November 1942, Roosevelt and his military advisors settled on a mobilization plan that called for building 107,000 military aircraft in 1943 (the United States built 299,293 military aircraft during the war) and focusing a naval construction program on aircraft carriers and amphibious shipping, but cutting an army mobilization to ninety divisions.[18] This technologically sophisticated operational concept and military force not only defeated the Axis powers, it greatly reduced US casualties compared with what they would have been with the prewar mobilization plan.[19]

Roosevelt and his advisors should get credit for beginning naval mobilization early, years before the war began. They should get additional credit for fashioning a highly competitive mobilization concept that matched America's technological and industrial advantages against the adversaries' vulnerabilities to tactical and strategic airpower and naval maneuver.

However, it is unfortunate that settling on this plan occurred over eleven months after the United States entered the war. This delay postponed the arrival of the massive fully mobilized and war-winning US military force until 1944, which added to the war's costs. Today's policymakers have an opportunity to learn from this experience and be fully prepared for this era's contingencies.

Finally, US policymakers should accept that even if they successfully deter a war against China, the geostrategic competition may last for the rest of this century. The strategy, operational concept, and preparatory mobilization policies these policymakers fashion should be acceptable to US society, find favor with both sides of the political spectrum, be affordable, be flexible during changing conditions, and thus be sustainable for an open-ended period. The concepts and mobilization program described in this chapter and the prior two, which match US competitive advantages against China's vulnerabilities, meet these criteria.

A Two-Year Action Plan

What actions should US and allied policymakers take now to prepare for a military mobilization against China?

1. US and allied policymakers and military planners should decide during a prospective prewar period on the military strategies, operational concepts, and supporting mobilization plans they would employ during alternative Taiwan defense contingencies. As discussed in chapters 7–9, these strategies, concepts, and plans should match enduring US and allied advantages against China's vulnerabilities and be economically and politically sustainable for an open-ended period. Establishing these policies in advance of need will strengthen deterrence and save time during a contingency, an important competitive variable.

2. US and allied policymakers and planners should meet with aerospace and maritime industry leaders to discuss preparations for mobilizing industry resources to achieve prospective wartime objectives, should it be necessary to do so.

3. The US Congress should appropriate funding to establish a second assembly facility for the B-21 Raider bomber aircraft, ideally at Tinker Air Force Base, Oklahoma, which is geographically separate from the primary assembly facility in California and is the designated site for the bomber's life-cycle maintenance

and sustainment.[20] Establishing a second assembly line for the B-21 will increase the production rate of the aircraft, provide additional capacity for allies such as Australia to obtain the bomber, and diversify the bomber's production at a facility farther from the reach of the PLA.[21] In a long military campaign against China, the US Air Force will need to add bomber production capacity, increase the campaign's tempo, replace inevitable aircraft losses, and provide sufficient bomber capacity to deter possible opportunistic aggression elsewhere.

4. The US Congress should increase funding for research and additional production capacity for weapon systems discussed in this chapter, such as air-to-surface munitions, unmanned autonomous air and undersea vehicles and weapons, and space-based communication and reconnaissance capacity. Funding for these systems in a prewar phase can expand production capacity, increase the pool of engineering talent, deepen supply chains, and support the creation of new entrants into the defense industrial base.

Summing up, US and allied leaders need to disabuse CCP leaders of the notion that China could win a mobilization competition or that China will possess more stamina in a long, even open-ended conflict. US and allied leaders will accomplish this when they establish during the prewar period their strategy for victory and a winning operational concept to achieve that. Perhaps the most effective deterrent action US and allied leaders can take is to prepare now for mobilization and display to CCP leaders that they are doing so. That would go a long way toward convincing China's leaders that they do not possess useful military options for seizing Taiwan.

NOTES

1. Geoffrey Blainey, *The Causes of War* (New York: Free Press, 1973), 122–23.
2. Dan Reiter, *How Wars End* (Princeton, NJ: Princeton University Press, 2009), 220–22.

3. Phillips Payson O'Brien, *The Second Most Powerful Man in the World: The Life of Admiral William D. Leahy, Roosevelt's Chief of Staff* (New York: Dutton Books 2019), 116.

4. GlobalSecurity.org, "Ship Building 1933–1945: Roosevelt, Franklin D.," November 18, 2015.

5. Selective Training and Service Act of 1940, Library of Congress legislative database, n.d.

6. American War Library, "Vietnam War Allied Troop Levels, 1960–1973," December 6, 2008.

7. Defense Manpower Data Center, "DoD Personnel, Workforce Reports & Publications," n.d.

8. Selective Service System, "Induction Statistics," n.d.

9. Federal Reserve Bank of St. Louis FRED, "US CPI Inflation and Unemployment Rate, 1960–1973," graph, accessed July 21, 2023.

10. Teal Group, "The Global Aerospace Industry: Size and Country Rankings," July 16, 2018.

11. Joseph Trevithick, "Alarming Navy Intel Slide Warns of China's 200 Times Greater Shipbuilding Capacity," *War Zone*, July 11, 2023.

12. Mark F. Cancian, Matthew Cancian, and Eric Heginbotham, *The First Battle of the Next War: Wargaming a Chinese Invasion of Taiwan*, Center for Strategic and International Studies, January 2023, 129–31.

13. Congressional Budget Office, "The 2023 Long-Term Budget Outlook," June 28, 2023.

14. For supporting documentation, see Office of the Undersecretary of Defense (Comptroller), "Defense Budget Materials—FY 2024," March 2023.

15. Office of the Under Secretary of Defense (Comptroller), "National Defense Budget Estimates for FY 2024," May 2023, 169, 284.

16. O'Brien, *Second Most Powerful Man*, 201–10.

17. O'Brien, *Second Most Powerful Man*, 202–03.

18. O'Brien, *Second Most Powerful Man*, 206–09.

19. Phillips Payson O'Brien, conclusion to *How the War Was Won: Air-Sea Power and Allied Victory in World War II* (Cambridge, UK: Cambridge University Press, 2015).

20. Mark Gunzinger, *Understanding the B-21 Raider: America's Deterrence Bomber*, Mitchell Institute for Aerospace Studies, March 2023, 31.

21. Robert Haddick, "Save the AUKUS Partnership—Share the B-21 Bomber," *The Hill*, November 2, 2022.

PART IV

Japan's Job Now

CHAPTER 10

Japan as the "Swing Vote"

GRANT NEWSHAM

A Taiwan emergency is a Japanese emergency, and
therefore an emergency for the Japan-U.S. alliance.

—FORMER PRIME MINISTER SHINZO ABE

Introduction

A key aspect of Xi Jinping's assessment will be Japan's posture and capabilities. Japan is a golden key to unlocking deterrence of Xi. And should the worst happen and deterrence fails, Japan's actions—both now and in the future—will likely determine whether Taiwan, along with the United States and the free world, wins or loses.

Unsatisfactory State of the Status Quo

The arrangement that has characterized Japan-US defense strategy for decades is the so-called shield and spear arrangement: Japan is the "shield" guarding bases, while the "spear" is the Americans going out and doing the fighting. Although US bases in Japan are essential for Western Pacific operations in general, and a Taiwan contingency in particular, Japan will need to do more than just provide US forces with bases and some limited logistics and defensive support.

A Chinese attack on Taiwan could be accompanied by "supporting" operations elsewhere in the region, if not globally. These might include North Korea starting hostilities on the Korean Peninsula, direct attacks on Japan, Chinese naval operations in the Malacca Strait, Russian moves against Japanese territory or provocations in Europe, and possibly Iranian moves in the Middle East.

The United States is limited in the number of simultaneous operations it can prosecute. Thus, capable allies who can defend themselves and also provide offensive support are required.

Japan needs to do more. This includes taking very specific actions to improve its military capabilities for Japan's own sake as well as to perform as a much more useful ally to the United States and other partners and, if necessary, to be able to do its share of the fighting.

More than anything, Japan has to demonstrate the *will* to fight. Without will, Tokyo cannot enhance deterrence, no matter how much high-priced hardware it has in the arsenal.

Tokyo can no longer maintain only a modest defense capability and remain coy about its intentions in a Taiwan contingency, in hopes of not offending the People's Republic of China. It cannot continue a policy of overreliance on the United States military. Instead, Japan must positively contribute to collective security. A more capable Japan Self-Defense Forces (JSDF) is essential and is a political statement by itself. Moreover, Japan's political class will need to marshal the citizenry and harness Japan's economic power toward bolstering national defense.

No doubt many policymakers—and even much of the public—in Japan will find a newfound Japanese forthrightness uncomfortable at first. But the more able and willing Japan is to fight, the less likely it will have to do so. And Japan should keep in mind that the more it demonstrates its own commitment, the more willing the United States, Tokyo's only formal ally, will be to fight on Japan's behalf.

Indeed, the chief of Japan's Joint Staff, General Yoshihide Yoshida, revealed a keen understanding of this dynamic—and of what Japan needs to do—in a recent interview with *Nikkei Asia*:

So far, we have been able to count on U.S. deterrence should there be a crisis. But if we rely too much on the U.S., there will be voices there [in the United States] questioning whether its alliance with us is worth the cost. We will bolster the alliance's capabilities by increasing the things Japan can do on its own.[1]

The Japanese public has a good understanding of national defense and the need for Japan to defend itself and to be a useful ally—when the matter is explained to them. When then prime minister Shinzo Abe pushed for revised interpretations of "collective self-defense," it is true that there were some public protests and that the public seemed skeptical of the need (and particularly the means) to significantly raise defense spending. Yet Abe and others continued to push for these changes even out of office, and by the time Prime Minister Fumio Kishida was in power just a few short years later, Kishida was able to push through all those agenda items with hardly any public opposition.

Sixty Years of the US-Japan Defense Relationship

Mike Mansfield, the US ambassador to Japan from 1977 to 1988, regularly said the US-Japan relationship was the "most important bilateral relationship, bar none."[2]

That is still true today. A solidly linked United States and Japan—not just militarily but politically and economically and psychologically—underpin freedom and security in the Asia-Pacific region.

China's rapid military buildup and increasing assertiveness over the last quarter century have given Mansfield's words new life. Beijing's objectives for regional domination include taking the Japanese-administered Senkaku Islands and undermining Japan's indisputably sovereign control over the Ryukyu chain. Mao's dictum that "power grows out of the barrel of a gun" is on display.

Many JSDF officers appreciated the China risk many years ago, using the phrase "Taiwan's defense is Japan's defense." If Taiwan were to fall, China would control the sea-lanes in the South China Sea through which most of Japan's trade and energy flows. People's Liberation Army (PLA) ships, submarines, and aircraft operating from Taiwan could easily isolate, harass, or surround Japan.

Admiral Yoji Koda, for example, then commander of the Japan Maritime Self-Defense Force Fleet (and author of the next chapter in

The China Coast Guard has promised to keep its vessels in Japanese territorial waters surrounding the Senkaku Islands for 365 days in 2024—an unprecedented increase in frequency from previous years—in support of Xi's declaration that the PRC "will never let even 1 millimeter of our territory [be] taken." *Kyodo News Stills via Getty Images*

this book), was sounding the alarm about Chinese island-building in the South China Sea—and the threat it posed to Japan—long before it became accepted wisdom in Tokyo or Washington, DC.[3]

Starting around 2010, the Chinese threat became hard for even the optimists to completely ignore—especially after China began turning up the heat around the Senkaku Islands. The People's Republic of China (PRC) started to use constant China Coast Guard and Chinese fishing boat incursions, along with PLA Air Force incursions, that tended to wear down if not overwhelm Japan Coast Guard ships and other JSDF resources in the area. It is an attempt to take over almost by osmosis, similar to Beijing's largely successful South China Sea strategy. Many Japanese fishermen no longer visit traditional fishing grounds in the area for fear of Chinese harassment.

In addition to China's mighty coast guard and maritime militia force, PLA Navy ships—sometimes operating with Russian Navy ships—intrude in Japanese waters and even circumnavigate Japan in shows of force.

Just one data point: the PLA Navy has more than 370 submarines and surface ships (and is expected to have nearly 400 by the end of 2025), compared with the Japan Maritime Self-Defense Force's approximately 154 total ships that have to cover all of Japan—and also keep an eye on North Korea and Russia.[4]

Not surprisingly, Japan Coast Guard and Japan Maritime Self-Defense Force (JMSDF) officers have occasionally admitted a sense of feeling "overwhelmed." The Japan Air Self-Defense Force (JASDF) is similarly overstretched by the high tempo of People's Liberation Army Air Force (PLAAF) incursions into the region.

And the Chinese military buildup is multifaceted—to include naval, airborne, and amphibious units; space, cyber, electronic, and nuclear weapons; and thousands of long-range missiles, to go with a long-standing political warfare campaign directed against Japan. Without Japanese support, the United States has slim hopes for successfully defending—and thus deterring—an attack on Taiwan. But without the Americans, Japan has no chance at all of defending itself.

Japan harbors long-standing doubts about US commitment, both conventional and nuclear. Observers note Japanese worries shifting between "Japan bashing" (asking Japan to do too much defense-wise) to "Japan passing" (the Americans and the Chinese cutting a deal that leaves Japan out in the cold to fend for itself). Nowadays, Japan doesn't worry about being "drawn into American wars." Rather the concern is about the reliability of the United States in defending Japan.

The Japanese and US Militaries: Except for the Two Navies, Basically Strangers

The US-Japan defense alliance has existed for over sixty years. One would think that the two militaries would be intimately familiar with each other and able to "take care of business." To be sure, there are pockets of good news: first, missile defense and second, the US Navy and the JMSDF. The United States and Japan have done a good job of combining missile defense capabilities and improving them.

The two navies also have a solid operational relationship. In the event of a fight over Taiwan, coordination between the JMSDF and the US Navy's Seventh Fleet, based in Yokosuka, could serve as a pillar of strength.

Despite these notable exceptions, the JSDF and US forces are no-where near as capable of combined operations as they should be after this many years of proximity.

Indeed, this was borne out in 2011 after the massive earth-quake and tsunami hit northern Japan. Except for the US Navy and the JMSDF—which promptly fell in with one another and went to work—other components of Japanese and American forces scram-bled to establish the most rudimentary cooperation and seemed to know almost nothing about each other's capabilities. Joint-combined operations—that is, operations involving troops from more than one military service from each nation's forces—were even more of a chal-lenge. And this was on Japanese territory, with no one shooting at them.

An ad hoc "joint US-Japan task force" was established for the first time in 2011 to deal with the earthquake and tsunami. In the thirteen years since Operation Tomodachi, progress has been halting.

In 2015, Prime Minister Abe successfully engineered a reinterpreta-tion of "collective self-defense" and the US-Japan Defense Guidelines to allow US and Japanese forces to train and operate together robustly. He also established an Alliance Coordination Mechanism (ACM) that has potential but is vague and unwieldy and would be of little real use in an actual conflict or contingency. The Japanese and US militaries now conduct more bilateral exercises and are trying to "join" their command and control more than in the past. But progress has been slow with few concrete outcomes in combined planning, including for a Taiwan contingency.

The Japan Self-Defense Forces

The Japan Self-Defense Forces are rated in some estimates as the fifth most powerful military power in the world. The JSDF has about 250,000 personnel: 150,000 for the Japan Ground Self-Defense Force (JGSDF) and about 50,000 each for the Japan Maritime Self-Defense Force (JMSDF and the Japan Air Self-Defense Force (JASDF). They have modern, effective hardware overall and personnel are profes-sional. Yet the whole may be less impressive than the sum of its parts.

The JSDF was essentially built as an adjunct to the US military. It provides specific capabilities that can contribute to US operations, but it is not a balanced force that can prosecute multi-domain, combined arms warfare. Chief of Japan Joint Staff Yoshida was asked in August 2023 whether the JSDF currently possesses the capability to defend Japan. He replied: "We cannot maintain Japan's security with our current capabilities."[5]

Over the last decade the JGSDF has begun shifting away from heavy, immobile units geared to fight off a Russian invasion of Hokkaido to more mobile forces able to operate in the maritime environment of southern Japan—where the Chinese threat is the highest. This required cooperating with the JMSDF, particularly as the JGSDF established its first amphibious force, the Amphibious Rapid Deployment Brigade.

Japan's JMSDF is highly professional and has excellent niche capabilities at submarine and antisubmarine warfare, surface warfare, maritime surveillance, and mine warfare. Since 2011, in addition to starting to develop joint operational capabilities with the JGSDF and the JASDF, the JMSDF is mastering the art of amphibious operations.

Nonetheless, despite some impressive capabilities, a foreign senior military officer with experience working with the JMSDF noted that it isn't equipped or trained in "multi-domain fleet actions," like those that could be required for effective combat against China. He added: "It is not a well-rounded force and is lacking in a fleet air arm, except for anti-submarine capabilities."[6] It also struggles to maintain sufficient personnel levels—much less to expand them as is needed. Recently, the JSDF even considered transferring five hundred JGSDF personnel into the Japanese navy to provide crews for two potential new destroyers.

The JASDF is another professional yet understaffed force. It too often tends to operate in isolation from the other services. The JSDF certainly needs more money, and the Kishida government (and previous ones starting with Prime Minister Abe in 2012) recognized this. In fact, plans are afoot to double defense spending over the next five years or so. And in 2025, Japan will establish a Permanent Joint Headquarters that will command the operations of the three JSDF services for the first time.

Importantly, Japan's previous self-imposed restriction on conducting "offensive" operations appears to have faded away. Tokyo now acknowledges the need for longer-range lethal capabilities, potentially even targeting enemy territory, in the context of a larger strategic defense campaign.

Within its military modernization plans, Tokyo must prioritize JSDF personnel as much as hardware. The JSDF has missed recruitment targets by about 20 percent for years and thus is an older and understaffed force. The problem is not just Japan's well-known shrinking population. Terms of service in the JSDF feature low salaries, dilapidated housing, and substandard medical care for family members. Yet there is public support for the JSDF, as attested by the popularity of base open-house days and other exercises that are open to public viewing.

The JSDF is a professional force that has the potential to be a first-rate military in short order—with the right force development policies and investments.

Urgent Recommendations

In late 2022, the Japanese government updated its three baseline national security documents: the National Security Strategy, National Defense Strategy, and Defense Buildup Program. They cover the waterfront and are clear about the threats facing Japan, naming China in particular. The following recommendations address the most urgent deficiencies in Japan's defensive capabilities set.

They are designed to deliver quick operational benefits that would improve the JSDF's capabilities and its ability to be a full partner "on the firing line." But they are also designed to have political benefits, like demonstrating resolve to China—and to other countries, in the region and around the world—as well as shaping the Japanese public's thinking.

These recommendations aim to follow former prime minister Kakuei Tanaka's advice, delivered to US interlocutors in 1970 when Washington was considering asking Tokyo if the US Navy could station an aircraft carrier at Yokosuka naval base. He advised the Americans to "tell us what you need and don't back down."

Steps by Japan on Its Own

1. Speak loudly from the highest levels of political leadership about the threat and Japan's defense deficiencies. Once the Japanese people understand the risks, they will support the policies with less complaint. Continue, or even increase, the JSDF's good work publicizing and exposing Chinese (and Russian) military and other malign activities around Japan. Beijing will help make the case for Tokyo. In 2022, for example, Beijing's reaction to US House Speaker Nancy Pelosi's visit helped push Tokyo's three new defense documents across the finish line.

2. Publicly emphasize that Taiwan is Japan's problem. Instead of suggesting that the United States must defend Taiwan in support of the US-Japan alliance, Japanese pundits should be asking how Japan can contribute more to Taiwan's defense.

3. Prepare the JSDF and the Japanese people, physically and psychologically, for a war over Taiwan. Japan cannot remain on the sidelines providing logistics support and guarding bases.

4. Provide the appropriate authorities to Japan's new joint operational headquarters, set to open in 2025, so that it can effectively improve JSDF readiness. There is concern that once it is set up it won't do much. The new joint headquarters needs budget approval among other authorities over the individual JSDF services. It needs teeth to enforce jointness in organization, capabilities, and equipment. Make the JASDF participate, even if it doesn't want to.

5. Broaden a "fighting mind-set" within the JSDF by allowing more risk and providing more range space and resources for realistic and effective training. The JSDF should not have to go to Australia to conduct serious training. Establish amphibious training areas in Japan. JSDF training needs to be more realistic and without the excessive safety restrictions that keep the services from professionalizing. Let the JSDF take risks.

6. Ensure adequate munitions stockpiles, combat logistics, casualty handling, and reservists who can replace combat casualties. Japan simply is not ready to fight a war. As for civil defense, Japan has a strong foundation given its long-standing and well-established local networks for responding to natural disasters. That needs to be built upon to prepare for a wider range of contingencies.

7. Harden bases and facilities (especially, but not only, in Japan's southern islands) and prepare to operate while getting hit by the enemy. Be able to make repairs quickly. This needs to be practiced through frequent, realistic drills.

8. Send JSDF medical personnel to Eastern Europe, such as Poland or even Ukraine, to assist and to learn about combat casualty handling and treatment.

9. Build the JSDF reserve into a useful and effective force. While doing so, determine which active-duty activities and missions would need immediate support in a contingency and make that the priority for reservist deployments.

10. Prioritize the JMSDF Mine Warfare Force—for both defensive and offensive mine warfare operations. Coordinate with South Korea to keep corridors open in a future contingency.

11. Expand overseas security assistance, especially with the Philippines. Expand Pacific Islands support too, especially in Palau, the Marshall Islands, and Tuvalu—the three countries in the region that still recognize Taiwan. There are operational benefits that can come from supporting these countries. It also shows that countries can derive benefits from supporting Taiwan. Prioritize energy, transportation, and communications. Coordinate efforts with the United States, South Korea, Australia, Taiwan, India, and others.

12. Launch a focused counterintelligence push against Chinese subversion and fifth-column efforts in Japan. This includes China-sponsored support for antimilitary, anti-base groups in Okinawa and elsewhere. Investigate the purchases of property in Japan and especially near sensitive locations and in sensitive industries.

13. Relax training restrictions for partner nations. US military units often leave Japan to train to defend Japan. These restrictions can and should be removed quickly. Also, continue hosting other friendly foreign militaries in Japan for meaningful exercises.

14. Address JSDF recruiting shortfalls through increased pay, benefits, and public messaging. Political and cultural leaders should talk up the benefits of serving in the Japanese military and remind people that it is a respectable profession. Encourage movies that increase morale (the *Top Gun* effect).

15. Reorganize the JGSDF along functional lines. Create bases for helicopter forces, infantry, and other specialties for efficiencies. Get rid of the dozens of penny packet bases with small units that do little more than have cherry blossom festivals with the local populations. The Japanese government may argue that this is how they keep the JSDF in touch with the local populace. If that is the case, these units have underperformed, judging by the severe restrictions still imposed on JSDF training.

16. Adopt NATO standards in the JSDF. Australia can provide an example of a non-NATO force that has seen the benefit of adopting NATO standards.

Steps by Japan in Cooperation with the United States

1. Establish a US-Japan joint operational headquarters in Japan. Simultaneously stand up a US-Japanese Joint Task Force Nansei Shoto (referring to Japan's "southwestern islands," including the Ryukyus) and headquarter it in Okinawa. These commands should conduct detailed, combined Taiwan contingency planning. Consider also putting a combined presence on the Senkaku Islands.

2. Open up more Japanese civilian airfields (of which there are over a hundred, most of them underutilized) for use by JSDF and US forces and other partner militaries.

3. Restart the US use of air and naval firing ranges on and near the Senkakus—and include the JSDF. These were used extensively

by US forces through the 1970s, and the United States still has the right to use them under its defense treaty with Japan.

4. Allow the Taiwan military to conduct training on Japanese territory, as it already does on US territory. This would foster interoperability and demonstrate political will.

5. Expand missile defense cooperation beyond the United States to include South Korea and Taiwan.

6. Raise information security protocols to Five Eyes standards and then increase intelligence sharing with US and other partners.[7] Given that it would probably take a long time to set up a government-wide security-clearance system, start with strict controls to allow small groups of Japanese civilian and military personnel to receive US classified data related to Taiwan contingency planning.

7. Implement Admiral Koda's ship-repair scheme where US Navy ships formally utilize Japanese shipyards and repair facilities in peacetime and wartime. The Japanese are highly skilled at this kind of work and US shipyards are thousands of miles away.

8. Prepare to offer full medical support, including through civilian hospitals, to US and allied forces in wartime. Casualties might be in the tens of thousands.

9. Procure more counterstrike and long-range missile capabilities. Integrate relevant intelligence, surveillance, reconnaissance, and targeting systems with US forces. China's military would fear the linking together of Japanese and American missile capabilities.

10. Continue to improve relations, especially in defense, between Japan and South Korea with the help of trilateral diplomacy led by the United States.

11. Ensure that long-standing US commitments to "extended deterrence"—the protection of Japan under the US nuclear weapons umbrella—remain solid and well understood by the Japanese people and by America's enemies. Tokyo and Washington should arrange for the United States to bring nuclear weapons into Japan aboard US Navy ships and, if the Japanese government requests it, store such weapons in Japan.

12. Open all US bases in Japan to become joint bases with Japanese troops based on them and providing security.

13. Implement a US advisor program to mentor, coach, and train key counterparts in the JSDF. US liaison officers are already established in each JGSDF army, for example. Expand these offices with soldiers, Marines, military Foreign Area Officers, US Army Special Forces, and others with specialties in ground, fires, logistics, and aviation.

14. Dispatch US war planners to directly assist JSDF planners in understanding the requirements—both hardware and operational capabilities—needed to fight a war and to be most useful to US forces. This will have the added benefit of ensuring that Japan's increased defense spending is spent wisely.

Unilateral Steps by Japan to Help Taiwan

1. Break Taiwan out of its diplomatic isolation. Visits to Taiwan by senior Japanese politicians representing the incumbent Liberal Democratic Party have been useful, but more needs to be done. Japanese government officials should visit and welcome reciprocal visits by Taiwan officials.

2. Pass a Japanese version of the Taiwan Relations Act (TRA), similar to the 1979 US law by that name that affirms Washington's support for Taiwan's defense. This would help shape thinking in Japan and serve as an authoritative statement of Japanese concern about Taiwan's fate.

3. Establish commercial transportation links between Taiwan and Yonaguni and other southern islands.

4. Hold Taiwan-Japan security talks at government-to-government levels. Include the Americans if that is desired. Taiwan has been asking the Japanese for this for years. Start these talks and it will demonstrate "will."

5. Send active-duty officers to Taiwan as full-fledged attachés and also as training advisors. Taiwan officers go to Japan in return. Media reports claim that Japan will be sending a "defense

official" to Taiwan to serve in addition to the retired military "attachés." This is a good move, but it is only one person—and is probably a civilian. That is not enough.

Conclusion

Potential is the operative word. More needs done both by Japan itself and in conjunction with the Americans and Japan's other friends. Fortunately, even as many political elites dithered, Japanese patriots—civilian and uniformed—quietly went about building and developing a military over the years that could potentially defend the nation when the time came and be an essential ally to the United States in its quest to deter or, if necessary, win a war against China.

If leaders find the will to do the things described in this chapter, we will find a more capable Japan—one that is able and willing to fight and solidly linked with US forces. That would have a stabilizing effect at a time when China seems to be revving up its war machine. Military capability improvements have attendant political and psychological effects that further enhance deterrence.

If Japan gets things right and addresses the threats it faces head on, it will indeed serve as the "swing vote" that prevents conflict over Taiwan.

NOTES

1. Yoshihide Yoshida, "Japan 'Cannot Maintain' Security at Current Capabilities: SDF Chief," interviewed by Naoya Yoshino, *Nikkei Asia*, August 29, 2023.
2. John V. Roos, former US ambassador to Japan, Statement Before the Senate Foreign Relations Committee, 111th Cong. (2009).
3. Admiral Yoji Koda, conversations with author.
4. Idrees Ali and Michael Martina, "What Is Most Significant in the Pentagon's China Military Report?," ed. Leslie Adler, Reuters, October 20, 2023.
5. Yoshida, "Japan 'Cannot Maintain' Security."
6. Author's private correspondence with a military officer familiar with Japan's military.
7. Five Eyes is an intelligence-sharing alliance that includes Australia, Canada, New Zealand, the United Kingdom, and the United States.

CHAPTER 11

"The Sun Also Rises"

YOJI KODA

There are three nations challenging the security and stability of East Asia and the Indo-Pacific region: China, North Korea, and Russia. All three harbor revanchist territorial objectives, share disdain for prevailing international norms and customs, and operate authoritarian—even totalitarian—political systems. All three have nuclear arsenals. And all three are neighbors of Japan.

Of the three, China casts the longest and darkest shadow and will probably continue to do so for the foreseeable future.

The United States, now wise to China's crafty security strategy, shifted its conciliatory attitude into a tougher and more competitive set of policies beginning in 2017, after China's illegal land reclamation and base building in the South China Sea was mostly complete. President Donald J. Trump, channeling widespread frustration and discontent over China's unfair trade practices, launched a trade war in 2018, further inflaming the US-China relationship.

Thus, the intense confrontation and strong rivalry between the United States and China has grown into a serious security concern with a large potential to escalate into real security crises and conflicts between the two strikingly different values of democracy with free society and authoritarian/autocracy with controlled society, focused on Taiwan and its surrounding waters.

This chapter recommends roles for Japan in helping deter Beijing from pursuing a war to subjugate Taiwan. It lays out steps Japan should pursue urgently to demonstrate that it has the political, logistical, and combat wherewithal to support its key ally, the United States, in the event of a war. Roles for Japan's Self-Defense Forces include securing airspace, strengthening ballistic missile defense systems, protecting sea lines of communication (SLOC), and providing airborne and maritime intelligence, reconnaissance, and surveillance (ISR) beyond the Japanese homeland to encompass the Ryukyu Islands, the Sea of Japan, and the East China Sea. The Japanese government should also coordinate a plan to support a dramatic increase in the number of US troops stationed on or passing through Japanese territory. This requires identifying areas that could quickly be developed into airfields, training grounds, and storage facilities for fuel and ammunition.

The chapter also recommends that the JSDF coordinate with South Korean and US forces to prevent adversaries, such as North Korea and Russia, from opening new fronts in a Taiwan scenario.

Taiwan: Center Stage for a US-China Confrontation

The question of Taiwan's status is often misinterpreted as a purely territorial matter for Beijing. It would be easy to draw that conclusion when Beijing has asserted for decades that Taiwan is an "inalienable" part of China and has cast the matter as an "internal" one with no space for foreign intervention. Xi Jinping, who holds paramount power as general secretary of the Chinese Communist Party (CCP) and as chairman of the party's Central Military Commission, has vowed multiple times, including at the 20th National Congress of the CCP in October 2022, that Taiwan's "unification" with China is "inevitable."

But the implications are far larger than that. From an international security point of view, Taiwan's fate is linked to a rivalry for global leadership between free and democratic nations on the one hand and closed, autocratic ones on the other. This is why the competition between the United States and China has become so prominent and increasingly intense since the turn of the century. In this respect, Taiwan is *center stage* in the drama for how this US-China strategic rivalry plays out.

Xi Jinping unequivocally reserves the right to use the People's Liberation Army (PLA) to "solve" what Xi calls "the Taiwan question." If China's moves on Taiwan militarily, there is a strong possibility the United States would intervene with its own military. Japan, as the United States's most important ally, would likely provide support to US military operations and would therefore be subjected to PLA attacks. In such a scenario, Japan's Western Islands chain, from Yonaguni Island through Okinawa to Kyushu, as well as the western half of Japan's mainland, Honshu, would be in the heart of the area of operations. The same is true for the northern half of the Philippines.

From a planning standpoint, the United States should posture its force deployment toward Taiwan based on an assumption of the most difficult scenario—a PLA operation to invade and seize Taiwan.

At the same time, a crisis may not be limited to the "center stage" of Taiwan. North Korea may be tempted (or even encouraged by China) to open a second front on the Korean Peninsula. In such a case, the United States might need to spread its force allocation across both fronts to defend Taiwan and South Korea simultaneously. The United States should preemptively develop allied strategies and operational plans with Japan and South Korea and perhaps with Australia and the United Kingdom. Other allied and like-minded nations could also participate as the geopolitical situation unfolds in real time.

In this scenario, South Korea should be prepared to assume as much of the Korean Peninsula's defense as possible, allowing the United States to allocate as many forces as possible to a Taiwan campaign. Similarly, this type of strategic mission planning would also be effective in a Taiwan-only crisis scenario, where a strong South Korean posture will deter North Korea from opening a second front.

Lessons from the Battle of Okinawa

One example of an island seizure operation that holds lessons today is the 1945 Battle of Okinawa. Though the defenders were defeated in that battle, it nonetheless holds cautionary lessons for Beijing and reasons for hope for Taiwan. The first condition for island seizure operations is to establish sea and air control near the objective island, as well as reliable logistic supply routes at sea. US forces during the Pacific War had established almost perfect sea and air control through two and a half years of combat, from mid-1942 to early 1945, that led to the annihilation of the Imperial Japanese Navy and Army forces in the Pacific. This provided the attacking US forces the freedom to conduct landing operations. The only means of resistance left for Imperial Japan was "Kamikaze" aircraft attacks against the US amphibious landing forces. The size of defending Japanese forces at the beginning of the battle was 60,000 regular forces and 50,000 locally recruited forces. The strength of US attacking units was 180,000 landing forces (US Army and Marines) and 350,000 support forces (US Navy and Army Air Corps). Logistic routes from forward US supply areas were also secured except for occasional Japanese submarine attacks. Yet even with this overwhelmingly favorable situation at Okinawa, it took almost three months for attacking US forces to seize the small island.

In the case of Taiwan, it may not be easy for the PLA to establish and maintain air and sea control, not only in the Taiwan Strait but also across the ocean areas around Taiwan, where US forces and Japan Self-Defense Forces (JSDF) might intervene. Then, the topography of Taiwan is strikingly different from Okinawa. The land area of Taiwan is roughly thirty times Okinawa's, and its population is nearly fifty times what Okinawa's had been in 1945.[1] Finally, Japan in 1945 was thoroughly isolated. Today's Taiwan has many friends, especially the United States and Japan.

This history underscores the difficulty faced by Chinese planners today. To successfully invade Taiwan, China would have to surge PLA forces and deploy almost a million PLA personnel for various relevant joint operations, including, at minimum, establishing sea and air control; destroying Taiwanese, US, and Japanese forces; bombarding Taiwan heavily; and conducting an amphibious invasion to seize the island itself. So for China, a Taiwan invasion is not an easy task but rather a massive and laborious operation that will need in-depth political-military coordination, precise planning, intense training, sufficient material preparation, and a resilient logistic support posture for all PRC forces.

Japan's Role in a Taiwan Crisis

In a Taiwan crisis, Japan and its self-defense forces will have to bear basic responsibilities for both national defense and protection for surged US reinforcements from Hawaii, the US mainland, South Korea, and perhaps elsewhere. Regarding Japan's national defense, in addition to overall homeland and airspace defense, protection of the southwestern islands, ballistic- and cruise-missile defense, protection of sea lines of communication, and control of maritime choke points (such as the Bashi Channel between Taiwan and the Philippines) are minimum essential missions.

But there are other tasks for Japan too. One will be full-scale logistical support to large numbers of US forces surged to the region: for example, basing hundreds more US military aircraft and providing and distributing fuel, supplies, medical care, and ammunition for surged US forces in a timely manner. Without adequate infrastructure in Japan, actual operations of US forces in a Taiwan crisis scenario are not possible.

Below is a list of Japan's responsibilities to enable surged US forces during a Taiwan contingency:

1. Fundamental JSDF missions as a national defense force:

   - Homeland defense, homeland airspace defense, sea lines of communication (SLOC) defense, and ballistic missile defense (BMD)

2. Additional JSDF missions in a Taiwan crisis:

   - Islands defense and control of choke points in the Southwest Islands chain
   - Sea control in the Western Pacific for the safety of surged US forces
   - BMD against the PLA's DF-21/26 antiship ballistic missiles, for the safety of surged US forces
   - Air and maritime surveillance of the Northwest Pacific and East China Sea (ECS), as well as Sea of Japan (SOJ)

3. Government of Japan tasks to enable combat operations by surged US forces:

- Provide enough airfields for aircraft
- Provide enough precrisis and pre-hostility storage facilities for ground-support equipment for aircraft
- Provide sufficient port facilities to berth naval units
- Provide enough wartime supplies storage facilities for various units
- Provide sufficient ship repair facilities for maintenance and combat damages repair
- Provide enough storage for fuel and ammunition for the wartime expenditures of both naval and air units
- Guarantee timely transportation and distribution of required materials from storage and depot facilities to frontline units, including afloat naval units
- Provide sufficient berthing facilities for US service members near their deployed bases
- Provide primary healthcare facilities for US service members

4. Government of Japan tasks to enhance overall logistics support for surged US forces:

- Provide twenty-four-hours/seven-days-a-week (24/7) operating load and off-load ports and airports for US military supplies and materials
- Provide sufficient 24/7 operational, practical, and realistic combat training ranges within Japan and surrounding waters
- Authorize Japan Maritime Self-Defense Force (JMSDF) ships to escort at-sea US Navy vessels that shuttle between Japanese ports and frontline US Navy units
- When necessary, provide logistic support to US Navy units by JMSDF logistic ships
- When necessary, provide air-refueling support to US Air Force (USAF) units by Japan Air Self-Defense Force (JASDF) air-refueling tankers

These are the overall tasks and missions for Japan as the principal ally of the United States. If Japan cannot execute these responsibilities, US operations to deter or defeat the PRC over Taiwan would be hindered and might fail. Japan's support roles and responsibilities in a Taiwan contingency will be many times larger than routine operations today.

One way to describe Japan's logistical support role is that it would bear responsibilities and perform tasks similar to what Saudi Arabia did to support US and other allied forces during operations Desert Shield and Desert Storm more than three decades ago.

Regarding Japan's current posture, the scorecard is mixed. The missions stated in parts 1 and 2 of the list are fundamental to the JSDF's current operational posture and concept in accordance with Japan's existing security laws, even under the "pacifist" constitution. However, there are also many deficiencies. These include combat sustainability and resiliency capabilities, as well as the logistical support posture of the JSDF. These big deficiencies are the areas where the government of Japan should place the highest priority in its future-force building.

The tasks in part 3 of the list are closely related to civilian infrastructure in Japan, and unfortunately, almost no governmental assessments have been made. In this regard, it is fair to say that Tokyo has no plan to accommodate and enable large numbers of US forces in Japan during a Taiwan crisis. The silver lining is that there are about one hundred nonmilitary airfields with runways longer than 8,000 feet (2,500 meters) capable of handling any type of US military aircraft, and numerous ports deeper than 60 feet (20 meters) in Japan. Tokyo, however, has yet to determine the operational requirements. To correct these deficiencies, the Japanese government will need to take necessary measures, including legislative actions, in the immediate future. Time is of the essence.

Owing to the small land area of Japan and relatively large population (about 120 million), sites that could be allocated for use of add-on fuel and ammunition storage facilities are extremely limited. So, Tokyo will need to convince many local communities to cooperate on this issue.

The tasks listed in part 4 are key operational but not direct combat support tasks like those listed in part 3, but Tokyo has likewise not taken any concrete measures to resolve them, except for logistic support to US units by JSDF units.

In summary, missions and tasks mentioned in this section are the urgent responsibilities of the government of Japan to prepare for a Taiwan crisis. Tokyo has much to do beyond pursuing its recently announced ambitious JSDF force buildup program.

North Korea: The Wild Card

Would the Democratic People's Republic of Korea (DPRK), on its own or in coordination with China, start military actions amid a Taiwan crisis? The odds are hard to estimate. The possibility of DPRK adventurism increases if the DPRK judges that the United States cannot allocate sufficient forces to the Korean Peninsula due to an overconcentration of US forces to counter China around Taiwan.

Yet the DRPK's military capability, other than its robust missile and rocket forces, looks weak in terms of sustainability and resilience—poor indicators for its ability to fight a prolonged war, given its poor economy and malnourished population. Knowing these weaknesses, the DPRK would have to depend heavily on its first strikes against South Korean and US forces on the peninsula in a fight. But these problems will be its Achilles' heel in future prolonged operations. In addition to this, DPRK's naval and air forces will be incapable of fighting a high-end war against Republic of Korea forces and US Forces Korea.

In the case of a Korean Peninsula crisis, either on its own or simultaneous with a Taiwan contingency, South Korea's role remains the same. Like Taiwan, South Korea must be prepared to survive the DPRK's massive first missile and rocket strikes. These efforts should include fortification of key military facilities and immediate counterstrikes to neutralize the DPRK's follow-on attack capacity.

In addition, South Korea should locate and destroy the DPRK's "tactical" nuclear-armed submarine in the Sea of Japan. Owing to the short distances to Seoul and Tokyo, the DPRK's submarine-launched ballistic missiles, potentially with nuclear warheads, would prove

Black stars indicate where the Tsushima, Tsugaru, and Soya (La Pérouse) straits lie (bottom to top). *Peter Hermes Furian/PIXTA*

difficult to intercept. Japan and South Korea should therefore conduct coordinated antisubmarine warfare patrols in the Sea of Japan on a continuous basis to mitigate this threat.

This new strategic situation in the Sea of Japan will generate a new burden of creating a new JMSDF Antisubmarine Warfare Task Group for 24/7 antisubmarine warfare operations in the Sea of Japan.

Containing a Russian Surprise

Russia may also take supportive military actions in coordination with China's Taiwan operations. However, eastern Russia is bordered by the

Korean Peninsula and the islands chain of Japan, as well as the Kuril Islands chain and Kamchatka Peninsula. Russia's Pacific Fleet, home-ported at Vladivostok, is therefore geographically contained in the Sea of Japan. There is another large Russian naval base at Petropavlovsk-Kamchatsky, on the east coast of the Kamchatka Peninsula, which is a strategic nuclear ballistic missile submarine base, so this force can make only limited contributions to China's Taiwan operations.

Japan should be prepared to contain the Russian fleet in the Sea of Japan by blocking the three strategic straits in Japan—that is, the Tsushima, Tsugaru, and Soya (La Pérouse) straits. This posture could prevent Russia from intervening in support of China's Taiwan operations.

Conclusion

A Taiwan contingency would not be an easy military operation for either the United States or China. For the allies, there are many urgent tasks ahead to deter China and to prevail if deterrence fails. However, the allied nations of the United States, Japan, and South Korea do not yet have a combined operational plan, or even a common strategy, to deal with a Taiwan contingency. Japan, as the United States' most im-portant ally in a Taiwan contingency, will play a critical and irreplace-able role in a Taiwan crisis. There are many tasks that Japan must be prepared to assume for which it is not prepared today.

The US and Japanese governments must develop detailed combined operational plans for Taiwan crisis scenarios today. If not, China will remain in an advantageous position to exploit delays, confusion, and inefficiencies in alliance operations during a contingency.

NOTES

1. Carl H. Marcoux, "Final Conflict on Okinawa," Warfare History Network, May 2004.

PART V

Australia's and Europe's Jobs Now

CHAPTER 12

Australia's Job Now

ROSS BABBAGE

In war, the victorious strategist only seeks battle after the victory has been won.

—SUN TZU, *THE ART OF WAR*, CHAPTER 4

Principles for Maximizing Australia's Deterrence Power

In Australia the goal of deterrence is mostly pursued in an ill-disciplined and incoherent manner. The selection, scaling, and operational employment of defense and other strategic systems are usually driven by the need to replace current capabilities, operational habits, a military service's preference, and domestic political imperatives or by budgetary allocations. Almost as an afterthought, selected options are often said to enhance deterrence. This behavior is flawed if one's primary goal is to deter military action by a major power.

There is a need for greater precision, especially when Australian decision makers consider how best to deter specific events, such as a Chinese assault on Taiwan. Planning to maximize combat power or achieve other goals may be laudable, but it is not the same as preparing to optimize deterrence. Deterrence involves using one's actions to deliver the strongest possible psychological impact on the opposing decision-making elite so as to persuade them to desist, delay, or other-wise alter their operations to one's advantage. To maximize impact, de-terrence operations need to focus on credibly placing at risk things that the opposing leadership values highly or considers especially sensitive. Such threats or pressures do not necessarily need to be overt or direct. Nor do threatening capabilities always need to be displayed. In some situations, it may be sufficient simply to assert or imply the existence of a capability that can threaten a high-value target for an opponent to be deterred.

For a medium power such as Australia, applying strong deterrence power against an opposing decision-making elite is a sophisticated form of signaling. It is the communication of a compelling message often using a combination of military and nonmilitary instruments so that the opposing decision makers become deeply concerned about the consequences that would flow if they act against the interests of Australia and its allies.

Not all types of deterrence work the same way. There are two main categories. First is offensive deterrence that, in its most basic form, threatens this way: "If you hit me, I will hit you back harder and you will regret hitting me in the first place." This might be called "cobra deterrence." The second main category is defensive deterrence. This in-volves sending a strong message: "If you strike me, you will get such a bloody arm that you will regret striking me." This might be called "por-cupine deterrence." Both categories are relevant to Australia's security challenges, but careful planning is needed to get the balance right.

Also relevant is the leverage rating—or power—of a particular instrument or action to force an opponent to change course. How strong a leveraging effect will a particular initiative have on the oppos-ing decision-making elite? When wishing to deter a Chinese attack on Taiwan, will "Option A" have a stronger psychological impact on Xi Jinping and his colleagues than "Option K"? It is important to note here that the views of the Chinese leadership should not be assumed to mirror-image those of allied leaders. The Chinese Communist Party's key players have mind-sets that are markedly different from those of Australian and other allied security planners and so any decision in this area needs to be made with great care. Assessments of options for delivering deterrence power should be made using the advice of expert analysts who follow the Chinese leaders' actions closely, can mimic their values and much of their thinking, and can accurately predict their next moves.

Then there is the question of the intensity rating of a particular deterrent measure and the manner in which it is expressed. For instance, if an Australian government document mentions that in the event of a military attack on Taiwan practical support would be delivered to the Taiwanese armed forces, the deterrence intensity rating might score 1 out of 10. However, if such a commitment to defend democratic Taiwan were publicly stated with strong emotion several times by the Australian prime minister, the intensity rating might rise to 3. Then, if such a commitment were delivered simultaneously with strong coordinated statements from the US president and the Japanese prime minister, the intensity rating might rise to 7 or 8. So in weighing the deterrence power of various Australian options, it is not only the specific action that is relevant but also the way it is expressed or delivered and by whom.

Other important factors in weighing deterrence options are cost-effectiveness and the ease and speed with which they can be implemented. Some options would clearly be more demanding of human and financial resources than others. Preferred options may draw on extant skills and other resources and offer strong deterrence power quickly at modest cost.

A final and critical consideration when rating deterrence options is the level of shock that an action can deliver to authoritarian state decision makers by suddenly short-circuiting their offensive plans. Is there an option that could take the opponent by surprise by rendering a key pillar of its strategic stance crippled or useless? Do Australia and its allies have an option that unexpectedly changes "the rules," negating a key part of the opponent's defense in a way that cannot be effectively countered? In other words, does Australia, in partnership with its allies, have a "third offset" option—analogous to the American-led "first offset" in the 1950s and the "second offset" strategy in the 1980s?[1]

If the answer is "probably yes," then this should be a core goal of Australian deterrence-led strategy.

What this discussion makes clear is that maximizing Australia's deterrence of a war over Taiwan would not be simple. It is unlikely to be achieved by accident. It requires a careful weighing of the type of deterrence, the leverage power and the intensity of a wide range of options, the cost-effectiveness of those options, the speed with which they can be delivered, and their potential to psychologically disarm the opponent's key decision makers.

Many deterrence options would require the involvement of not only Australia's defense organization and the country's national security agencies but also other government departments, business leaders, elements of broader Australian society, and, in most cases, allies and security partners. In contrast to Australia's military commitments during the last half century, maximizing deterrence of an expansionist China will require much more than contracting the task out to the Australian Defence Force to manage. It will need careful analysis of new multi-domain options, the fostering of a more innovative and fast-moving culture, a reshaping of some organizations, and operation within a society that is well informed, very supportive, and actively involved.

All this is possible, but it is far removed from current practice. This chapter considers briefly a menu of ten investment options that if delivered well could contribute significantly to Australia's deterrence of a Chinese assault on Taiwan and its potential escalation to a major Indo-Pacific war. A key question is which mix of recommendations promises the strongest deterrence power in a cost-effective and timely way.

1. Clarification of Goals and Disciplined Implementation of Strategy

Australia's *2020 Defence Strategic Update* states that the country's Defence Strategic Objectives are to shape the country's strategic environment, deter actions against Australia's interests, and respond with credible military force, when required.[2] The *Defence Strategic Review* of 2023 endorsed these objectives but stated that they needed to be viewed through the lens of a strategy of denial.[3]

Although this statement of strategic objectives is useful, it provides only the most general guidance. In particular, the logic for prioritizing investments to achieve optimal effects—especially maximizing deterrence—is missing.

More specific advice is needed to facilitate capability selection and employment for the primary categories of contingency. How are decision makers across government, industry, and civil society to judge what is needed urgently and what is of lower priority? Very little, if any, of this advice is currently being provided either formally or informally.

If deterrence is a primary Australian strategic goal and the national strategy is to be denial, there is a need to explore what this means not only for the Australian defense organization but also for other parts of government, for business, and for broader elements of society. The country's security challenges are multidimensional and so Australia's deterrence planning needs also to be multidimensional, engaging whole-of-nation and, in many cases, whole-of-alliance assets.

This is because deterring through a strategy of denial means not only blocking an opponent from physical, electronic, and other access but also denying the opponent's achievement of broader campaign goals, such as disrupting Australian and allied economies, undermining international supply chains, and damaging essential communication systems. If an opponent is to be deterred from launching such intrusive and disruptive operations by the specter of dismal failure or by the threat of disarming retaliation, carefully crafted plans are needed to develop these counters and then communicate the threat they pose to authoritarian opponents in appropriate time frames.

For example, one potentially powerful generator of Australian deterrence is the outsized strategic leverage provided by the country's role in international trade. Australia has some trade vulnerabilities of its own. But the country's role as a leading producer of many strategic materials (especially iron ore and natural gas) has produced a situation in which China has become heavily dependent on uninterrupted imported supplies.[4] Were trade from Australia and other partners to cease, some

Chinese industries would slow within weeks and the economic impact could be far-reaching within months. Even a hint that a Chinese assault on Taiwan would bring such disruption could encourage the regime to tread cautiously.

If the deterrence of a major authoritarian power requires many parts of government, business, and Australia's broader society to be marshaled, means must be found to properly brief the community and help relevant parties understand the types of actions that may be needed and when. Some countries do this very effectively, especially in Scandinavia. Australia has much to learn from them.

Very little of this whole-of-nation planning, preparing, testing, and demonstrating deterrence and denial capabilities has been done in Australia thus far. A primary reason is that political leaders in Canberra and some other allied capitals have not wanted to disturb their electorates by discussing the risk of major conflict and the need to prepare. Some special-interest groups have also complicated the situation by working to prevent the diversion of budgetary, human, and technical resources to deterrence priorities. So until the national leadership takes the initiative, explains the need for these measures, and initiates practical steps, Australia's deterrence of a major Indo-Pacific crisis will be handicapped and unnecessarily weak.

Further clarifying the country's strategic goals and initiating a number of organizational and process steps have the potential to send a strong signal internationally that Australia is preparing itself to reinforce allied deterrence power. Some of these initiatives could surprise authoritarian leaderships and give them new reasons to be cautious.

2. Establish a Permanent Australia-US (and Other Allied) Strategic Planning Group

Australia, the United States, and other close allies have well-established mechanisms for strategic and operational consultation and cooperation. Coordination is close in many areas, personnel are routinely posted to serve in each other's organizations, and the level of trust is high. There is little doubt that the defense and broader security systems of the United

States, Australia, the United Kingdom, and a number of other allies can operate effectively together at very short notice when required.

However, the coordination of contingency planning does have limitations largely because the political leaderships of each ally are hesitant to precommit their countries to conflicts well in advance. In Australia's case, political leaders appreciate that the circumstances of future crises will vary greatly and they want to decide how best to act in the national interest in the particular circumstances of the time.

Although this stance is understandable, it does place constraints on the speed and effectiveness with which some allied deterrence operations can be launched. It can also constrain the extent to which contingency plans can be developed and tested across the allied community prior to a crisis arising.

If Australia and its allies wish to maximize their deterrence of a Chinese military assault on Taiwan, there is a need for more extensive combined planning of contingent operations, and of deterrence signaling in particular. Political leaderships would always retain the right to approve campaign goals, generic deployments, rules of engagement, and suchlike, but there is a need for allied military commanders and other security leaders to be authorized to develop combined planning well in advance. They need to be well placed to move quickly and with strong effect should a crisis threaten with no warning. This would be achieved most effectively by establishing a permanent Australia-US (and potentially other allied) strategic planning group.

A public announcement of this combined planning group not only would strengthen allied operational coordination, but also would signal to potential opponents that the allies are united in the Indo-Pacific and are well organized and prepared to counter any authoritarian state adventurism immediately and in ways that are truly formidable.

3. Strengthen and Demonstrate Regional Security Partnerships

One activity that has the potential to help shape the Indo-Pacific in positive ways and also contribute to stronger Australian and allied deterrence is a further development of security partnerships with like-minded states across the region.

Successive Australian governments have worked hard to build networks of countries willing to stand together to resist authoritarian state subversion, coercion, and territorial intrusions. The emerging Indo-Pacific architecture is a layered series of overlapping partnerships tailored to specific needs and fully respecting local sensitivities. At the highest and most intimate level is Australia's exceptionally close alliance with the United States and the other Five Eyes partners: the United Kingdom, Canada, and New Zealand. Not far behind is the Quad, linking Australia with the United States, Japan, and India. Then there is a broader network of trusted relationships with other formal allies of the United States, especially South Korea, the Philippines, and the member states of NATO. There are also special partnerships with most members of the Association of Southeast Asian Nations (ASEAN) and the island states of the south and central Pacific. Beijing's aggressive international behavior during the last decade, its seizure and militarization of most of the South China Sea, its repeated intrusions across India's and Bhutan's northern borders, and its staunch support for Russia's invasion of Ukraine have accelerated the development of these counter-authoritarian networks. This has troubled the Chinese leadership, fanning fears of being surrounded and internationally isolated.[5]

Working closely with its allies and partners, Australia could further strengthen these counter-authoritarian partnerships and simultaneously warn Beijing of much worse to come if it launches a war to seize Taiwan. Early steps could include coordinated counters to Beijing's lawfare in the South China Sea and along India's northern borders. China's information warfare offensives could be thwarted more effectively by combined regional action. Other possibilities include sustained programs to prevent China's manipulation of international agencies. Upgrades could also be considered for more conventional security cooperation, especially intelligence sharing, exercise and training programs, the supply of military equipment, and the development of new security technologies.

One of the most powerful contributions to deterrence within this framework would be for Canberra to publicly assure key regional neighbors and friends that in the event of their facing direct coercion and territorial incursions, Australia will stand with them to do whatever it can to support them in their time of need. Reinforcing this strong declaratory support, Australia could offer to work closely with regional governments to strengthen their defense resilience against authoritarian state attacks. Beijing would certainly notice this growing regional security cooperation and China's leaders could be brought to realize that if they attacked Taiwan, a likely consequence would be a much stronger antiauthoritarian alliance and a more complete isolation of China from most of the world.

4. Accelerate the Large-Scale Deployment of American and Other High-Leverage Allied Military Capabilities to Australia

One option that potentially offers much stronger deterrence of a Chinese assault on Taiwan is to accelerate programs to welcome American, British, and other allied forces in much larger numbers to Australia. This requires many things to be done quickly, including substantial expansions of military and dual-purpose facilities across the country.

For the United States, this would relieve the pressure on its long-standing basing structure in the Western Pacific and provide exceptional opportunities to disperse high-value assets across a relatively secure landmass of comparable size to the continental United States. Once these assets are located in Australia, extensive support would be available from well-educated, supportive communities. Australia offers the United States a very strong southern anchor of great strategic depth for its military operations in the Western Pacific.

When viewed from Beijing, the growing allied military presence in Australia creates a stronger immediate response capability to any Chinese adventurism in East Asia and also a new level of logistic resilience and sustainability for prolonged allied operations in the theater. Moreover, senior Chinese decision makers realize that forces operating from Australia can readily swing their focus from the Western Pacific

On March 13, 2023, Australian prime minister Anthony Albanese, US president Joe Biden, and UK prime minister Rishi Sunak met to announce the specifics of submarine acquisition set forth by AUKUS. *Official White House photo*

to operations across the Indian Ocean to help control maritime traffic west of the Indonesian straits, support India's northern defenses, and, potentially, threaten sensitive parts of Southern and Western China. There are serious concerns in Beijing about the threat of encirclement and of potentially needing to fight on more than one front.[6] A buildup of allied forces in Australia would underline the risk that launching an assault on Taiwan could quicky escalate into a much larger conflict in which the Chinese Communist Party might be placed under great pressure in unexpected ways and locations. This could have serious consequences for the regime.

The Australian, American, and other allied governments have already agreed to expand military operations on and from Australia. As part of AUKUS, the 2021 security partnership between Australia, the United Kingdom, and the United States, the US Navy plans to increase submarine visits to Australia starting in 2023 and the British Royal Navy will do the same in 2026.[7] Then, starting in 2027 the US Navy will routinely operate up to four nuclear-powered attack submarines from Australia, and the Royal Navy one similar submarine.[8] In the early 2030s the Royal Australian Navy is expected to commission its first three nuclear-powered submarines to supplement US and British subsurface operations in the theater, with a further five boats joining the force in the early 2040s.[9]

In addition to this, key airfields are being upgraded across Northern Australia to support more substantial US and allied air operations, and the US Army is planning to stockpile stores of military equipment in Australia to equip much larger numbers of troops should they need to be flown into the theater.[10]

These and related initiatives are already sending strong signals to Chinese political leaders that should they launch a major assault on Taiwan, the United States and its allies have strong capabilities close at hand that are able to intervene on short notice. Were Australia to further accelerate these programs, the risks of an immediate and very strong allied intervention could be elevated to higher levels. The deterrent effects on the Chinese leadership could be substantial.

5. Strengthen Australia's Role as a Fully Integrated C4ISR Hub and Theater Headquarters

A potentially powerful way for Australia to strengthen its deterrence of a Chinese assault on Taiwan is to offer to host one or more allied theater headquarters, complete with the full range of advanced communications, command, control, computer and intelligence, surveillance, and reconnaissance (C4ISR) systems.

This option builds on a long-standing strategic logic. During the early stages of World War II, Australia was seen in the United States as being an ideal location for the allied Pacific theater headquarters. Operations launched from Australia into the Western Pacific, Southeast Asia, and adjacent maritime areas were far easier and quicker than those launched from the continental United States. Because of Australia's vast size, terrain diversity, and strategic depth, it was considered a formidable bastion. It was politically reliable, shared America's war aims, and possessed a well-trained English-speaking workforce.[11] It was an ideal command location, and this remains the case in the twenty-first century.

Since the 1950s Australia and the United States have built an extensive array of regional surveillance, intelligence, and space support facilities across the continent, and further developments in these fields are now underway. In July 2023 a program of Enhanced Space Cooperation was announced "to increase space integration and cooperation in existing operations and exercises."[12] Agreement was also reached to establish a Combined Intelligence Center–Australia within Australia's Defence Intelligence Organisation by 2024.[13] When these are added to the wide range of US, Australian, and other intelligence assets already operating in the theater, Beijing will face increasingly strong deterrence by detection and direct observation.

Australia has the option of further enhancing these capabilities and making it crystal clear to key Chinese decision makers that they will have diminishing scope for achieving surprise and information superiority should they decide to launch a major assault on Taiwan. If done well, this has the potential to make the Chinese Communist Party leadership rethink its campaign plans.

6. Accelerate the Deployment of High-Leverage Military Capabilities

When developing the Australian Defence Force (ADF) during the coming five to ten years, Australia should place much stronger emphasis on "game changing" and other high-leverage deterrence options than has been done in the past.

Australia's 2023 *Defence Strategic Review* addresses part of this logic when it states:

> Maximising the deterrent effect and response options from ADF capabilities is critical. To achieve the maximum benefits from our capability investments, the ADF force structure must become not only focused, but also integrated.[14]

The *Defence Strategic Review* then says that the ADF must harness effects across all five domains (maritime, air, land, cyber, and space) by applying the following ten "critical capabilities":

- undersea warfare capabilities (crewed and uncrewed) optimised for persistent, long-range sub-surface intelligence, surveillance and reconnaissance and strike;
- an enhanced, integrated targeting capability;
- an enhanced long-range strike capability in all domains;
- a fully enabled, integrated amphibious-capable combined-arms land system;
- enhanced, all-domain, maritime capabilities for sea denial operations and localised sea control;
- a networked expeditionary air operations capability;
- an enhanced, all-domain, integrated air and missile defence capability;
- a joint, expeditionary theatre logistics system with strategic depth and mobility;
- a theatre command and control framework that enables an enhanced *Integrated Force*; and
- a developed network of northern bases to provide a platform for logistics support, denial and deterrence.[15]

Each of these capabilities could contribute significantly to meeting Australia's defense challenges. And, as a group, they could also help field a fully integrated force. However, not all these capabilities carry strong deterrence power.

What is needed is a sharper assessment of the investment options that have the potential to stop even a major power in its tracks. Particularly valuable are high-leverage investments that can be revealed in whole or in part prior to any kinetic conflict so as to undermine the opposing leadership's confidence that they can prevail on the battlefield.

Australia has some options that potentially possess strong deterrence leverage, and it should have even more when it plans combined operations with the United States and its other close allies. This chapter argues that these special capabilities deserve a disproportionate share of investment attention if the country is serious about maximizing its deterrence of serious threats in the period ahead.

7. Develop Australia as the Indo-Pacific Arsenal for National and Allied Needs

Australia has the potential to redevelop and markedly expand its munitions manufacturing and servicing capabilities, not only to provide priority weapons for the Australian Defence Force, but also to contribute significantly to the supply of munitions to US and other partner forces operating in the Indo-Pacific theater.

Australia has been able to manufacture a range of munitions since World War II, including several types of small- and medium-caliber ammunition, artillery rounds, aircraft bombs, a few guided munitions, and a range of special-purpose weapons.[16] Building on this foundation, the Australian government announced in March 2021 the creation of a new and much expanded Guided Weapons and Explosive Ordnance Enterprise with a substantial initial budget.[17] Raytheon Australia and Lockheed Martin Australia were subsequently announced as the initial strategic partners for this program.[18] The intent is to manufacture a suite of advanced munitions starting with coproduction of Guided Multiple Launch Rocket Systems by 2025.[19] Regulatory, intellectual property, and other constraints are being removed in Washington, and production of other systems, including some sourced from other partner countries, is expected to follow promptly. Most Australian-manufactured munitions are planned to fully meet allied standards and to be interchangeable with those manufactured in the United States.

This and related military industrial initiatives have the potential to significantly boost the strategic contribution Australia makes to allied operations in the Indo-Pacific. In particular, these investments should add depth to America's hard-pressed munitions production base and substantially boost the resilience and endurance of forward-deployed allied units.[20]

From Beijing's perspective, accelerated Australian investments in large-scale munition manufacturing will heighten concerns that Washington and its allies are moving rapidly to reinforce their strategic posture in the region and their capabilities to engage with powerful force both at the outset of any major conflict and through its full duration. In combination with other initiatives, this program has the potential to undermine any Chinese view that allied forces would run out of munitions within days. As Australian and allied munition initiatives accelerate, China's leaders will be forced to face the reality that in any major war in the Indo-Pacific, they are unlikely to have an easy or quick path to victory. Launching such a war in the face of this changing strategic outlook will be an increasingly daunting prospect.

8. Accelerate Restructuring of Strategic Supply Chains to Underpin National and Allied Resilience and Endurance

During the first two decades of this century, the United States and its allies drove for greater economic efficiency by exporting many of their materials-processing-and-manufacturing capacities to lower-cost countries—most notably to China.[21] This process of globalization and sweeping deindustrialization of the West has resulted in America's manufacturing output falling from more than twice that of China in 2004 to only about half that of China in 2020.[22] A key consequence is that the United States and its allies lost control of the supply chains of many strategically important products—from steel to pharmaceuticals and machine tools to laptop computers. American and allied governments and businesses voluntarily delivered a substantial strategic advantage to Beijing. In the event of major war, the allies' loss of industrial supremacy could play a key role in determining the side that prevails.

Some important remedial steps have now been taken in Washington and other allied capitals, but many more are needed. The United States, Japan, South Korea, the Netherlands, and a number of other countries have already moved to restrict the transfer of advanced semiconductor and other sensitive technologies to China.[23] The Biden administration has also placed curbs on American investment flows into Chinese companies seeking leading-edge semiconductors, quantum computing, and artificial intelligence.[24] These restrictions will likely be extended further, and additional countries can be expected to enact similar restrictions in coming years.

At the same time, the United States and several of its allies have started to encourage the onshoring and friend-shoring of strategically important supply chains for key raw materials, material processing, priority manufactured goods, and system support capabilities.

In order to coordinate and accelerate these processes, Australia has worked closely with the United States and twelve other countries to establish the Indo-Pacific Economic Framework (IPEF) Supply Chain Agreement that authorizes the creation of a "world class Crisis Response Network." This network is tasked to

> facilitate faster collective responses to critical shortages and supply chain disruptions. This will help ensure . . . access to critical goods and reduce market instability. . . . In addition, an IPEF Supply Chains Council will start work on action plans to address vulnerabilities and chokepoints. This will provide a lasting platform to mobilise investment and boost value-adding opportunities for . . . industry in areas such as critical minerals and clean energy technologies, strengthening our economic resilience.[25]

If these and related initiatives can overcome political resistance in their home countries, they stand to insulate the allies from the threat of supply shocks imposed by Beijing.

Australia has a particularly important role to play because of its abundant reserves of rare earths, lithium, copper, silver, and many other strategic minerals and the country's potential to process these resources economically. With modest international investments, Australia could markedly reduce the allies' current dependence on China for a wide range of priority products. This would be a key step in removing Beijing's effective control of an array of strategic supply chains, and it would help restore the industrial strength and resilience of the allies and their trusted partners. This rapid recovery of the allies would send a strong signal to Beijing that in a major crisis or war, it could no longer expect to have sustained industrial dominance. To the contrary, within a few years it is possible that coordinated action by a range of allied and partner countries could result in China's industrial base stalling and becoming more vulnerable to international pressures.

9. In Close Partnership with Allies, Demonstrate a Next-Generation Ballistic Missile Defense System

One of the key features of China's military forces is its strong and sustained investment in short- and medium-range ballistic and cruise missiles, a large proportion of which are based in China's coastal provinces.[26] In the event of a large-scale assault on Taiwan, many of these weapons are likely to be launched against leadership, command and control, and other targets, not only in Taiwan but also potentially against American, Japanese, and other allied bases in the region. The People's Liberation Army's Rocket Force is structured to incapacitate and effectively disarm key Taiwanese and many allied units in the first hours of a kinetic war.[27]

For Washington and its allies, this large Chinese missile force poses a serious threat but also a strategic opportunity. If the allies could effectively counter this force of ballistic and cruise missiles, Beijing would lose much of its offensive power and be forced to halt most types of offensive operation.

Although the prospect of countering China's theater missile forces might be enticing to the allies, such a "game-changing" advance would be difficult to achieve. Shooting down ballistic missiles is akin to shooting down bullets in flight. Moreover, China's ballistic and cruise missile programs are some of the most active in the world, with several types of hypersonic missiles (i.e., Mach 5+) and other advanced systems currently being introduced into service.[28] Nevertheless, this has not dissuaded American, Australian, European, and other allied defense organizations from working intensively to develop capable missile defenses.

Some capabilities to intercept and destroy short-, medium-, and intermediate-range ballistic and cruise missiles are already deployed in the region. They include SM-3 and SM-6 missile systems aboard American ships and SM-3 missiles aboard Japanese ships. Advanced Patriot missile systems are operational in Japan and South Korea, and Terminal High Altitude Area Defense (THAAD) missile defense systems are deployed in South Korea and Guam.[29] These systems are useful, but now strong efforts are being made to develop a new generation of advanced ballistic and cruise missile defense systems that promise to be far more cost-effective.[30]

Modern wide-area ballistic and cruise missile defenses typically include prelaunch detection capabilities, then in-flight tracking and categorization systems that are mostly space based, and, finally, missile or directed-energy interception systems. Australia possesses extensive experience in several of these fields and has been working closely with the United States on hypersonic missile and defensive technologies for decades. There is thus some prospect that Washington and its allies may be able to progress a much more effective missile defense system into advanced development and test in coming years. The demonstration of such a capability, followed rapidly by initial deployments, would undermine China's advantage in theater ballistic and cruise missiles and seriously complicate, if not prevent, any large-scale Chinese military offensives for several decades. If assessed to be practical, this type of development should be prioritized as a "game-changing" deterrent.

10. Threaten to Expose Leadership Corruption

The extreme concentration of political power in China has generated an extreme vulnerability. There have been periodic reports over more than a decade of senior Chinese leaders gaining unexplained wealth and squirreling large sums in "bolt-hole" investments overseas.[31] If Australian and/or allied researchers were able to verify these stories and gather other evidence of leadership corruption and illegal and/or immoral behavior, they would have produced a powerful deterrent. The public release of this information, or the threat of doing so, may deter international adventurism by the most determined authoritarian leader.

As Grant Newsham and others have argued, the exposure of flagrant corruption by the Chinese Communist Party's most senior leaders is not likely to be tolerated in Beijing for long.[32] Were Western researchers, intelligence agencies, or others to signal that they hold such highly incriminating evidence and that they are ready to broadcast it to ethnic Chinese communities globally if Beijing launches an attack on Taiwan, the regime would be forced to recalibrate its tolerance of risk. Regime leaders may conclude that the release of such damaging information to the international community might trigger serious domestic unrest, a revolt, and, potentially, the demise of the Chinese Communist Party regime itself.

This type of deterrence option need not be linked directly to the Australian, American, or any other allied government. But some Australian and American journalists have shown themselves to be dogged pursuers of the truth over the origins of COVID-19, the incarceration of large numbers of Uyghurs and Kazaks in Western China, the suppression of dissent in Tibet, and other sensitive stories. There is certainly potential for Western researchers to uncover deeply incriminating information about the behavior of China's leaders. This material might be a powerful and cost-effective deterrence option for Australian security planners to hold in their arsenal.

Getting the Job Done

In Australia there has long been a gap between official statements on defense strategy on the one hand and the strategic and operational capabilities that are actually delivered on the other. The government's declaration that the nation's security will be driven by deterrence viewed through a lens of denial will be of little account unless it is implemented with sincerity, rigorous analysis, strong discipline, and sustained determination.

There is a great deal at stake. If Australia and its close allies carefully select and then fully develop a powerful set of deterrence options, they should be capable of preventing a Chinese invasion of democratic

Taiwan and a rapid escalation to a major war between China and its supporters on one side and the United States and its allies and partners on the other. This would save the world untold suffering and the probable loss of many thousands of lives. It deserves to be much more than an afterthought. The performance of Australia's entire national security system should be judged in large part on whether powerful deterrence is actually delivered.

Difficult decisions on resource allocations will be necessary. Strong cases can be made for investments in capabilities that have not been mentioned in this chapter. There is an array of new technology opportunities, logic in strengthening the sizes of permanent and reserve forces, a strong case for modernizing and expanding mobilization planning, and obvious needs to strengthen national infrastructure. All these and other possibilities may warrant significant funding. But if the government is to be true to its chosen strategy, all options must be shown to have strong potential to change the mind-set and planning of China's leadership elite.

Whatever deterrence options are chosen, a planning framework of this kind cannot be operationalized without extensive involvement by many government agencies, large parts of industry, and much of the broader Australian community. So for deterrence through denial to be more than a bumper sticker or just a convenient catch-all label for government reports, national leadership must explain openly the international challenges the country faces and the need to take precautionary steps. The hesitancy of successive governments to take the community into their confidence and encourage citizens to work together to build the country's security preparedness is unnecessary and counterproductive. Australians have a track record of responding well to such frankness, taking up the cause and working as a team to reinforce the nation's security. But until government ministers explain the need and the broad framework for action, little of substance will change. The ball is firmly in their court.

NOTES

1. The first American offset strategy was President Eisenhower's decision in 1953 to deploy tactical nuclear weapons to Europe to counter the Soviet Union's overwhelming conventional military advantage in that theater. The second offset strategy was the US decision to demonstrate Assault Breaker and Follow-on Forces Attack capabilities in the late 1970s and early 1980s that could defeat any attempted Soviet military assault into Western Europe. For further discussion, see Robert Work, "The Third U.S. Offset Strategy and Its Implications for Partners and Allies" speech delivered by the deputy secretary of defense, Washington, DC, January 28, 2015.

2. Commonwealth of Australia, *2020 Defence Strategic Update*, Department of Defence, Canberra, 2020, 24–25.

3. Australian Government, *National Defence: Defence Strategic Review*, Canberra, 2023, 37–40.

4. For details, see the table in Ross Babbage, *The Next Major War: Can the US and Its Allies Win against China?* (Amherst, NY: Cambria Press, 2023), 186.

5. For further discussion, see Chris Buckley, "The East Is Rising: Xi Maps Out China's Post-Covid Ascent," *New York Times*, March 3, 2021.

6. Buckley, "The East Is Rising."

7. For details, see Senator Penny Wong, Minister for Foreign Affairs, "Joint Statement on Australia-United States Ministerial Consultations (AUSMIN) 2023," July 29, 2023.

8. Wong, "Joint Statement on Australia-United States Ministerial Consultations."

9. Wong, "Joint Statement on Australia-United States Ministerial Consultations."

10. Wong, "Joint Statement on Australia-United States Ministerial Consultations." See also Charles Edel, "The AUKUS Wager: More Than a Security Pact, the Deal Aims to Transform the Indo-Pacific Order," *Foreign Affairs*, August 4, 2022.

11. For further discussion, see Peter Edwards, "Curtin, MacArthur and the 'Surrender of Sovereignty': A Historiographical Assessment," *Australian Journal of International Affairs* 55, no. 2, July 2001, 175–85, and Peter Edwards, "From Curtin to Beazley: Labor Leaders and the American Alliance," lecture, John Curtin Prime Ministerial Library, Curtin University, October 2001.

12. For details, see Wong, "Joint Statement on Australia-United States Ministerial Consultations."

13. Wong, "Joint Statement on Australia-United States Consultations."

14. Australian Government, *National Defence*, 54.

15. Australian Government, *National Defence*, 54–55.

16. For details, see Chris Coulthard-Clark, *Breaking Free: Transforming Australia's Defence Industry* (Kew, Victoria: Australian Scholarly Publishing, 1999), 37–90.

17. Hon. Scott Morrison MP, "Morrison Government Accelerates Sovereign Guided Weapons Manufacturing," media release, March 31, 2021.
18. Hon. Peter Dutton MP, "Australia Takes Next Step to Delivering Guided Weapons and Explosive Ordnance Enterprise," media release, April 5, 2022.
19. For details, see Wong, "Joint Statement on Australia-United States Ministerial Consultations."
20. For details on the stresses facing US munitions production, see Mark F. Cancian, *Industrial Mobilization: Assessing Surge Capabilities, Wartime Risk and System Brittleness*, Center for Strategic and International Studies, 2021; Joe Gould, "Lockheed, Aiming to Double Javelin Production, Seeks Supply Chain 'Crank Up,'" *Defense News*, May 9, 2022; Conrad Crane, "Too Fragile to Fight: Could the U.S. Military Withstand a War of Attrition?," *War on the Rocks*, May 9, 2022; Gordon Lubold, Nancy A. Youssef, and Ben Kesling, "Ukraine War Is Depleting U.S. Ammunition Stockpiles, Sparking Pentagon Concern," *Wall Street Journal*, August 28, 2022.
21. These issues are discussed in Babbage, *Next Major War*, 101–08.
22. Babbage, *Next Major War*, 101–08.
23. "US to Expand Semiconductor Export Controls on China," *Kyodo News*, June 23, 2023.
24. Andrew Duehren, "US Bid to Hamper China's Military," *The Australian*, August 10, 2023.
25. Senator the Hon. Don Farrell, Minister for Trade and Tourism, "IPEF Supply Chains Agreement—More Resilient Supply Chains for Uncertain Times," joint media release with the Hon. Ed Husic MP, Minister for Industry and Science, Canberra, May 28, 2023. See also US Department of Commerce, "Ministerial Statement for Pillar II of the Indo-Pacific Economic Framework for Prosperity," September 9, 2022, https://www.commerce.gov/sites/default/files/2022-09/Pillar-II-Ministerial-Statement.pdf.
26. Office of the Secretary of Defense, *Military and Security Developments Involving the People's Republic of China 2020: Annual Report to Congress*, US Department of Defense, 57.
27. These issues are discussed in Babbage, *Next Major War*, 29–31, 48, 49, 131–39.
28. Holmes Liao, "China's Development of Hypersonic Missiles and Thought on Hypersonic Defense," *China Brief*, October 21, 2021.
29. For details, see International Institute for Strategic Studies, *The Military Balance 2023* (Abingdon-on-Thames, UK: Routledge, 2023), 47–49, 259, 268.
30. US Department of Defense, "Missile Defense Agency Officials Hold a Press Briefing on President Biden's Fiscal 2024 Missile Defense Budget," March 14, 2023.

31. See, for example, Marina Walker Guevara, Gerard Ryle, Alexa Olesen, Mar Cabra, Michael Hudson, Christoph Giesen, Margot Williams, and David Donald, "Leaked Records Reveal Offshore Holdings of China's Elite," International Consortium of Investigative Journalists, January 21, 2014; Celia Hatton, "Panama Papers: How China's Wealth Is Sneaked Abroad," BBC News, April 6, 2016.

32. Grant Newsham, "The Way to Take On China Is to Make It Personal," Fox News, August 3, 2023.

CHAPTER 13

Europe's Job Now

**ANDERS FOGH RASMUSSEN AND
JONAS PARELLO-PLESNER**

"Ukraine today, Taiwan tomorrow." Such ominous messages flooded Taiwanese social media immediately after Russia's full-scale invasion of Ukraine on February 24, 2022. The Taiwanese were filled with concern for both Ukraine's future—and their own.

For the Taiwanese, the parallels with Russia and Ukraine are hard to ignore. Living next door to an aggressive authoritarian regime is a dangerous place to be. Russia's war in Ukraine has destroyed the last remnants of naïveté about the threat posed by dictators like Vladimir Putin. For years Putin denied Ukraine's right to exist beyond Russia's sphere of influence. On February 24, we saw the reality of those words.

In the Taiwan Strait, Xi Jinping has been equally clear about his intent to take over Taiwan by whatever means necessary, including a military assault. Since the onset of war in Ukraine, the Chinese navy and air force have ramped up exercises around Taiwan. Chinese warplanes enter Taiwanese air space on an almost daily basis. These sorties are both to degrade Taiwan's capabilities and to undermine the country's morale.

Despite the words of China's leaders and the actions of its military, many European leaders continue to ignore the peril Taiwan faces. Even at the NATO summit in Vilnius in June 2023 where Europeans went further than usual in their China strategy, Taiwan remained a taboo word.

In terms of value systems, Taiwan and China are night and day. After more than a decade in power, Xi Jinping and his autocratic state ideology—"Xi Jinping Thought on Socialism with Chinese

Characteristics for a New Era"—has made China increasingly repressive. Meanwhile, Taiwan has become a beacon of democracy in the region, scoring 94 out of 100 in the Freedom House index—higher than most EU members.[1] As Taiwanese president Tsai Ing-wen stated: "Democracy has become a non-negotiable part of our identity."[2]

Like Putin, however, Xi is clear in his ambitions to reunite the motherland—which, for him, includes Taiwan—by whatever means necessary. Over the last decade, the Chinese military has massively ramped up spending, expanding its footprint and attempting to neutralize American military strength in the region.

European leaders must not make the same mistakes with Xi Jinping that they did with Vladimir Putin. To prevent Taiwan from becoming the next Ukraine, it's time that NATO and European Union (EU) member states stand up for their values and help a small democracy face an aggressive autocratic neighbor. They have the power to do so—but only if they act now.

There are three key themes upon which to draw lessons from the war in Ukraine and to prevent one happening in the Taiwan Strait.

1. Finding Europe's Strength in Economic Deterrence

Ultimately it is the United States that has the military strength and global reach to prevent a Chinese attack on Taiwan. However, there is more than one way to influence Beijing's calculations and deter a war. Together with the global democracies of the Group of Seven (G7) and beyond, European leaders should signal that any Chinese military aggression would be met with forceful sanctions, just as they did with Russia following the invasion of Ukraine.

In such a scenario, China would see itself cut out of the globalization that it has benefited from. The threat of economic sanctions will carry greater weight with Chinese Communist Party leaders than it did with their Russian counterparts, as the party's legitimacy rests on continuously rising living standards. China's growth has been fueled partly by exports, leaving it far more reliant on global supply chains than Russia. That is why it is vital that EU and NATO members state clearly the severe economic consequences of any attack. There should be no ambiguity—any attack on Taiwan would come at an immense cost for China.

For Europe, this means starting a frank conversation with the business community. Many European companies have now pulled out of Russia entirely, going beyond what's legally required by sanctions. Most were taken by surprise when Putin launched a full-scale war of aggression, and some, particularly in the German business community, still dream of a return to the world of yesterday.

Fortunately, at least some German politicians have woken up to the new reality. Foreign Minister Annalena Baerbock said it clearly in September 2022 in a speech aimed at German industry dealing with China: "Simply keeping our fingers crossed and thinking it won't be all that bad with these autocratic regimes is a mistake we can't afford to make a second time."[3]

This matters because Germany accounts for almost half of the EU's exports to the Middle Kingdom, with cars, machinery, and chemicals leading the way.

European reliance on Chinese imports is an even greater concern. We cannot end our nefarious dependence on Russian gas only to end up reliant on China to power the green transition. From solar cells to batteries for electric cars, China has used immense state subsidies to dominate new industries. The current battle line is on electric vehicles and windmills where Chinese state-driven companies seek to dominate the European market, much as China's subsidized solar-panel industry was fatal to European players. Meanwhile, Chinese control of critical raw materials leaves Europe in a position of weakness.

As a response, in the EU and among other democratic countries, we must establish our own internal supply chains that reduce dependence on China. This does not mean ending all trade. But Europeans must have secure supply chains for sensitive technology, critical infrastructure, and access to vital raw materials. This should be based on allied circulation and on free trade among free nations.

That is the direction that Ursula von der Leyen, president of the European Commission, proposed in a speech on EU-China relations on

March 30, 2023. She called for Europe to "de-risk" its trade and investment relations from China. The term has even caught on in Washington policy circles, a rarity for Brussels-bubble terminology. De-risking—if done well—spells a much-needed farewell to starry-eyed economic dependence on autocratic China.[4]

European companies should recognize this new reality and adapt their supply chains accordingly in concert with the United States and other democratic partners globally. Any company with significant dealings with China needs to have contingency plans for a potential future attack on Taiwan.

China is also preparing to sanctions-proof its economy, denominating a growing portion of its trade in yuan in an attempt to de-link China's financial system from the US dollar. US and European sanctions in 2024 might not have the same impact in 2027 and onward. A Taiwanese military expert has told us that in his estimation China might not venture to attack Taiwan until 2035, when it expects to have secured its energy independence through Russia and other land-based sources.

The major difference between Russia's invasion of Ukraine and a potential war in Taiwan would be the size of the economies at play. Chinese trade flows dwarf those of Russia, meaning the economic reverberations would be enormous. This would be damaging for the West but catastrophic for China itself, which still relies heavily on export-led growth. This makes it even more important to put China on alert now, so that the threat of economic carnage can act as a deterrent.

Some still dream of European neutrality, to shield or at least mitigate the damage to our economies. This is deeply misguided. In the event of a conflict in the Taiwan Strait, Europe would immediately feel the economic consequences. Because almost 50 percent of global maritime trade passes between mainland China and Taiwan, significant disruption there would send shock waves around the world. Meanwhile, Taiwan's position as the global leader in advanced microchips means that an attack on the island would affect all of us who use the latest iPhone or technological device in our work or private life. The same goes for supply chains weaving through China. Ultimately, there is no mouse hole big enough for Europeans to crawl into to escape the economic consequences. Far better to act and prepare now.

Are European populations more prepared for this reality than companies? Would they back curbing trade with China if the country launched an attack on Taiwan? According to some polls, yes, they would. In a major annual survey conducted by the polling company Latana on behalf of the Alliance of Democracies Foundation, a majority of respondents in half the countries surveyed favored cutting economic ties with China if it were to invade Taiwan.[5] These countries include many of China's top trading partners, such as the United States, Japan, South Korea, and Germany, which collectively account for over 53 percent of China's annual trade, or $2.3 trillion.

That's a clear message of unity that should compel Chinese leaders and military planners to think twice. European leaders should listen to their populations. They should begin planning for this scenario and make sure that China understands what the full consequences of its actions could be.

Being caught off guard by Russia's invasion of Ukraine was bad enough, but repeating the mistake would be unforgivable.

2. Ensuring Ukraine Wins and Stepping Up European Security Burden Sharing

Another important way to deter a Chinese move on Taiwan is to ensure a Ukrainian victory over Russia in the current war.

If Russia can permanently gain territory and establish a new status quo by force, it will set a precedent. Dictators everywhere from Beijing to Tehran will conclude that ultimately military aggression works and that the democratic world chooses appeasement over confrontation.

The lesson we learn from history is that appeasing dictators does not lead to peace. On the contrary, it leads to war and conflict.

That is why Europe should make sure that Ukraine wins by providing the country with all the arms and munitions it needs for a military victory with no "ifs," "ands," "buts," or caveats. Ukrainians continue to demonstrate their will to fight despite hundreds of thousands of casualties on each side of the war; we must give them the means to do so. Ukrainians are not just fighting for their own freedom; they are fighting for all of ours.

All those who believe in a democratic Taiwan and a rules-based international order must work to ensure that Ukraine prevails. That is also the reality some young Taiwanese felt when they joined the Ukrainian foreign legion to fight for Ukraine in 2022. "If we don't stop them, we will be next," as Jack, a young Taiwanese volunteer soldier, told the Copenhagen Democracy Summit in May 2023.[6]

Europeans are now supplying most of the military assistance to Ukraine. The value of European military aid reached $53 billion while US military aid accounts for $44.2 billion as of November 2023, according to Kiel Institute for the World Economy and the US Department of State.[7] Regarding total contributions, Europeans have spent a total of $140 billion, which includes the recently approved $53 billion Ukraine Facility by the European Union. Total contributions from the United States stand at approximately $113 billion as of September 21, 2023, according to the Committee for a Responsible Federal Budget.[8]

A surge of American military assistance to Israel following the Hamas terrorist attacks of October 7, 2023, and the rising threat of a Chinese attack on Taiwan mean that Europe needs to shoulder an even greater part of the burden for Ukraine. NATO and EU allies of the United States should expect Washington to reallocate military platforms, troops, and munitions to Asia from Europe in the event Beijing initiates a crisis in the Taiwan Strait. That would entail European forces stepping up in their own neighborhood. A similar revised burden sharing also applies to NATO commitments in Europe, where Europeans should expect to pay more overall in defense expenditures and to contribute more to European exercises and joint operations.

We have no illusions that Europe—apart from France and potentially Great Britain—will have the military capabilities to play a significant military role in the Taiwan Strait. In the event of a Taiwan war, it would be Taiwan and the United States and Washington's Pacific allies Japan and Australia that would play the primary military roles.

Right now, Europeans are not adequately preparing for that scenario, as the British Parliament's Defense Committee pointed out in a report in October 2023, warning bluntly that "China intends to confront Taiwan" and that "the UK's regional military presence in the Indo-Pacific remains limited and the strategy to which it contributes is unclear."[9]

Europe would play a minor role in any military scenario due to lack of capabilities. Yet its contribution to economic deterrence combined with military burden sharing in Europe would amount to a substantial contribution.

3. Urging an Audacious Taiwan Policy from Europeans

Just as the United States has shown itself essential to European security, European countries must work more closely with the United States, Taiwan, and democracies in the Indo-Pacific.

Although European countries maintain "one China" policies that extend diplomatic recognition to the People's Republic of China, there is room to maneuver to increase support for democratic Taiwan.

European politicians should be much clearer and provide unequivocal support for Taiwan being given the opportunity to maintain its democratic system and its free way of life. That should be our value-based starting point, especially when Taiwan is peaking at the top of global democracy rankings and China descends further into autocracy and repression. That reality needs to be spelled out to citizens across European countries.

In Europe, there is a vanguard of leaders prepared to stand up for Taiwan. These hail primarily from Central and Eastern Europe. Lithuania's prime minister Ingrida Šimonytė and foreign minister Gabrielius Landsbergis led the way and were willing to risk the country's entire trade with China to increase interaction with Taiwan in 2021. Even after strong Chinese trade sanctions, Lithuania stayed on this course. In October 2023, the Lithuanian speaker of Parliament led a large delegation to Taiwan to the consternation of the Chinese government and party apparatus.

Under President Zuzana Čaputová, Slovakia has also increased its cooperation with Taiwan. However, the election of the pro-Moscow and pro-Beijing prime minister Robert Fico will likely torpedo this progress. There are more positive signs in neighboring Czechia, where President Petr Pavel has taken large steps toward a rapprochement with Taiwan. He was elected in January 2023 and shortly afterward did something unprecedented for a European leader. He spoke with Taiwanese president Tsai Ing-wen and promised to meet with her at a later stage. China condemned the conversation, accusing the president of violating China's "one-China principle." Pavel signaled clearly that he was elected in a free country and has the right to talk to whomever he wants. The Czech government has also invited the Taiwanese foreign minister to visit and expanded military exchanges. Czech officials also tell us that the years of courting China led to little economic benefit. Taiwan is a bigger investor in Czechia than is China.

Pavel's example should set the standard for the European Union's Taiwan policy so that everyone is clear about the democratic right to free exchanges with Taiwan. It must not be the autocratic leaders in Beijing who decide the yardstick for elected politicians in Europe on their interactions with Taiwan. The former British prime minister Liz Truss also brought that message when she visited Taiwan in May 2023 as the first former UK prime minister to visit the island since Margaret Thatcher.

Some people allege such actions and statements are "provocative" toward China. In reality they are stabilizing because they demonstrate how much Taiwan matters, economically and geopolitically, to world order. Publicly affirming the importance of Taiwan and its security is a prerequisite to effectively deterring Beijing.

Despite these positive examples, Europe is still not speaking with one voice when it comes to China and Taiwan. That was made abundantly clear by the state visit of French president Emmanuel Macron to China in April 2023. While enjoying the pomp and pageantry laid on by Xi Jinping, Macron conspicuously failed to bring up Taiwan with the Chinese leadership. This was even more galling given that China announced renewed military exercises around Taiwan while the

An honor guard greets President Emmanuel Macron during his stay in Beijing in April 2023. *Ng Han Guan—Pool via Getty Images*

president was visiting. Asked by *Politico* about his stance on Taiwan during the trip, President Macron said it was important that Europe "did not get caught up in crises that are not ours."[10]

President Macron's comments rightly caused outrage on both sides of the Atlantic. In the United States, politicians questioned why Washington should continue to subsidize European security when its leaders undermine US interests in the Indo-Pacific. In Europe, leaders from Poland, Czechia, and Lithuania all reaffirmed their support for Taipei. Even in Germany, Chancellor Olaf Scholz was clear that Beijing would face consequences if it attempted to change the status quo in Taiwan by force. Foreign Minister Baerbock also paid a speedy follow-up visit to Beijing with the same warning message to China.

President Macron did eventually qualify his remarks, but in many ways the damage was already done. Rather than a strong show of unity, China got what it wanted—a weak and divided response from the democratic world. You cannot declare yourself neutral when it comes to the front line of freedom—in Donbass or in the Taiwan Strait.

Macron should have learned from his diplomatic efforts with Putin regarding Ukraine that with dictators only military and economic deterrence have an impact, not diplomatic coffee chats.

With democratic values and the rules-based international order increasingly under threat, the democratic world needs to draw closer together, not pull itself apart. The war in Ukraine has shown that when we are united, the free world remains a formidable force. In the face of an increasingly aggressive China, we need a similarly unified approach.

Nowhere is that clearer than in Taiwan. If we want it to be based on freedom, then we must show resolute support for Taipei's democracy and speak clearly to Beijing. If we fail to do so, the world's dictators will gain ground. As Chinese military activity increases around Taiwan, the danger of escalation or miscalculation grows. If we send mixed signals, we heighten these risks.

Even if European troops were not directly involved in a war in the Taiwan Strait, any conflict there would have huge ramifications for our continent. That is why it is vital that Europe takes actions now to deter any attempt by China to change the current status quo by force. If Europe can shoulder more of the burden for its own defense, lay out the economic consequences of an attack on Taiwan, and speak clearly and with one voice to Beijing, it will lessen the risk of conflict. That is not just in Taiwan's interest but in the entire world's.

NOTES

1. Freedom House, "Taiwan," Freedom in the World 2022, accessed November 21, 2023.
2. Tsai Ing-wen, "Taiwan: An Integral Partner of the Global Democratic Alliance," speech, Office of the President Republic of China (Taiwan), Taipei, June 10, 2022.
3. Annalena Baerbock, "Speech by Foreign Minister Annalena Baerbock at the Business Forum of the 20th Conference of the Heads of German Missions," Federal Foreign Office, Berlin, June 9, 2022.
4. Ursula von der Leyen, "Speech by President von der Leyen on EU-China relations to the Mercator Institute for China Studies and the European Policy Centre," European Commission, Brussels, March 30, 2023.

5. The Democracy Perception Index, the world's largest annual study on democracy, covers more than fifty countries representative of more than three-quarters of the world's population; Alliance of Democracies, "Global Democracy Poll: Western Support for Ukraine Holds, Democracy at Home Is under Pressure," press release, May 10, 2023.

6. Alliance of Democracies, "Global Democracy Poll."

7. Pietro Bomprezzi, Yelmurat Dyussimbinov, André Frank, Ivan Kharitonov, and Christoph Tresbesch, "Ukraine Support Tracker," Kiel Institute for the World Economy, accessed November 22, 2023; Bureau of Political-Military Affairs, "U.S. Security Cooperation with Ukraine," US Department of State, November 20, 2023.

8. Committee for a Responsible Federal Budget, "Congress Approved $113 Billion of Aid to Ukraine in 2022," blog, January 5, 2023.

9. UK Parliament, House of Commons, Defence Committee, *UK Defence and the Indo-Pacific*, October 2023.

10. Jamil Anderlini and Clea Caulcutt, "Europe Must Resist Pressure to Become 'America's Followers,' Says Macron," *Politico*, April 9, 2023.

ABOUT THE EDITOR

Matt Pottinger is a distinguished visiting fellow at the Hoover Institution and chairman of the China Program at the Foundation for Defense of Democracies. He served as US deputy national security advisor from 2019 to 2021 and, previously, as the National Security Council's senior director for Asia from 2017 to 2019. Pottinger spent the late 1990s to mid-2000s in China as a reporter for Reuters and the *Wall Street Journal*. He fought in Iraq and Afghanistan as a US Marine during three combat deployments between 2007 and 2010.

ABOUT THE CONTRIBUTORS

Dr. Ross Babbage has worked on Australian and international defense and security issues for over four decades. He has held senior positions in the Australian Department of Defence, the intelligence community, at the Australian National University, and in the corporate sector. Babbage currently leads two companies that work on the tough security challenges confronting Australia and its allies and is also a nonresident senior fellow at the Center for Strategic and Budgetary Assessments in Washington, DC. His latest book is *The Next Major War: Can the US and Its Allies Win against China?*

Gabriel B. Collins is the Baker Botts Fellow in Energy and Environmental Regulatory Affairs at the Center for Energy Studies at Rice University's Baker Institute for Public Policy. At Baker, he coheads the Program on Energy and Geopolitics in Eurasia. Collins received his BA from Princeton University and his JD from the University of Michigan Law School. He is still teased by his family for joining a commodity hedge fund right before the 2008 market crash. Collins reads Mandarin, Russian, and Spanish well enough to use them in his research, speaks each just well enough to get himself in trouble, and is licensed to practice law in Texas.

Dr. Andrew S. Erickson is a professor of strategy (tenured full professor) in the US Naval War College's China Maritime Studies Institute (CMSI) and a visiting scholar in residence in Harvard University's Department of Government. A core founding member of CMSI, he helped establish and stand it up officially in 2006 and has played an integral role in its development; from 2021 to 2023 he served as its research director. Erickson has advised and supported other research centers whose creation was inspired by CMSI and is an associate of the China Aerospace Studies Institute. He received his PhD and MA from Princeton. His research website is http://www.andrewerickson.com.

Robert Haddick is a visiting senior fellow at the Mitchell Institute for Aerospace Studies of the Air & Space Forces Association. He is the author of *Fire on the Water, Second Edition: China, America, and the Future of the Pacific*, published by US Naval Institute Press. Haddick was a US Marine Corps officer and served in the Western Pacific and Africa, with duties ranging from security force assistance to nuclear command and control. He was a contractor for US Special Operations Command and performed research for the Pentagon's Office of Net Assessment. Haddick was a national security columnist at *Foreign Policy* magazine and has delivered lectures on strategy across the US government.

Isaac "Ike" Harris is vice president, government strategy, at Exiger, where he directs the integration of strategy to deliver state-of-the-art supply-chain risk-management technology. Harris is a leading expert in technology competition and policy. He has two decades of experience as a US Navy officer serving at sea and across the Washington, DC, area, including in the Pentagon and Congress. Most recently, he served as an advisor to the under secretary of defense for policy on matters relating to China and technology competition. His final operational tour as a surface warfare officer was as the commanding officer of USS *Ramage* (DDG-61), deploying to Europe and the Middle East.

Michael A. Hunzeker is an associate professor at George Mason University's Schar School of Policy and Government, the associate director of the Schar School's Center for Security Policy Studies, and a senior nonresident fellow at the Center for Strategic and Budgetary Assessments. He served in the US Marine Corps from 2000 to 2006 and holds an AB from the University of California–Berkeley, as well as an AM, MPA, and PhD from Princeton University.

Ivan Kanapathy is an adjunct professor at Georgetown University's School of Foreign Service (Asian studies), a nonresident senior fellow with the Center for Strategic and Budgetary Assessments, and a nonresident senior associate with the Center for Strategic and International Studies (Freeman Chair in China Studies). A retired US Marine, he previously served as the deputy senior director for Asian affairs on the National Security Council staff, the deputy chief of liaison affairs at the American Institute in Taiwan, and an F/A-18 strike fighter tactics instructor at the US Navy Fighter Weapons School, better known as TOPGUN.

Vice Admiral Yoji Koda is a graduate of the National Defense Academy of Japan, the Japan Maritime Self-Defense Force (JMSDF) Command and Staff College, and the US Naval War College. He served as commander of the JS *Sawayuki* (DD-125) and the Fleet Escort Force. His on-shore duty included service as director general in the Plans and Programs and System Programs divisions of the Maritime Staff Office of the JMSDF Programming Center, Tokyo. After retiring from JMSDF as commander in chief of the Self-Defense Fleet in 2008, he spent two years conducting research on China's naval strategy at the Harvard University Asia Center. He served as an advisor to the Japanese national security secretariat from 2014 to 2016. His publications about security include *The US-Japan Alliance: Responding to China's A2/AD Threat*, published by the Center for a New American Security.

Elaine Luria graduated from the US Naval Academy and served two decades in the US Navy as a nuclear-trained surface warfare officer. From 2019 to 2023, Luria represented Virginia's Second Congressional District, serving as the vice chair of the House Armed Services Committee and on the House Select Committee to Investigate the

January 6th Attack on the United States Capitol. In Congress, Luria consistently advocated for larger investments in defense and naval assets to meet challenges in the Pacific.

Kobi Marom is an expert on strategic situations on radical movements operating in the Middle East today. Marom is a decorated veteran who commanded rescue operations of Ethiopian Jews in the Sudanese desert in 1984. As the Israel Defense Forces' brigade commander for the Eastern Front in South Lebanon and as head of the Hermon Brigade, he supervised complex and varied combat units under conditions of duress and uncertainty. He is a respected scholar and a research associate at the International Institute for Counter-Terrorism of the Interdisciplinary Center in Herzliya, Israel. He is a popular media commentator and often speaks to Jewish communities, members of Congress, and diplomatic, political, and philanthropic delegations. Kobi received a master's in business administration and security studies from the National Defense University in Washington, DC, and a BA in political science from the University of Haifa, Israel.

Mark Montgomery serves as senior director of the Center on Cyber and Technology Innovation, where he leads the Foundation for Defense of Democracies' efforts to advance US prosperity and security through technology innovation while countering cyber threats that seek to diminish them. Montgomery also directs CSC 2.0, an initiative that works to implement the recommendations of the congressionally mandated Cyberspace Solarium Commission, where he served as executive director. Previously, Montgomery served as policy director for the Senate Armed Services Committee under the leadership of Senator John S. McCain, coordinating policy efforts on national security strategy, capabilities and requirements, and cyber policy. He served for thirty-two years in the US Navy as a nuclear-trained surface warfare officer, retiring as rear admiral in 2017. His flag officer assignments included director of operations (J3) at US Pacific Command; commander of Carrier Strike Group 5, embarked on the USS *George Washington*, stationed in Japan; and deputy director for plans, policy, and strategy (J5) at US European Command. He was assigned to the National Security Council from 1998 to 2000, serving as director for transnational threats. Montgomery has graduate degrees from the University of Pennsylvania and the University of Oxford and completed the US Navy's nuclear power training program.

Grant Newsham is a former US Marine, diplomat, business executive, and lawyer who lived and worked in Japan for twenty-five years. He was the Marine Corps's first liaison officer to the Japan Self-Defense Forces and was instrumental in creating Japan's amphibious force. He also served as the Marine attaché at the US Embassy, Tokyo, on two occasions and headed up the Sendai bilateral coordination cell during Operation Tomodachi, the recovery effort following the 2011 earthquake and tsunami. Newsham lived in Taiwan in 2019 researching the nation's defense capabilities, and he recently published a book: *When China Attacks: A Warning to America.*

Jonas Parello-Plesner is executive director of the Alliance of Democracies Foundation, which is dedicated to strengthening cooperation among democracies worldwide and which hosts the annual Copenhagen Democracy Summit. Parello-Plesner has a background as a Danish diplomat focusing on China and Taiwan. From 2013 to 2017, he was head of department for foreign policy at the Danish embassy in Washington, DC. He has also worked as a senior China fellow for think tanks in Washington, Brussels, and London. He writes for Danish and international media outlets, such as *Politico* and the *Wall Street Journal*, and has coauthored the books *China's Strong Arm* and *The Battle for Taiwan.*

Anders Fogh Rasmussen has been at the center of European and global politics for over three decades as a leading Danish parliamentarian, Danish minister of economic affairs, prime minister of Denmark, and secretary general of NATO. Upon leaving NATO, he founded the strategic advisory firm Rasmussen Global, which provides geopolitical and strategic consulting services. He is also the chairman of the Alliance of

Democracies Foundation, a nonprofit organization committed to the advancement of democracy and free markets across the globe.

Matthew Turpin, a visiting fellow at the Hoover Institution and a senior advisor at Palantir, previously served for nearly two years as director for China at the White House National Security Council and senior advisor for China to the secretary of commerce. In that role, he managed the interagency effort to develop and implement US government policies toward the People's Republic of China. Turpin previously served in the US Army for twenty-two years, the last seven focused on China at US Pacific Command and as an advisor to the chairman and vice chairman of the Joint Chiefs of Staff.

Enoch Wu is the founder of Forward Alliance, a Taiwanese nonprofit organization that focuses on civic engagement and national security. Previously, Wu served on Taiwan's National Security Council, where his portfolio included homeland security and critical infrastructure protection. Before that, Enoch led an Executive Yuan interagency task force under the direction of Premier Lin Chuan to review protective security policies for government affairs. Earlier in his career, Wu spent a decade in the financial industry, working primarily for Goldman Sachs in its Special Situations Group. He later served in the Republic of China (Taiwan) Army's Special Forces Command, from 2014 to 2015, and is currently a reserve noncommissioned officer. He is a graduate of Yale University.

INDEX

Note: The letter f following a page number denotes a figure.